Myth and Magic
in Heavy Metal Music

ALSO BY ROBERT MCPARLAND

*Science Fiction in Classic Rock:
Musical Explorations of Space, Technology
and the Imagination, 1967–1982* (McFarland, 2017)

Myth and Magic in Heavy Metal Music

Robert McParland

McFarland & Company, Inc., Publishers
Jefferson, North Carolina

LIBRARY OF CONGRESS CATALOGUING-IN-PUBLICATION DATA

Names: McParland, Robert, author.
Title: Myth and magic in heavy metal music / Robert McParland.
Description: Jefferson, North Carolina : McFarland & Company, 2018. |
    Includes bibliographical references and index.
Identifiers: LCCN 2018022606 | ISBN 9781476673356 (softcover :
    acid free paper) ∞
Subjects: LCSH: Heavy metal (Music)—History and criticism. | Music
    and mythology.
Classification: LCC ML3534 .M4717 2018 | DDC 781.6609—dc23
LC record available at https://lccn.loc.gov/2018022606

BRITISH LIBRARY CATALOGUING DATA ARE AVAILABLE

ISBN (print) 978-1-4766-7335-6
ISBN (ebook) 978-1-4766-3298-8

© 2018 Robert McParland. All rights reserved

No part of this book may be reproduced or transmitted in any form or by any means, electronic or mechanical, including photocopying or recording, or by any information storage and retrieval system, without permission in writing from the publisher.

Front cover: Venom guitarist Conrad "Cronos" Lant
during the Party.San Metal Open Air music festival
on August 8, 2013, at the Obermehler-Schlotheim airfield
in Germany (photograph by Jonas Rogowski)

Printed in the United States of America

McFarland & Company, Inc., Publishers
  Box 611, Jefferson, North Carolina 28640
    www.mcfarlandpub.com

Acknowledgments

A book like this that focuses on the enduring power of myth is only possible because artists and creators, devoted music fans, and a dedicated publishing team value imagination and recognize that it plays a significant role in human experience. The author would like to thank the many critics of heavy metal upon whose work this volume rests. Thanks also go to Donald Palumbo for his helpful feedback for an earlier book, *Science Fiction and Classic Rock: Musical Explorations of Space, Technology and the Human Imagination, 1967–1982* (2017). Inspiration has come from a thoughtful network of rock music enthusiasts who meet each year at the American Popular Culture Conference. Among this network of talented individuals are Tom Kitts and Gary Burns, who edit *Popular Music and Society* and *Rock Music Studies*, Nick Baxter-Moore, Alex Di Blasi, Steve Hamelman, Scott Henderson, Lawrence Pitilli, and the Maine poet Jim Mello. Their support and their insights into rock music are much appreciated.

Table of Contents

Acknowledgments v
Preface 1
Introduction 5

1. Led Zeppelin: Houses of the Holy, Myth and the Esoteric Tradition   17
2. Black Sabbath: Dark Symbolism   31
3. Power, Noise and Rebellion   44
4. Mythical Roots   59
5. Shadow Dreams: The Legacy of Gothic Romanticism   84
6. Iron Maiden: Mythology and the Ancient Mariner   103
7. Thor's Thunder: Norse Myth and the Gods of Valhalla   118
8. Sonnets to Orpheus: Journeys to the Underworld   136
9. Madness, Magic and Virtuosity   155

Selected Discography 177
Chapter Notes 181
Bibliography 186
Index 195

Preface

Rock has made its own myths and created heroes. Legends and tales have been transcribed in rock criticism for more than half a century. Heavy metal asserts power and sings about our situation now. Yet, its creativity relies upon the recasting of human experience in symbols, myths, and dreams. This is a book about those heavy metal dreams.

Heavy metal is in dialogue with our contemporary world. When in its discourse of power and imagination it appeals to ancient mythology heavy metal offers us fresh perspectives on our current situation. "Today rationalism is global, computer compatible everywhere. It is the international style of the mind's architecture," writes James Hillman (152). This book argues for balance. It calls for recognition of our human need for entertainment, fantasy, and mythical imagination. To embrace such imagination is to don wings like Icarus, to set sail with Charon on a journey across the border of the sacred and the scared. Mythic imagination attempts to make visible the invisible, to assert that intuition and imagination are necessary. Power, fantasy, wonder, and excess are the stuff of metal, as some critics have said. It takes us to fantastic sites, the decks of haunted ships, the cobblestones of ancient cities, the gates of hell.

Heavy metal is a voice in the modern world that recognizes the power of myth. Its expression of those myths is crucial to heavy metal's ongoing creativity and its longevity in a music business in which it has been appropriated and commercialized. The future of heavy metal depends upon its creators' desire to create powerful and authentic music alongside compelling imagery that rests upon archetypes. Such music speaks to human emotion and imagination.

When Christopher Booker gives us his archetypal analysis of the seven plots that underpin most literature he reminds us that plotlines like overcoming the monster, the quest myth, or voyage and return have been

Preface

present in stories from time immemorial. It follows that whenever an ambitious heavy metal song involves a narrative there is often a mythical impulse and an archetypal monomyth at work in it. Manowar's extended treatment of Achilles and Iron Maiden's *Rime of the Ancient Mariner* are examples of this. (Booker, who worked for more than thirty years on his book, identifies the major plots as Overcoming the Monster, The Quest, Rags to Riches, Voyage and Return, Comedy, Tragedy, and Rebirth.)

Myths seek to take us beyond ordinary perception. Mythic stories, however fantastic, connect with human experience. They are revised and retold across generations and these revisions bring the myths alive within each new cultural context. Myths, legends, and folk tales may be recited or sung for the delight of audiences. They are entertaining and also can be told for a serious purpose. Rock song lyrics are a form of popular literature that suggest attitudes or tell stories and continue myth's involvement in creating meaning.

"In the old days, rock music was a distraction from your studies; now it may well be what you are studying," Terry Eagleton points out (3). The literary critic Louis Menand, in a review essay in *The New Yorker* (July 31, 2017), recognized the trend of academics who are producing what he called "advanced pop." Commenting on Michael Robbins's book *Equipment for Living: On Poetry and Pop Music* (2017), he wrote that this form of criticism is "premised on the belief that you can talk about cultural goods loved uncritically by millions in terms originally developed to talk about cultural goods known mainly to an overeducated few" (64). This book applies some of that approach, arguing for something that listeners to heavy metal may feel viscerally: that myth, metaphor, imagination, entertainment, and passion remain crucial in our contemporary society. The best way to approach this mythological framework is to locate the lyrics and to listen to the recordings.

This study of myth and metal is an attempt to approach heavy metal primarily from a mythological and literary perspective. Previous book-length studies have tended to investigate heavy metal from the perspectives of sociology, musicology, or cultural studies. There has also been much work in psychology on the impact of heavy metal on youth. The reader is encouraged to turn to the ever-developing scholarship about heavy metal. The study of this field was opened by Deena Weinstein (1991) and Robert Walser (1993). Their pivotal studies were followed by books by Harris M. Berger (1999), Steve Waksman (1999, 2009), Susan Fast

Preface

(2001), Natalie Purcell (2003), Glenn Pillsbury (2006), Chris McDonald (2007), and Keith Kahn-Harris (2007). In recent years essays have been gathered into collections such as Gerd Bayer's *Heavy Metal Music in Britain* (2009), Donna Weston and Andy Bennett's *Pagan Metal* (2014), and Scott A. Wilson's *Music at the Extremes* (2015). Heavy metal is looked at in a global context in the essays gathered in *Metal Rules the Globe* (2011) from Jeremy Wallach, Harris M. Berger, and Paul D. Greene and in *Global Metal Music* (2016), edited by Andy Brown, Karl Spracklen, Keith Kahn-Harris, and Niall W.R. Scott. In *The Wall Street Journal* (2016) Neil Shah pointed to what he called "The Weird Appeal of Heavy Metal" as world music, or as the post about this on the Web put it: "Heavy Metal Becomes the Unlikely Soundtrack of Globalization." In that article Brian Hickam, a librarian/archivist at Wilmington College since 2015, reported that 224 academic articles on heavy metal were published between 2000 to 2011 and 63 more were published in the following year. The International Society for Metal Music Studies and their journal *Metal Music Studies* has brought more attention to the field during the past few years.

Storytelling and ritual have always been at the center of community. As Nelson Varas-Diaz and Niall Scott point out in their introduction to *Heavy Metal and the Communal Experience* (2016) heavy metal supplies a narrative among fans, a mythmaking that contributes to a sense of belonging: shared experiences, behavioral expectations, codes of dress, collective information outlets, joint discussion of the music and events (xii). Myths are invented about being rebellious or magical, or identifying with mythical heroes.

The timeless power of myth remains crucial in our own time. Following an introduction that sets out this theme, we will look at precursors of heavy metal. Among the most prominent of these bands were Led Zeppelin and Black Sabbath. The popular rise of metal came in the 1980s. During this decade heavy metal became further diversified: from the power metal of bands like Iron Maiden to thrash bands like Metallica, Megadeth, Slayer, and Anthrax, and from lite-metal (hard rock/pop) to black metal and death metal. Theoretical chapters on myth itself are important for an understanding of the ways that myth from Greek, Celtic, Sumerian/Akkadian, Egyptian, and other cultures have been used in heavy metal song lyrics and heavy metal iconography. This includes some explanation of the relationships between rock music and the rebellion of Romanticism: an artistic movement that embraced the use of myth and

Preface

asserted the importance of emotion, intuition, and symbolic expression. A consideration of Iron Maiden's music follows, with a close reading of bassist Steve Harris's adaptation of "The Rime of the Ancient Mariner."

The search for cultural roots and primitive originality in Romanticism appears in Nordic heavy metal, which makes use of Norse mythology. So, we will take a look at black metal and Viking metal and then move on to reflections on the archetypal figures of the Underworld and dreams and nightmares. In the final chapter, with reference to the work of some current heavy metal bands, we will again look at how heavy metal is an important cultural discourse that utilizes mythology as an imaginative voice of contestation and celebration in modern society. A bibliography and selected discography are provided for further reading and listening.

Introduction

The sky cracks open, shatters like dark glass, and a powerful pulse moves through the audience. An inarticulate growl rises to a scream, to a sustained wail that pierces sanity, convention, and common reality. Something wicked this way comes. The heavy metal concert is a ritual, the communal apex of a musical genre that is fundamentally based in myth, power, and rebellious energy. Heavy metal comes in many forms with sonic vitality and overwhelming loudness. When it is at its best it brings listeners to the ecstatic peaks of Dionysian revelry and down to the dark chaos of infernal depths, to the underworld. Listeners are swept into the apocalyptic battle of guitars, blistering bass, and pounding polyrhythms.

Heavy metal is a mythical genre of heroes, outlaws, ominous gods, grotesques, and monsters. It is a proud world of intense battles with chaos and confrontation with modern alienation. Heavy metal is charisma, cynicism, and prophecy. It is a musical path through this muddy vesture of decay that is an embodiment of rock music's persistent quest for transcendence. In the commercial arena, heavy metal music is a commodity: a product that makes money. It is entertainment that exists to be sold. Metal has also been found by some people to be offensive, revolting, or appalling. However, conjuring up that distaste seems to be the idea. For however commercial or imitative some heavy metal has become, there is much heavy metal music that remains edgy, rebellious, and provocative. As *Newsweek* observed in 1989, heavy metal, once the "scourge of the pop scene now dominates record sales" (148). Despite the many changes in the record industry since then, if heavy metal is considered broadly amid all of its wide variety, that statement remains just as true today.

Myth pervades heavy metal. Its visual elements draw upon the horror story or film, suggesting chaos and disruption. It calls forth images of

Introduction

Promethean rebellion and mythic heroism, adopting a proud and determined oppositional stance to the conventional. Heavy metal takes the world and paints it black. Its color schemes involve the blackness of darkness and blood red intensity. It often intends to appear ominous, threatening, and disturbing. The metal song is delivered with vocal toughness, gritty tenors and growling baritones that are emotional and powerful. The loud vocal is accompanied by fierce guitars, supported by an array of effects pedals, and loud, pulsating bass and drums that emphasize the heaviness of the heavy metal sound.

Heavy metal today is a variety of forms that continue to emphasize power, myth, force, and imagination. The sound of heavy metal is the aspect of it that stays with listeners most. Heavy metal fans tend to recall fragments of lyrics. When a listener has a favorite song, or is deeply committed to a band, that listener may have paid close attention to the lyrics. However, as Deena Weinstein puts it: "The words of a song function for listeners, in metal and in rock in general, more as isolated words and phrases than as integral poetic texts" (125). The symbols of chaos, danger, darkness, and outlaws are indeed "deeply rooted in Western mythology, as Weinstein recognizes (*Heavy Metal: The Music and Its Culture*, 128). These themes and visual images repeat throughout the heavy metal imagination. There are skulls, skeletons, daggers, snakes, dragons, and maces and chaos-monster figures abound (128). These images are present in band logos, on T-shirts, in album art, and on tattoos as signs of heavy metal culture.

The heavy metal concert is a gathering of collective energy in the enactment of a ritual. In its best moments, with the bonding of artist and audience there is an experience in which "time stands still and one feels that one belongs to a higher reality" says Weinstein (231). The heavy metal concert may be experienced as a sacred rite, as a space in which what mythologist Mircea Eliade called hierophanies may occur (232).[1] The performance accentuates the Dionysian and expresses the familiar codes of heavy metal, energy and power, taking listeners out of the mundane world (213). The concert appears to satisfy a human desire for transcendence: a desire for awe and wonder, to be shaken, charged, and lifted out beyond the ordinary. It floods the listener with sonic energy, rhythm, flashing lights, and thunderous sensory stimulation.

Heavy metal has its own auditory and visual codes. With its power chord changes, its chord inversions, changing time signatures, and con-

Introduction

trasting guitar and bass lines it expresses a unique auditory sensibility. Its sound is often harsh, direct, loud and its visual imagery, rich with mythical figures and grotesque representations, contrasts with other visual imagery in rock performance and art. Heavy metal can be distinguished from hard rock, or from lite metal bands like Van Halen, Aerosmith, Mötley Crüe, and Guns n' Roses. It is also different in attitude and approach from grunge bands that emerged from Seattle in the 1990s like Nirvana, Soundgarden, and Pearl Jam. Metal underscores the idea of power and pleasure. Grunge centers upon alienation, pain and hurt, anguish and sincerity (Weinstein 279). Lost in the universe, grunge seeks authenticity. In contrast, a band like Mötley Crüe is about hedonism and decadence. Metal plays with images of horror, with ancient myth, and with themes of apocalyptic struggle.

War is a common theme in heavy metal and the myths of ancient war fit well into an expression of conflict, resistance, and heroism. The intensity of war and the *agon*, drama, and noise of battle correspond with the heavy metal genre. Heavy metal storytelling emerges forcefully in these forays into history and mythological battles. The approaches vary from visceral horrors to bombastic glorification and from nationalistic and patriotic stances to criticism of war and the powers behind our modern conflicts. For example, Lamb of God's "Contractors" criticizes private military firms seeking profit from war. Metallica's "Master of Puppets" has a similar theme and "Disposable Heroes" points out how youth are used and wasted in war. These songs follow in the line of criticism set out by Black Sabbath's "War Pigs." Meanwhile, Metallica's "Search and Destroy" and other heavy metal music has been used in recent years during actual military patrols.

There is sound and fury, imagery and testosterone in songs describing historical or mythical battles. The storytelling of Iron Maiden has depicted the aerial battle between the RAF and the Luftwaffe, the muddy gore of the Third Battle of Ypres during the First World War, Alexander the Great's march, and the Charge of the Light Brigade. The battle has been an ample subject for an extended, energetic piece of music.

Across the years heavy metal has developed with increasing variety. Speed/thrash metal arose in California between 1981 and 1983. It is usually direct, is played fast with aggressive rhythms, and at times has some punk elements. It draws upon the theme of chaos. Bands range from Anthrax and Megadeth to Metallica. Some thrash metal bands may convey a sense of isolation and alienation. Death metal makes reference to horror movies

Introduction

and invokes dark images. It growls, snarls, gargles, screams, and will tear at your listening ears with a sense of misery. Black metal looks imaginatively to the underworld. It inverts Christianity. Its contrast is the Christian metal of bands like Stryper, which emerged in the 1980s with *Soldiers Under Command* (1985) and *To Hell with the Devil* (1987). The subgenre of glam-metal derives from the visual expression of bands like the New York Dolls, Kiss, and glam rock acts.

By the early 1990s, heavy metal seemed to be moving into another phase. Black Sabbath had dissolved and Ozzy returned to the stage with guitarist Randy Rhoads. Following their album *Painkiller*, Judas Priest vocalist Rob Halford sought a solo direction and Tim Owens became the new vocalist as the band tried to keep going. Bruce Dickinson left Iron Maiden for several years. Slayer produced their album *Divine Intervention*. Metal seemed to have declined during those years. However, it returned with a vengeance. Metallica, with its speed/thrash metal, became the darlings of pop radio airplay and MTV videos with their *Load* and *Re-Load* albums. Heavy metal prospered in Europe and it became a worldwide phenomenon as interest in it increased in Japan and spread to other areas of Asia.

Heavy metal may come to listeners in many styles and just which bands are metal is likely to be debated. Metal can come from *Billboard* charting bands like Disturbed or Metallica and can range from the dissonant edge of Korn to the art rock of Jane's Addiction and from the progressive sounds of Rush and Dreamtheater to Norwegian black metal and the demonic posturing of death metal. The heavy metal genre reaches deeply into the sources of myth. Heavy metal thrives on the idea of disorder. The heavy metal underground remains a Dante's Inferno of grotesque forms, tormented souls, death and decay. It is a voice for the supernatural and the diabolical, for energy and the assertion of full-throated power. It reserves an imaginative place in the modern world for the archaic and the archetypal, for the passionate and emotional, and for the mythical and the magical.

Music and Emotion

Heavy metal bands often play in festivals in which a variety of metal bands play across several hours for fans who gather in the communal

Introduction

concert setting. In this way, heavy metal expresses the carnivalesque: celebration, play, role reversals, inversion. Heavy metal produces a release of energy. It gives free rein to a variety of voices. Extravagance, myth, and mystery play with possibility and revive a sense of the heroic. At these events, heavy metal music moves emotions. The energy and sounds of heavy metal participate in a non-discursive "language" from which listeners make meaning. Fans share these meanings in their dialogue about heavy metal music. Myths are also engaged in this dialogue. Heavy metal connects myth as archetype and as metaphor with these fans through musical activity. This is a way of communicating imagination and generating meaning in a social context. Heavy metal songs become a discourse that is open to a variety of interpretations.

Musical knowledge is something different from the knowledge of science and language. The philosopher Ernst Cassirer has spoken of non-propositional realms of human experience. Susanne Langer, following Cassirer, stated her view that music is an expressional way of knowing. In her work *Philosophy in a New Key*, Langer explored our emotional experience. She made a distinction between the conventional symbols of mathematics and language and symbols in the expressional mode. These, she insisted, defy linguistic or propositional formulation. These symbols go beyond words. Langer writes: "The tonal structures we call music bear a close logical similarity to the forms of human feeling" (27). Langer's theories support the notion that music is connected with the capacity for expression and emotional awareness. These ideas lend support to the view that music helps us to understand the universe of feeling.

The musical knowledge of heavy metal performers may be looked at as a procedural form of knowledge. Performance is more than actualizing the possibilities of a piece of music. It is also a mode of knowing which is social. It is a self-actualizing expression that unfolds into knowledge of self and culture. The performer is aware and makes decisions while performing about what is going to happen next and what is happening musically. The performer is a discoverer who responds to the music and to the audience and pursues strategies concerning how to enhance what is happening. The social experience of the concert and a band's songs is shared. It is an interaction: a social field in which myths, ideas, themes, sounds are constructed, exchanged, and interpreted.

Music is often described in terms of emotions and heavy metal music stirs those emotions. "What heavy metal fans are experiencing is an

Introduction

emancipation of emotions," writes Gary Sinclair in "Heavy Metal Rituals and the Civilizing Process" (95–96). Sinclair says that one of these emotions is anger. Even so, a study of heavy metal's effects on arousal and anger, published by researchers William Neil Gowensmith and Larry J. Bloom in *The Journal of Music Therapy* (Spring 1997), showed that metal fans on the whole feel and express no more anger than those in the general population. Metal listeners did not show any startling levels of anger. Instead, some of those fans found metal music exhilarating and claimed that music gives them a high. The researchers also affirmed that listeners may have physical responses to music.

With *Emotion and Meaning in Music* (1956), Leonard Meyer set in motion a psychological literature on music and emotion which is complex. Meyer theorized that a listener hearing patterns in music anticipates the return of these patterns and figures and delights in the variations or changes in the music. These changes are experiences as pleasurable or as disruptive. Meyer wrote that an emotion is "aroused when a tendency to respond is arrested or inhibited" (19).

Considering how music may express emotion, Langer pointed out that "music is significant form, and its significance is that of a symbol, a highly articulated, sensuous object, which by virtue of its dynamic structure can express the forms of vital experience which language is peculiarly unfit to convey. Feeling, life, motion, and emotion constitute its import" (32).

The famed anthropologist Claude Levi-Straus, in *The Raw and the Crooked* (1970), spoke of "the surprising affinity between music and myth" (ii-iv). However, whether listeners can actually hear a story pattern in the music itself is questionable. Heavy metal music is often accompanied by lyrics which set forth mythical images. We may wonder if the music itself is able to tell a story. Philosopher Roger Scruton, in *Aesthetics of Music* (1997), contends that we never can pinpoint the plot of a story in the musical composition itself. Stories are extra-musical. In his view, a musical composition in itself is unable to convey a monomyth: a story of challenge and calling, initiation, journey and struggle, achievement and return. However, other critics and musicologists hold a different view.

Heavy metal is a discourse. Its powerful chords, propulsive rhythms, screams and screeches, and piercing guitar leads are part of its "language" by which it engages listeners. Music plays upon our tendency to anticipate what is coming next, observed Leonard Meyer in *Emotion and Meaning*

Introduction

in Music. Sometimes that pattern of music shifts, tricking us, delighting us, by going somewhere unexpected. That is not to say that the music, arousing our feelings, is telling a story. However, musicologists Susan McClary and Christopher Small both claim that the structural practices of Tchaikovsky in his *Third Symphony* spell out a plot, a narrative pattern that suggests his personal struggles. When we look to lengthy mythically based heavy metal compositions like Manowar's tale of Achilles, or Iron Maiden's adaptation of "The Rime of the Ancient Mariner," we encounter an extended narrative that resembles the monomyth. The bands repeat motifs or musical patterns and dramatic phrasing throughout these compositions. Similarly, the ancient bards utilized repetition to unify their stories and to convey them in memorable ways. When a modern translator offers a contemporary translation of *The Odyssey*, for example, that translator repeats key phrases, continuing that literary oral tradition.

With lights, pulse, power, and fire, heavy metal entertains with a spectacle of effects and with raw, harsh, gritty, rebellious energy. Its meaning arises in an experience that is shared. Songs mean a variety of different things to different people. The music is the center of a social activity in which myths appear in a system of symbols. In Iron Maiden's "Seventh Son," for example, ritual and myth suggests the quest for gnosis, or secret knowledge, through mythology, religion, and alchemy. A series of disjunctive images parallel their musical montage of tempo changes and rhythmic shifts, intricately coordinated. Metallica and Megadeth lyrics point out contemporary culture's anxieties. Angry, cynical voices critique society and swift changes in tempo reflect a fragmented modern world. For Venom, a band that pushed metal in the direction of punk, Satan was viewed as a mythical figure, a symbol of fascination (Waksman 194).

Heavy metal, in these instances, becomes a means of response to the impact of modernity. Myths revived and retold in a contemporary context take us beyond ordinary perception. Legends and sagas that have been handed down across generations are put to imaginative use in a world where globalization now represents waves of social, cultural, and institutional change. Heavy metal is involved in an expression of life, an assertion of wonder and emotion, and a search for meaning in collective interaction. Myths help us to structure our sense of the world, to escape inhibiting structures, and to seek new possibilities for heroism, community, and wonder.

Today's heroes are inspired by those of "yesteryear," asserted

Introduction

Manowar's Joey De Maio in an interview. Myths have been retold over thousands of years because they have inspired one person after another. He added that he views the past and present of heavy metal as intertwined. "There's a frame of metal that dialogues with our forefathers": Led Zeppelin, Black Sabbath, Deep Purple, Uriah Heep, Mountain. War and fight are metaphors for our tensions and struggles over the decisions we have to make in life, or our internal struggle with change. De Maio meditated on what it may be within a person that compels that individual toward action or sacrifice. Heavy metal, he said, is involved in the desire to do something special and to find "a spark of greatness" within oneself. It is possible, he added, to search for wisdom, like Odin in the Norse myths, and to seek reality in something more than in depressing television news. In the interview, De Maio noted Manowar's collaboration with German fantasy writer Wolfgang Holbein and the band's "ongoing quest to look to different cultures" and to their myths.

Iron Maiden's *The Book of Souls* is a double album that makes a similar exploration. It features the band's fierce guitars, the galloping bass of Steve Harris, and the vocals of Bruce Dickinson, who had experienced a series of cancer treatments before the album was recorded. The recording repeats Iron Maiden's interest in mythical and historical subject matter, which has had worldwide influence.

Heavy metal has gone global and so has its distribution of mythical discourse. In Europe we have heard mythical references and the introduction of symphonic sounds accompanying metal on Einherjer's *Dreamstorm* and Dimmu Borgir's *Serpentine Offering* (2007). On Einherjer's *Dreamstorm* we hear a guitar riff and then the guitar begins racing with the drums. "Conquerer" achieves the same speed and "Crimson Rain," which follows, is all energy. Odin still lives within these songs, as do dragons of the north. Dimmu Borgir's *The Serpentine Offering* has a symphonic opening. Their video for the song begins with an image of the Crusades. The band enters, with fast bass and guitar patterns that then return to the symphonic. The vocal is gargled like a monster from the deep. "Progenies of the Great Apocalypse" bursts out with a fast, driving bass and strong drums underneath. A second voice is more tenor and dramatic and rises over echoed drum and bass rolls. There is a bridge with piano and strings and the thunder of the drums and bass are joined with a symphony. All of this suggests that a continuing mining of resources of myth from the past and a variety of intersections of musical styles and sounds may be

Introduction

aspects of heavy metal's future. While some bands will persist in declaring their uniqueness with extreme metal, or with musical complexity, other bands, like Disturbed, will become more melodic and mainstream. Disturbed is David Draiman (vocals), Dan Donegan (guitar), John Moyer (bass), and Mike Wegren (drums). Upon realizing much commercial success with the debuts of albums high on the charts, from *Down with the Sickness* (2000), *The Sound of Silence* (2003), and *Ten Thousand Fists* (2005) to *Immortalized* (2015), Disturbed intends to last for a long time.

Mapping Our Mythic Journey: An Outline of This Book

In this book heavy metal is approached as the music of a self-referencing community that draws upon archetypes and the unconscious. From Black Sabbath to Metallica, there is a commercial appeal of heavy metal which plays a role in entertainment industries. However, at the root of these bands is their vigorous creative expression through symbols, power, dissonance, loudness, and mythmaking. Heavy metal invites its fans to join in ritual, imagination, and participatory community which offer them catharsis, connection, and a sense of wonder that helps them to, as Robert Walser says in *Running with the Devil*, "weather the strains of modernity."

To explore the beginnings of heavy metal the first section of this book will include an examination of the impact of the work of Led Zeppelin and Black Sabbath. Led Zeppelin's music is grounded in the blues and in myth deriving from the esoteric traditions, including ancient mythologies. We will explore Led Zeppelin's mythology across their albums and situate the band within their esoteric interests. The persona of Black Sabbath is connected with occultism, gore, death, hell, as well as protest of war and of convention. In their music we hear inversions, tri-tones, heavy bass, and dissonant chords. Black Sabbath initiates heavy metal orientations toward occultism and the imagery of horror, or otherworldliness.

The next chapter further addresses the topics of heavy metal power, the use of volume, and spectacle. Heavy metal is characterized by rebellion, non-conformity, opposition, and creativity. We will look at how this relates to mythical imagination in some of the bands that employ myth in their

Introduction

work. Heavy metal extends rock's rebellious stance into the twenty-first century. The development of a heavy metal sound from the blues emerged with power chords and dissonance. This chapter addresses the heavy metal genre's precursors. There is some dispute about this. However, it is clear that British metal and its roots emerge in Birmingham, and are connected with the hard rock of the 1960s and 1970s. Briefly considered here are the blues rock bands The Yardbirds, Cream, and the contributions of Jimi Hendrix to the soaring guitar solo playing style; the loud and direct styles of MC5 and Blue Cheer, and the influences of The Kinks, Steppenwolf, Iron Butterfly, Vanilla Fudge, Judas Priest, Alice Cooper, Kiss, and Deep Purple. Bands that treated and developed mythical constructs, such as Manowar and Iron Maiden are also discussed.

The dark dreams of Gothic horror, terror, and the sublime, which are the legacy of Gothic Romanticism, are explored next. By looking back at the legacy of European Romanticism we can see how it emphasized emotion, passion, the primitive and Gothicism. Heavy metal strikes a note of awe or shock. In "On the Sublime" Edmund Burke pointed to powerful experiences and emotions like terror, which open the mind to wonder. The argument of this chapter is that Romanticism, in its emphasis upon emotion, or feeling, myth and nostalgia, lives at the heart of much rock music and the legacy of Gothic Romanticism is directly related to heavy metal.

We then look at the uses of myth, medievalism, historic themes and romantic horror by the heavy metal band Iron Maiden by examining bassist Steve Harris's transposition of Samuel Taylor Coleridge's famous poem "The Rime of the Ancient Mariner" into what has been called an "epic" dramatic piece.

The myths of the Norse gods are at the center of heavy metal imagination, particularly in northern Europe. These have served as inspiration for speed, thrash, and death metal. The Nordic myths, which appealed greatly to the German romantic composer Richard Wagner, have been present in the work of a variety of metal bands. They have made references to Odin, Thor, and other gods. Their lyrics have elicited images of northern landscapes of rough and untamed nature, and power and adventure. Nordic metal has emerged forcefully since *Scandinavian Metal Attack* (1984) featured bands from Finland and Sweden. The extreme metal forms of black and death metal draw upon Viking imagery. Bathory, with *Blood Fire Death* (1988), *Hammerheart* (1989), and *Twilight of the Gods* (1990),

Introduction

and the UK band Venom stand as precursors to the Norwegian black metal movement. Other bands like Mayhem, Darkthrone, and Emperor contributed further, influencing bands in Norway and Germany. Dismember and Entombed came from Sweden. Sentenced and Amorphis appeared in Finland. All of these bands turned toward Nordic myths, the Vikings, and the Eddas, Scandinavia's early mythic literature.

Heavy metal mythology is fascinated by hell and the underworld. AC/DC sang about a highway to hell. Heavy metal bands draw upon the myths of an Underworld: a frightening region which recalls Greek mythology in Odysseus' journey to meet with Tiresius and the journey of Orpheus, the singer, in his quest to return Eurydice from this region of death. Hebraic/biblical, Egyptian, and Persian/Zoroastrian notions of the underworld are also discussed in relation to the many uses by bands of the imagery of hell and underworld. The apocalyptic strain persists in metal and is one of its key mythical features.

Of course, heavy metal has its dissenters as well as its fans. There are censors at the gates of hell and this was particularly true in the 1980s, as metal rose to prominence in popular culture. The heavy metal bands and lite metal bands of the 1980s included Twisted Sister, Megadeth, Mötley Crüe, Scorpions, Def Leppard, Quiet Riot, Dokken, Poison, Van Halen, and Whitesnake. As heavy metal became more prominent in the 1980s, its lyrics, aggressive music, and expression in performance aroused concern from parts of society that sought to limit, censor, or label it as dangerous or unsafe. Considering the rise of heavy metal in the 1980s, we will look at why its mythologies, fantasies, and approach to creative expression may have felt threatening for some of its critics.

In the 1990s and 2000s heavy metal had surely arrived. From the mid-1980s heavy metal had become one of the central forces in popular music. Response to heavy metal dipped in the early 1990s and there was then a resurgence of the form. The final chapters explore the mythical features sustained by heavy metal performance, like the image of the shaman, or magus: the charismatic performer, the front-man vocalist, and the exceptional guitarist. Heavy metal has diversified into several subgenres from speed/thrash to black metal, death metal, and glam-metal. The bands of the past decade retrace the symbolic representation in auditory and visual iconography of their predecessors. Myths and dreams continue in the sound, lyrics, and the ritual aspects of stage presentations. The 1990s and the new century brought bands that ranged from Korn, Tool

Introduction

and Slipknot to System of a Down, Five Finger Death Punch, and many others. The concluding chapter considers the continuing role of myth and archetypes in the images and music of current heavy metal bands. This book is an invitation to get to those MP3s, to load up those CDs, and to listen to the wide range of heavy metal creativity.

1

Led Zeppelin
Houses of the Holy, Myth and the Esoteric Tradition

Led Zeppelin, one of the most remarkably enduring rock bands, may be viewed as heavy metal precursors that embraced mythology and occult symbolism. References to myth appear throughout Led Zeppelin's catalog. Guitarist Jimmy Page was fascinated with occultism, mythology, and esoteric symbolism. Robert Plant was a reader of mythology and fantasy. Jimmy Page brought his esoteric interests to his music, matching this with the mythical lyrics of Robert Plant. Page was deeply interested in the hermetic tradition and he was a reader of the work of occultist Aleister Crowley and bought his estate at Loch Ness.[1] Led Zeppelin's fourth album includes symbols that are said to represent the four members of the band and Led Zeppelin is held to be the alchemy of the elements, according to Page: a combination of Led Zeppelin's four members.[2] The Hermit from the Tarot on the inner sleeve of *Led Zeppelin IV* has been identified as a variation of the Rider Waite of legend.[3]

Led Zeppelin presents a hermit-figure on the inside cover of *Led Zeppelin IV*: the hermit, the bearer of the lamp and light. The Led Zeppelin figure of pastoral peasant and crumbling modern city on the cover of *Led Zeppelin IV (ZOSO)* represents the dialogue between past and present, the mythical and the modern. Led Zeppelin's turn toward mythology, Celtic culture, and occultism was one expression of an exploratory venture for alternatives to a rational-institutional-technologically engineered society. Rock music artists like Page and Plant sought through the otherworldly for magic.

Led Zeppelin is one of many rock bands that emerged amid what rock music critic Lester Bangs recognized as the "new romanticism." Deena Weinstein comments: "Heavy metal is a child of 1960s counterculture with its interest in the occult, shamans, nature, and pre-modern [ways] of living" (*Heavy Metal Music and Its Culture*, 59). Led Zeppelin was a blues based band that infused the blues with high octane rock. Yet, they also ventured toward mysticism, or what Andy Bennett refers to as "pagan pop." Bennett points to the counter-cultural skepticism toward the rational-scientific way of life that had increasingly taken hold in the sixties. Commentators on the counterculture addressed this often. Theodore Roszak pointed to the dilemma of technocracy and to rationalized planning (5). Charles Reich, in *The Greening of America* (1971), dreamed that Consciousness III, as he called this new awareness, would move society toward the goal of transformation. A turn toward the spiritual, toward nature, aesthetic sense, and criticism of 20th century horrors like the Holocaust and world wars, characterized this movement. In the lyrics of many songs, Led Zeppelin often seems to be forever travelling on a quest for a more idyllic and ethereal realm.

While Led Zeppelin is one of the fundamental sources for the development of heavy metal, *Led Zeppelin I* was a blues based album.[4] "That was not heavy metal," Robert Plant has said. "There was nothing heavy about that at all…. It was ethereal."[5] Led Zeppelin recorded two blues covers on that album. That ethereal musical journey was also the beginning of a mystical and mythical one. In Led Zeppelin's blues-based songs we encounter lyrics that speak of darkness and light, illumination, angelic-power, mystery, magic, and alchemy.

"Myths are Big Stories that tell poetic truths about humanity and its role in the cosmos," writes Erik Davis in his book on *Led Zeppelin IV*. He suggests that "Stairway to Heaven" might be regarded as a myth and recognizes that this song has become "part of our minds" (Introduction, ii). Musically and lyrically the song suggests a kind of passage and the hero's journey. "Stairway to Heaven" proceeds from its pastoral opening to the energetic driven conclusion. Robert Walser sees in this "contradictory sensibilities without reconciling them." Susan Fast says that the song has been a marker of "spiritual life" among teens that "stays with them … probably for the rest of their lives." Led Zeppelin provides "one expression of living mythology in contemporary culture and fan responses to this are a clear indication of the necessity of such mythology in people's lives," observes Fast (50). She concludes that the band "consciously constructed a kind of mythology" and utilized "the spirit of mythological discourse by using "poetic, formal, or slightly archaic language" (50).

1. Led Zeppelin

Led Zeppelin developed a signature sound while also creating a diversity of treatments. Page brought his guitar work across many moods: heavy, driving blues, ethereal acoustic patterns, Celtic mysticism, mid-East and Eastern sounds. His piercing lines and shimmering solos included some of the most memorable phrases in rock music: the powerful blast into "Whole Lotta Love," that ringing D suspended followed by the lyrical, aggressive solo at the end of "Stairway to Heaven."

Robert Plant dived into myth with allusions to *The Lord of the Rings*. "Misty Mountain Hop" and "The Battle of Evermore" recall J.R.R. Tolkien's mythical landscapes. In Plant's lyrics, the mythic aspect of Led Zeppelin's songs is inescapable. Rock critics, academic writers, and fans have commented on it frequently. It is one of the aspects of Led Zeppelin that make this blues based rock band a precursor of heavy metal. "Page is a "creator of powerful archetypal symbols" and Plant is the force behind "poetic lyrical symbols," observes Randell Auxier (127). He asserts that Led Zeppelin has "mythic power" and that past and present are connected by "symbolizing power. Auxier also points out that a belief in magic is one of many expressions of mythic consciousness that have "provided the basis for human civilization (123)."

"Ramble On" on *Led Zeppelin II* recalls J.R.R. Tolkien's *The Lord of the Rings*. "Ramble On" is a song about leaving and seeking an ideal woman. The lyrics recall the stories and imagery of Tolkien. Mordor and Golum enter the lyric for "Ramble On." The speaker laments that he was in Mordor's depth and darkness in the days when there was magic. The evil golem took his lover away. "Ramble On" describes a relentless journey that includes the memory of a quest to find a dream-queen. It is a tale that could be told by a knight, as in the poet John Keats' "La Belle Dame sans Merci" about a knight who awakens on a cold hillside from a dream and a disturbing encounter with an enchanting but merciless lady. The second verse of the song tells the story of how the speaker found a fine maiden in a magical time in the deepest and darkest realm of Mordor. The reference to the mythical world of Tolkien continues. For we hear that it was then that the evil Golem sneaked in and took the maiden away from him. We are introduced to Golem in the first book of the trilogy of *Lord of the Rings*: "He was a loathsome little creature" paddling a boat, "peering with pale luminous eyes" and strangling the fish that he caught (26). Golem possessed a ring of gold. (This is an image that is directly related to the Nibelungenlied of Nordic-German mythology.) In "Ramble On" the singer remains on his interminable journey and he has to continue on. The structure of this song rests upon an alternation of E and A chords. It is in the melody and Plant's vocal that the story lives. His vocal rises on the hook of the title and his reference to singing his song and the band rocks and rambles on with him.

In some contrast to the driving, edgy rock of "Whole Lotta Love," with its climactic break, the vocal on "What Is and Should Never Be" is set in a slow blues. Plant sings directly to someone he says that he will take to a castle. Here is another subtle suggestion of a wistful medieval realm like that of which nineteenth century British writers once dreamed. In the Victorian mirror of history those poets imagined an almost prelapsarian pastoral world in which there was knightly honor and beauty now lost to the modern world. We see this in Tennyson's *Idylls of the King*, William Morris's designs, John Ruskin's apologetics for the Gothic age. There were also the pre-Raphaelite painters and Robert Browning's poetic embrace of monastic figures, painters in early Renaissance Italy. Led Zeppelin, likewise, imaginatively reaches back in the mists of time for a more idyllic and mythical world that contrasts with the modern present.

On *Led Zeppelin III*, "Immigrant Song" is clearly mythical and magical. Immediately the listener hears the name of the god Thor and hears of Valhalla. "Immigrant Song" suggests a world of primeval Vikings and tells the story of Viking warriors seeking new lands. Opening with Plant's striking primal wail, the "Immigrant Song" invites us into the Nordic mythical imagery of Thor's hammer, the hammer of the gods, a land filled with ice and snow. We are told of the epic journey of Viking oarsmen traversing across ice and snow. They seek the western shore and a green landscape that whispers stories of blood and gore and stories of bringing peace after war. To reconstruct society from the ruins trust will be needed, a passion to rebuild and to sail toward the future. The guitar riffs off F sharp minor and the song moves harmonically upward stepwise (E-F sharp minor-A-B) along with the exhilarating vocal.

The song pulses rhythmically through Viking imagery of threshing oars and a call to overcome war and rebuild the ruins in peace. Page's guitar is firmly anchored within the blues but bursts out with energy and Plant's vocal travels melodically, always with that edge we hear in his singing. Andy Bennett notes Plant's "wandering phrasing" and almost chant-like vocalizing to the "relentless chopping" of bass, rhythm guitar and drums.

1. Led Zeppelin

The guitar solo that begins "Since I've Been Loving You" shifts the mood. "Gallows Pole" follows with its A-A minor and foreboding warning and folk-tale quality. "Bron-y-Aur Stomp" has a sense of the Celtic in the tile. Bron-yr-aur was an 18th century country cottage at Machynlieth in Wales. Bron-yr-aur means "breast of gold," or "hill of gold," or "golden hill." Plant used Bron-yr-aur as a family vacation home. Led Zeppelin stayed in that rural setting while composing *Led Zeppelin III* in 1970. Several songs were begun in the farmhouse: "Over the Hills and Far Away," "The Rover," "The Crunge," which would appear on *Houses of the Holy* and "Down by the Seaside," which would appear on *Physical Graffiti*. The name of the place was misspelled as "Bron-Y-Aur Stomp" on *Led Zeppelin III* and an acoustic instrumental by Page was later played for *Physical Graffiti*.

Led Zeppelin presents fantasy-like production in songs like "The Song Remains the Same" and songs on *Houses of the Holy* like "Dancing Days." Archetypes appear in "All My Love," "The Battle of Evermore," "Kashmir," and "Achilles Last Stand." On side two of the original pressing of *Led Zeppelin III* we hear the phrase "So mote it be," which was used in rituals of *Ordo Templi Orientis* (The Order of the Oriental Templars).

Led Zeppelin IV immediately cranks out blues power with "Black Dog." The lyric for "Four Sticks" expresses a need to get away and we hear of a blue eyed-merle. However, it is in "Stairway to Heaven" where the lyric becomes most mythical and the musical textures and transitions have become a most memorable part of popular culture.

Picture Plant and Page sitting near a fireplace. Page is strumming a few chords, playing a pattern on his guitar. Plant starts randomly scribbling words about a lady. Suddenly, like a drop of inspiration from the ether, a lyric begins to form and the song "Stairway to Heaven" begins to take shape. On record, "Stairway to Heaven" moves from its lilting medieval-Renaissance woodwinds introduction through a ballad form to its energetic conclusion. After several verses, there is a pause and a bridge section follows. D chords descend to a C and overdubbed guitars. Page's guitar cuts in with his solo, repeating a figure eleven times. The guitar rings out on suspended chords and the band blasts into the song's familiar Am-G-F conclusion: a rock pulsing section with Plant's vocal climbing and Page's guitar rising into a searing lead.[6]

In "Misty Mountain Hop" the speaker declares to someone that he will leave and go to a more imaginative place. The lyric begins with the narrator reporting that he went to a park where many people gave him advice. He saw a policeman and other signs of the contemporary reality of the streets. Now he is going to pack his things and go away across the hills, out of town, into the misty mountains where the spirits can fly free. Some have suggested that he wanted to get away from the policeman and from drug busts (Wall, 241). The mention of misty mountains reflects Tolkien's dream world of Middle Earth. In the Prologue we read that the hobbits dwelled between Greenwood the Great and the Misty Mountains. In their wandering days, men and elves lived between the Misty Mountains and the mountains of the northland (18).

After that signature song "Stairway to Heaven" we also hear the rollicking assertion of "Rock and Roll," with its blues rock in the key of A bounding along. The dreamy "Going to California" takes us to the wistful myth of a West Coast land where there is a girl with flowers in her hair: a place of dreams, where a queen awaits that needs a king. Like some Dionysian dreamer smoking his stuff, drinking wine, he imagines this mythical place. The modern world seems to intervene in the dream when the singer meets modernity. To get to California the singer has to fly on a jet plane, each of which are all the same: just another excursion of monotony. The airy acoustic pattern, alternating G and D chords, underlies the narrative of the journey toward children of the sun. The gods of some mythical land seem to awaken. Earth itself seems to respond by shaking. The vocal rhythm picks up in eighth notes and the verbs in the lyric suggest the awakening. At the end of a musical phrase, the word "sinking" is embedded in reverb.

Led Zeppelin's "The Battle of Evermore," also on *Led Zeppelin IV*, begins in a pattern of A minor to G and A minor to C, followed by the D chord and it stays with this harmonic pattern throughout. The vocal melody then jumps to A, an octave from the note on which the song began. The lyric begins with an interplay of light and dark; there is a queen of light and a prince of peace. There are agrarian images of hoes, plows, and apples, a rich and well cared for land that is spoiled by tyranny and war. The lyric tells us of a thunderous sound and waiting upon Avalon's angels: a mythic image of an ideal land. We are given an imagery of a castle, battle, bows and arrows flying, a dragon of darkness, magic runes and a world that must be brought back into balance.

"The Battle of Evermore" brings us one of Robert Plant's most developed mythical narratives.[7] With romantic medievalism the lyric draws upon Tolkien. Plant presents the archetypal figures of a Queen of Light

1. Led Zeppelin

and a Prince of Peace who is walking out into the dreariness of the oncoming night. He anticipates the appearance of a dark lord who will ride forth. The speaker warns his listeners of the doom that is to come. Toss away your tools with which you work the field and lock your doors, he tells them. He can hear the powerful approach of the horses. Still, he dreams of a new day: one of Avalon, angelic appearances, dawning light and hope: an ethereal land where the earth is treated tenderly. But no—the horrors come: the withering apples, the angry tyrant, the winds of war. He encourages the people: Put aside your ploughshares and pick up your swords. Heroically raise your bows and shoot more surely than you ever have before. There will be war's pain and its resulting sorrow.

In *The Lord of the Rings* there are great wars against Morgoth. The siege of Gandor and the Battle of Pelannor Fields appear in *The Return of the King*. "The Battle of Evermore" reflects that mythic framework. Plant takes the story in new directions. The contrast in the lyric between pastoral place and war's dark claims is striking. Despite battle there is the chance that a new dawn of warming fires, dance, and magic runes may return balance to the kingdom. Robert Plant told *Record Mirror* (March 1972), "Albion would have been a good place to be, but that was England before it got messed up.... You can live in fairy land if you read enough books and if you're interested in it as I am—the Dark Ages and all that" (240).

The Lord of the Rings and Celtic myth gave Robert Plant material for his own mythic journey in his song lyrics. J.R.R. Tolkien's *The Lord of the Rings* tells of an epic struggle between darkness and light, symbolic quest for awakening. We witness the evil Sauron atop his tower and the array on monsters sent against humanity. We see the misty mountains, the wise man Gandalf who represents maturity and guidance, the young Frodo and Sam in search of a ring, which at first seems so harmless but which becomes so important to the quest. An older man is returning home from exile in *The Return of the King*. The story has all the markers of the monomyth. The heroes are called to adventure, encounter exhilarating fortune, initiation, and serious obstacles, and are assisted by helper figures across the various thresholds of their encounter with trials and destiny. There is *nostos*, or return, and the two storylines converge. Life re-emerges and light returns.

Houses of the Holy is "Led Zeppelin V." The production brings a new sound as the album opens with "The Crunge" and "D'Yer Mak'er." The song "Over the Hills and Far Away" mentions the open road and of course Plant, Page, Jones, and Bonham are traveling widely at that time. The title also recalls the perspective in *The Lord of the Rings* of people gazing outward to that place they imagine that is far away. "The Rain Song" never answers who might be those who tender the fire or who may be the keepers of gloom. In "No Quarter" we hear that the winds of Thor have come with some news beckoning the speaker to venture forth. The forest has "no quarter" for anyone who trudges across snow in this unforgiving place where the devil is mocking the traveler and dogs of doom howl at him.[8]

On *Presence*, Robert Plant sings a story of Achilles, a prominent character of *The Iliad*. However, the Iliad does not focus on Achilles' final stand or his death. There is no heroic Achilles finale. The epic begins with the wrath of Achilles: with his standoffish refusal to participate in the wars because King Agamemnon has kept a woman Breisius from him. He considers this woman rightfully his as among the spoils of war. While Achilles is indeed a great warrior there is little that is heroic about him if one applies the values of the 5th century to him. He is proud. He is selfish. He gloats to see his comrades die. He rejects all offers of the generals and wise men (Nestor and Odysseus among them) that are sent to him to coax him to fight in the war against the Trojans. He does not possess the arête of the Trojan prince Hector, who has the courage and willingness to fight for his people and his city. Achilles is nearly invulnerable because his mother once dipped him into a pool that would make him so. Unfortunately, she had to hold him by his ankle as she dipped him down into that pond that made him invincible. Thus, he had that weakness we call the Achilles heel. In Book 7 Hector reflects on what the people of the future will say of the heroes of the Trojan War. He arrives at the idea of a future of permanent glory. (We see this idea repeated in medieval King Henry V's grand speech at Agincourt.) Achilles, on the other hand, only comes to battle after Patroclus, wearing his armor, is killed and his armor is stripped off the body and taken away by the Trojans. When he finally meets Hector outside the walls of Troy he is merciless.

Plant takes his lyric in a different direction. Achilles becomes Albion, the hero of William Blake's poetry, as in "Milton," "The Four Zoas," or "The Dance of Albion." He has become a British mythic figure. The lyric becomes vague, referring to summer and a child and to the figure of Atlas who holds the world, or the universe. Plant himself as narrative storyteller

1. Led Zeppelin

seems to embody the myth and the heroic pose. The mythical journey to Troy seems like a metaphor for Led Zeppelin's own tour.

Traveling on tour, Led Zeppelin entered the storied history of the minstrel, the wandering troubadour who was associated in legends with the devil. We see this image in the painter Hieronymous Bosch's visions of Hell where minstrels play on instruments that look like torture devices. The medieval minstrel seldom knew the kind of esoteric literature that Jimmy Page absorbed. "The minstrel lacked real knowledge. He did not understand the speculative aspects of *musica*, its theological context, or the rational and theoretical principles of order that lay at its roots" (Hammerstein, 266). So this minstrel, untrained in theory, was considered more earthy, more irrational animal, and was related to numerous depictions in art of devils, or pre-Christian music-making animals. It is in these figures that we see "the inverted, demonic-diabolical minstrel aspect of the Christian order in general and of music in particular" (266). The lusty Sirens also are portrayed in this art. In Led Zeppelin's music the dancing days are here again: the dance music that was once called diabolical.

The Led Zeppelin travelers covered Robert Johnson's "Traveling Riverside Blues." They covered Howlin' Wolf and other blues players: those wandering singer-songwriters of the Delta. "You Shook Me" and "I Can't Quit You Baby" were Chicago blues standards. Robert Plant, who clearly has wide musical tastes, liked the West Coast troubadours of 1970 Joni Mitchell and Crosby, Stills, Nash, and Young. He was well-anchored in blues metaphors and the work of modern minstrels. Plant and Page were young troubadours, fueled by amplified blues and rock, by drugs and esoteric myth. Page told Led Zeppelin biographer Stephen Davis: "Magic is a system of will and strength. I can't produce material magic, real magic, so what we offer is the illusion of magic" (161).

Occultism and Hermeticism

Aleister Crowley identified as a magician and founded Thelema, a religious cult. For many years he was part of the Order of the Golden Dawn, which emerged from a Freemasonry secret society, including interests in the occult and in Egyptian myth. Before long, Crowley then developed his A.A.: Arentinum Astrum. He was also a member of Ordo Templi, the English branch of a German based esoteric group. He may have indeed been a Satanist and he certainly was a libertine, experimenting with sex, with drugs, and with occultism.

The Irish poet William Butler Yeats, arriving in London in 1887, also participated in the hermetic order of the Golden Dawn and knew Crowley. He studied the occult and the paranormal and wrote *A Vision*, in which he expressed a system of spirituality, an interest in contact with spirits, and his curiosity about ghosts, telepathy and automatic writing. Freemasons and Rosicrucian members William Robert Woodman, William Wynn Wescott, and Samuel Liddell MacGregor Mathers were founders of the Golden Dawn. Their founding documents were known as the Cipher Manuscripts and they were involved with spiritualism, astrology, tarot, alchemy, and Kabbalah. In 1888 the Urania Temple was founded in London and the group began to include women. Mathers and Crowley soon were at odds with other members and took a different direction. Yeats left the Golden Dawn in 1901. Crowley formed Arentinum Astrum in 1905. He asserted that "do what thou wilt" would align one with the will of the universe.

Yeats was a poet whose work was partly based in the Irish revival of myths and legends and the renaissance of the Irish theater. He was interested in the poetry and Rosicrucian themes of Edmund Spenser, with his Red Cross Knight in *The Faerie Queene* (1590). He was intrigued by Percy Bysshe Shelley's romanticism and rebellion. Like Page and Plant, he was interested in the nineteenth century painters known as the Pre-Raphaelites. His verse and vision was inspired by Hinduism and by the thought of Emanuel Swedenborg. In 1911, he joined The Ghost Club.

Hermeticism is concerned with humanity's relation to the cosmos. The human individual is a microcosm of the macrocosm of the universe. This hermetic approach to life can focus on alchemy, or on something more than the transmutation of metals: the shaping of the soul. Giordano Bruno was burned at the stake for such views. Pico della Mirandola viewed man as magus and saw Renaissance magic as a key to understanding. Henry Cornelius Agrippa wrote of magic and the cabbalists, suggesting that there was a lower world of the human and a celestial world that included music, mythologies, and numerology. The mysterious John Dee, a secret agent for Queen Elizabeth and an earlier inquirer in celestial "mechanics," was intrigued by astrology and cabbalist numerology. Sir Edmund Spenser wrote his greatest poem with a background of Rosicrucian thought.

1. Led Zeppelin

Perhaps most mysterious of all was one they looked to: Hermes Trismegistus, an alchemist who was thought to have been an Egyptian priest. The early modern hermetical tradition, as a search for understanding, has sometimes been seen as a prelude to modern science.

Led Zeppelin in Popular Culture Criticism

In his introduction to *Led Zeppelin and Philosophy* (2009) Scott Calef reflects on the album *Presence* and on alchemy. In a footnote he explores whether the swan song figure on the cover art for *Presence* is Apollo, god of music and poetry. The figure might be the mythical Icarus who flew too close to sun. Or it might be Lucifer. John Stone-Mediatore addresses the sublime in the first chapter (1–16). He notes that the words astonishment, obscurity, privation, vastness, magnitude, darkness, gloom, confusion, violence, overpowering light and loudness all appear in the classic statement on the sublime by the conservative thinker Edmund Burke. All of these words—suggesting the shock that takes us out of ourselves—can describe heavy metal.

What critic Louis Menand has called "advanced pop criticism" (*The New Yorker*, July 31, 2017) has frequently trained its sights on Led Zeppelin:

- Robert Walser provides one of the finest discussions of Led Zeppelin's "Stairway to Heaven" in his book *Running with the Devil: Power, Gender, and Madness in Heavy Metal Music* (Wesleyan University Press, 1993, 158–59.) The creative "magic" of musical performance by Led Zeppelin is discussed by Randall E. Auxier when he writes of "history and re-enactment" in their blues tributes. "The magic happens when a musician is playing" and is in the zone and is able to "get out of the way" (118).
- Scott Calef discusses Led Zeppelin's use of symbols in *Led Zeppelin and Philosophy*. He was bothered by their cover photo of a suburban family gathering around a kitchen table until he explored the possible meanings of the black obelisk at the center of the table. One interpretation is that this oddly placed figure is a hole, or nothingness, at the center of modern life. Perhaps it is a black hole in space (136–37).

Myth and Magic in Heavy Metal Music

- Theodore Gracyk writes that "Plant verbalizes his Viking and Lord of the Rings fantasies over Page's riffs."[9] Astrological interests also connect with Led Zeppelin's music, Chris Welch notes in an interview with Jimmy Page (Welch in Wall, 263). Page has a sense of talismanic magic, observes Theodore Schick (97). With embroidery on his stage clothing at that time, Page was a public figure, not a reclusive one.

In one of the more thorough accounts of Led Zeppelin, Susan Fast notes that what fans seem to be saying is that Led Zeppelin's lyrics, imagery, discourse and music may suggest "the sacred" (53). Fast then cites Paul Ricouer's view that the sacred and myth are linked. The "symbolic function of myth is its power of discovering and revealing the bond between man and what he considers sacred" (53).[10] "Definitions of myth and epic are highly contested among scholars of this genre," Fast observes. Of course it can be said that "myth" and "epic" are not readily distinguished by most rock fans. "Epic," for most, tends to mean how long or how "big" the song is. Fast has pointed out that the Led Zeppelin audience felt a sense of unity and a "feeling of connectedness." She points to Victor Turner's reflections in *From Ritual to Theatre* on ritual and performing myth and "symbolic enactment" (54). Fast cites Christopher Williams's assertion that this is transformative experience for fans and is ritualistic (56). That ritual enactment and sense of community is central to the life of heavy metal.

When we look into Led Zeppelin, observes Randall Auxier, we begin to learn "why myth is so pervasive in human history and in our present experience" (115). Auxier rejects the cynical notion that Led Zeppelin conjured up myth and magic to attract an audience and sell more records. Rather, they were creative and curious about magic and myth. We see in Plant and Page "parallel quests for their roots" (115). The rationalist view regards magic as superstitious, a matter of quaint belief in an "ill informed past." However, an historical approach will tell us otherwise. The alchemical quest preceded modern science and is a metaphor for the search for an understanding of humanity's place in the cosmos. It is the recognition of creative processes at work in us and in this world and a metaphor for discovery in science and in art.

The other point Auxier effectively makes is that there is "magic" in music. (Or, as Auxier puts it, for any music listener: "what makes you head

1. Led Zeppelin

hum and why?" Where do you find the magic?) Musicianship is learned and technique is practiced. However, there may be an aha moment when the musician enters the music and it takes off. Page and Plant knew of this spontaneous breakthrough moment, this peak experience of "being there" in the music. A musician has to practice and prepare to be ready. Likewise, a listener to music is prepared through previous listening. Then, as Plant sings in "Stairway to Heaven," if one calls the tune, the piper of inspiration might lead the listener and the music maker to join him and make that something happen.

The fascination of Led Zeppelin with myth and occultism coincided with the late sixties hippie era in which quests like those of Hermann Hesse's *Siddhartha* and Tolkien's *The Lord of the Rings* became part of popular reading. By the time that the film version of the *Lord of the Rings* trilogy appeared in 2001 and 2003, Led Zeppelin themselves were legendary. Cutting edge computer technology brings alive film and television extravaganzas that are fully anchored in age-old archetypes: the *Lord of the Rings* trilogy, the Harry Potter films, Marvel comics films, and *Game of Thrones* are among these. Their appeal lies not only in dramatic effects but in the deep springs of storytelling: the stories of strong or frail honorable humans thrown into mythic landscapes to face evil, deformed human monsters and undead white-walkers, the bringers of darkness, destruction and death. They are men and women defended by magic or by dragons, who are also forced to rely on their own resources of courage. They face the power of Sauron, blazing atop his tower: the narrow-minded one-dimensional curse of the world. In *The Lord of the Rings*, Frodo achieves his quest and Aragorn returns to throw out the imposters and regain his kingdom. Heavy metal reflects all of these figures: humanity's battle with modernity, the fall of the World Trade Center and the war with Iraq, the vanquishing of Osama bin Laden, the shadows that are projected by Trump and by a pudgy North Korean as they voice tough rhetoric and play with the risk of nuclear calamity.

"Kashmir" plays. The music recalls an exotic culture, an ancient landscape. Kashmir is today a place in India toward which China has carved out a threatening path. Led Zeppelin's music takes us away from that political reality for a while. It suggests energy, a genie in a bottle, a magic carpet, a means of musical transcendence. The distinctive vocal of Robert Plant floats on high. The rhythm section of John Paul Jones and John Bonham stays steady with the layered guitars of Jimmy Page. The past arises and

Myth and Magic in Heavy Metal Music

Plant's vocal streams out into the air from a car that drives down suburban streets out onto the interstate highway. That edgy, wailing voice calls to the evening sun. The mythical is sustained like a suspended chord and Led Zeppelin endures in the minds of new generations. Amid a world of difference and change the song remains the same.

2

Black Sabbath
Dark Symbolism

Black Sabbath was dark, in name and in symbolism. With heaviness and tri-tones and references to the devil they are recognized as precursors of the heavy metal sound. Shadowy, visceral, and loud, wearing black and wearing crosses, they could appear almost demonic. The sound of the band, with their use of modes rather than blues chords, the heavy bass pulse, the assemblage of chord structures, set out musical characteristics that would later identify the heavy metal sound. Some critics, like Andrew Cope, are intent upon distinguishing the proto-heavy metal sound of Black Sabbath from the blues of Led Zeppelin and regard the musical syntax of Black Sabbath, rather than that of Led Zeppelin, as the foundation of all things heavy.[1] Whereas Led Zeppelin's rock was blues-oriented, eclectic, and sometimes dreamy, Black Sabbath more clearly established the musical codes for heavy metal bands that followed. Thematically, they were dark, morbid, and somewhat scary. They emerged from the industrial Midlands with the weight of the world on their shoulders and a burdened edge to their music. Black Sabbath titled their albums *Paranoid, Masters of Reality, Sabotage, Heaven and Hell*, and *Sabbath Bloody Sabbath*. There was chaos and dread in that sensibility.

In 1968, founding members of Black Sabbath Tony Iommi and Bill Ward had a band called Mythology. They performed in Halifax, Chester, and Manchester. Butler listened to The Who, The Beatles, and Cream and Jack Bruce to develop his bass playing. Mythology dissolved after a police raid backstage busted them for pot. Vocalist Ozzy Osborne joined them when his band Rare Breed dissolved and they re-named themselves Earth. They then became Black Sabbath. The Black Sabbath sound was created collectively. Part of the sound emerged from Tony Iommi, their guitarist, and bassist Geezer Butler. They emphasized the bass or bottom of their songs. Iommi, with two of his fingers shaved shorter by an industrial accident, tuned down his guitar a half step from the low E that is usually where guitarists have their top string to E flat. He was joined in this tuning down by Geezer Butler. They then began to tune down a minor third to D flat. Boosting treble and distortion, Black Sabbath developed their heavy, power chord driven sound. Tuning down made the music darker and made it sound heavier. The songwriting stayed in that murky down-tuned zone, with dark and compelling imaginative lyrics.

Black Sabbath set out to be unique and disturbing. Their sound emerged along with their dark underworld mythology and suggestions of chaos and madness. *Paranoid* (1970) and *Black Sabbath* (1970) were recorded in standard 440 tuning. *Black Sabbath* was recorded October 1969. During the recording, left-handed Iommi changed from a Fender Stratocaster to a Gibson SG, which he played upside down. The album provided the first expressions of paganism, the occult, and H.P. Lovecraft-like horror. The first song begins on a tritone interval played on guitar by Iommi. This is three adjacent whole tones. Harmonically, this is often considered unstable.

Geezer (Terry) Butler wrote the lyrics. These were often a satirical critique of humanity. For some listeners, the band's references to the devil stood out. However, it was in the music, built modally on intervals, that the band's sound distinguished itself. Musically, the guitar riffs of Tony Iommi led the way. Bill Ward was the percussionist who loved jazz as well as rock and he set out a strong, definitive rhythm that itself was an unmistakable hook for several songs.

Black Sabbath appeared with two albums in 1970: the self-titled *Black Sabbath* and *Paranoid*. They wasted no time in introducing a figure in black in their opening tune. The singer says that he has been chosen by this figure with eyes of fire. Immediately, the listener recognizes this as a reference to Satan. Amid the foreboding sound there is fear and angst. He is coming. The record opens with a funeral bell and weighty chords. The music is heavy slow rock, with G5 and C#5 chords grounding the tune. The tempo picks up with the G minor chord and triplets. The bridge rides on that G minor chord as the vocal jumps one octave G to G, then descends to C-B flat in a key signature of E flat. Satan is coming around the bend and Sabbath's nightmare has begun.

The second song brings a contrasting mystical figure: the wizard.

2. Black Sabbath

From misty clouds he comes: the wizard with his spells. He spreads hope and power that can cause demons to disappear and run away when he comes. Fears turn to joy. Black Sabbath holds these two images in tandem: the figure of evil in the modern world and the figure of magic and hope, the music that casts a spell and unites. In Black Sabbath's song the wizard is an ambiguous figure: mysterious and hopeful, an enchanter who is both sage and trickster. In touch with the supernatural, the magician is a keeper of gnosis, or a secret knowledge. He is a wanderer who is just now arriving. Potentially transformative, he casts a spell like the band does on its audience. The wizard is potentially a hero whose appearance suggests that he will change something.

According to mythical lore, the wizard uses supernatural methods to achieve concrete goals. Distinctions have been made between black magic and white magic, even if there are no distinct boundaries between them. (Ozzy raises the specter of the modern magus Aleister Crowley on his first solo album in his song "Mr. Crowley.) *Pharmakon*, or drugs, is related to this magic and shares in this ambiguity: the drug may be poison or medicine. A goal of white magic is protection against mishap, or a search for healing, sometimes using amulets. This magic is a metaphor for the proto-metal music of Black Sabbath: a performance focused in secret sources of power. Strangeness, spells, uncanny phrases, and repetition are characteristics of the magical practice. The music is intended to have power and force. The heavy metal performance is quasi-liturgical: a communal celebration, a magical dynamic and achievement of power, what Mircea Eliade has called a hierophany.

Cloaked in ambiguity, the members of Black Sabbath are heroes/villains. The hero is "a myth with a human face," the author of *Les Miserables*, Victor Hugo, once said. The members of Black Sabbath make themselves mythical. They are like the metal workers of Greek myth (or modern Birmingham) who knew magic. They are Orpheus as a magician, or the witch Circe who casts spells and tricks Odysseus. They are sorcerers: a word that has dark connotations.

"Behind the Wall of Sleep" may refer to the drug that lifts the spirit and the drug that clouds it. With reference to a poison or potion, a chill comes that is turning your body to death and sleep. Yet, despite the imagery of death there comes a resurrection of light from the sun and an awakening. We stretch out across a landscape of sun, stars and moon on "N.I.B." and in that landscape of the universe a figure beckons. He has an alluring power. The voice of Satan entices, urges the listener to look into his eyes and to join with him hand in hand. He announces that his name is Lucifer. Presumably, the listener is enthralled by now—or a bit freaked out, as some were, by the repeated devil references.

The evil image next is one of a woman—call it misogynist if you will. This is one wicked femme fatale, with evil in her eyes. Ozzy's vocal declares that this witchy woman plays games with him. The evil woman is an ancient archetype that extends into popular music in songs like those of Santana, ELO, and The Eagles. In ancient Greek theater, Euripedes' Medea becomes the evil woman: witchlike, conjuring a plan to kill her children to punish her unfaithful husband Jason. Cursing him to damnation, she is both victim and manipulator, demon and tormented avenger. The evil woman that Ozzy Osborne sings about has been a bad experience he seems unable to shake and get rid of. Ronnie James Dio picks up the theme again in a later Black Sabbath song on the *Heaven and Hell* album (1980). In Dio's "Lady Evil" he sings of a temptress who kills. This is set in a witches' valley. Rain turns to blood. When the thunder comes it causes the sky to bleed. There is a fantasy darkness like in Samuel Taylor Coleridge's poem "Cristabel." Dio's character is an evil muse.

It's a wicked world we live in today, the next song lyric begins. It is a world of conflict and it is worse overseas. Politicians are criticized in the second verse for having the ability to send a man to the moon while they do nothing to care for people with disease here on earth, or for the lonely child who has been abandoned. Black Sabbath's politics is at last given voice and it will rear its angry claims in "War Pigs."

Protest rose from this band's roots. Black Sabbath emerged from a place in which a Birmingham factory future held little promise. Heavy metal related to adolescents with no future jobs who felt alienated and sought community. Black Sabbath connected with their blue collar community. Black Sabbath, like a horror film unfolding, stood in opposition to the "greening of America" dreams and consciousness of the sixties youth movement. They represented Altamont more than Woodstock. They made overt the anxieties of society in 1970. They set a foundation for heavy metal with symbolic rebellion. Black Sabbath was a response to the collapse of that 1960s youth culture and "the cultural marginalization of the working class," as Deena Weinstein has observed (114).

There was the derogation of Black Sabbath by rock critics in 1970,

2. Black Sabbath

just as there has been dismissal of myth by rationalists. Robert Cristgau is representative, calling Black Sabbath "a dim-witted, a-moral exploitation." The *Rolling Stone Album Guide* called Black Sabbath: "Stoned out, dumb, clumsy, soulless, overamplified, and ugly" (Kot, www.bbc.com). Critics viewed heavy metal negatively and "metal's appropriations were interpreted ... as retrograde" (Weinstein, 110). However, for dark romanticism myth was a mode of power and seeking truth. Black Sabbath, like the Grimm Brothers, seized upon the inversion of stories into fear, anxiety, deviltry and darkness. They were involved with a use of dark Gothic myth as an attack on mechanism, industrialism, and the mind forged manacles of a rationalized society. Their response was to be blue collar masculine with tattoos and leather and black. They would not engage in glam play with gender. Rather, they would assert aggressive maleness and embrace the primitive in the world. There were those damned 5th chords and distortion instead of clean major chords. Lester Bangs referred to Black Sabbath as "the John Milton of rock 'n' roll" (*Main Lines,* 78) Milton in his epic poem *Paradise Lost* developed a dramatic Satan character, appreciated by Romantics like Percy Bysshe Shelley for his vigorous rebellion. Black Sabbath may be likened to Milton's rebel. Milton's term "darkness visible" suggests a paradox that is an attempt to describe the infernal *and* the ineffable: "Dark with excessive bright thy skirts appear" (*Paradise Lost*).

Black Sabbath highlighted the bad boy image in rock music that extends back to Elvis and was underscored in The Rolling Stones. The outlaw theme connected with biker gear in Judas Priest. That biker image—denim jeans, leather jackets and studs, tattoos and iconography—became part of proto-heavy metal. Blue Cheer's manager was a Hell's Angel member. Steppenwolf's "Born to Be Wild," including the words "heavy metal" in the lyric, was released in 1968 and gained more attention on the soundtrack of film *Easy Rider* the next year. One might look at this play of fantasy through the lens of romantic irony. Cervantes' Don Quixote is a figure who dreams of heroism. We may understand him through irony and wit, as did the German critic Friedrich Schlegel in his review of Ludwig Tieck's translation of *Don Quixote* (1799). Likewise, we may listen to Geezer Butler's lyrics and Ozzy Osborne's vocals as ironic expression.

The narrator of the title cut, "Paranoid," sounds more depressed and alienated than genuinely paranoid but he does speak of his worry about the state of his mind. He senses that no one can help him—certainly not the woman he addresses with his plea. She cannot help what is going on in his shattered mind, where he feels no satisfaction, no peace. He asks the listener to help him to find the things that he can't find: that elusive happiness, or whatever else it is that he seeks.

"Electric Funeral" and "Hand of Doom" glare at a broken modern world: its artificiality and its wars. "Electric Funeral" portrays a fearful day on which the atomic bomb will explode. At the start, there is a theme of transformation: a storm and death are coming. The robot minds live among flowers that are plastic and unnatural and they lie behind the problem. (These mechanical, detached men would be in the poet Blake's terms bound by "mind forged manacles.") There will be radiation, buildings falling, evil souls lined up and going to hell. "Hand of Doom" trains its focus on the Vietnam War draftee sent into combat. In a world of disillusion the needle brings drug escape. The images of death linger.

"Planet Caravan" is poetic. The imagery of a universe unfolding and the moon in the trees is accompanied by Mars, the god of war, arising. Yet, the song does not burst into conflict. Mars does not overwhelm. The song is a reprieve from intensity. That intensity awaits in the song "Iron Man."

With "Iron Man" Black Sabbath mythologize themselves. They are the alienated working class kids, the men who work with steel in Birmingham who are fed up with the smoke and the machine. The iron man becomes a mythological monster figure who will vent his rage. He is a Frankenstein who has awakened and arises from numbing industrial slumber. The Iron Man wears leaden boots and has turned to steel. The steel suggests coldness or hard-heartedness as well as an armored invulnerability. The archetypal psychologist James Hillman addresses the evil in "coldness" with stories about Hitler's rhetoric: praising the coldness of his General Rommel and speaking of coldness as he faced his final doom in a bunker as Allied forces entered Berlin. The Iron Man refuses to be defeated by his environment. He will travel across time—like a mythical figure. Alienated, like the contemporary terrorist, he is determined to create havoc and cause dread.

An apocalyptic future war is imagined on "War Pigs" which denounces the powers that be that propagate war for their own purposes. The song announces the power E chord. A siren sounds about thirty seconds into the song. Black Sabbath produces a bleak, desperate, and dark art that

2. Black Sabbath

argues against the darkness in humanity. They contest "robot minds." In singing about darkness and evil, fantasy intersects with this critique. Robert Walser observes: "Osborne plays with signs of the supernatural mystery because they evoke a power and mystery that is highly attractive to many fans" (*Running with the Devil*, 148).

Ozzy Osborne was a satyr figure, a doomsday reflection of one the mythical creatures which one classical scholar describes as "unrestrained in their desires for sex and wine" (639). Were not his eyes—the windows of the soul—at times like glazed semaphores from a stoned abyss? Ozzy became mythical: a name painted on a water tower in Alabama by a fan; the scrawl on a wall in a Passaic, New Jersey, park that read "Ozzy Is God."[2] The classics critic writes that one sees "the satyrs as grotesque hedonists and yet the immortal companion of a god, cruder than humans and yet somehow wiser, combining mischief with wisdom, lewdness with skill in music, animality with divinity" (Seaford, *Oxford Classical*, 639).

In 1978 working with Ozzy Osborne had become impossible for the members of Black Sabbath. In the 1980s Ronnie James Dio toured and recorded as the vocalist with the band. The band then split over tensions between the ego-driven Dio and strong-willed Tony Iommi. There was a reunion of Black Sabbath with Dio in 1992, including the *Dehumanizer* album. By then Ozzy Osborne had recorded a half-dozen albums as a solo artist, for a time supported by the guitar work of Randy Rhoads. Beginning with *Blizzard of Ozz* (1980), he followed with the best-selling *Diary of a Madman* (1981) and *Bark at the Moon* (1983). On the red cover of *Ultimate Sin* (1986) we see Ozzy as a monster-demon from hell caricature: the comic-trickster character. In 1999, Black Sabbath reunited for a tour and the *Reunion* album with Ozzy Osborne. Some critics argued that there was nothing new in Iommi's guitar playing or in Ozzy's vocal but Black Sabbath had indeed arisen, however zombielike, and unlike in their earlier career they were, for a time, wildly popular. Ozzy had become an icon long before he emerged as a slightly daft figure on a reality television show.[3]

Black Sabbath's criticism of the contemporary world rests upon a mythology of darkness. Some would call that evil a reality in our world. They rejected the peace and love platitudes that flow from fine musicians like Ringo Starr like well wishes on a Hallmark card. Black Sabbath's fantasy has a mythological— and perhaps a theological and cultural—basis. Their music is nasty. Their images are archetypal.

Myth and Magic in Heavy Metal Music

Gothic Art of the Disturbed

Art can be disturbing. The writhing, twisted figures of Picasso's *Guernica* break in cubist fragments on his canvas: reminders of the agony of war. The dark folk tales collected by the Brothers Grimm lead us into an imaginative fairy-tale woods of horrors. Black Sabbath is scary, heavy, and their nightmare songs likewise wrestle with a broken world. There is a curious ambivalence in the Black Sabbath lyrics of Geezer Butler. They tell of hell but wonder about heaven. This is not merely a dualism, a Manichean vision of good/evil. The songs seem to say that this world is an intersection of the two: a place where one can, in Sabbath's very first song, meet that dark figure. The protest we hear in songs like "War Pigs," in which "people of the lie" engineer the fate of many, is directly connected with the evil that Black Sabbath sees in the world. Like heavy metal bands that would follow them, Black Sabbath defiantly declares their position: "I am not your facts. I will not let what is strange in me, about me, my mystery, be put in a world of fact" (Hillman, *The Essential*, 180–81).

Black Sabbath was constructing a mythical discourse, a rhetoric that would serve heavy metal in the future. They were engaged in a "bridge burning act" that shifted perception and reconstituted identity in their audience. There was a kind of "frame alignment" in which the public could work out meanings. They were not only producing shock value for sales, although there must have been some of that. They were expressing a Bakhtinian carnival in which irony, humor, masquerade, symbol and story upend the order of things. They were branding themselves as bad boys, denizens of hell, but also addressing social problems. They were spitting into the void, pointing to the heart of darkness, to non-being and gaps in society's soul.

Upon listening to Black Sabbath's first albums, rock critic Lester Bangs wrote that they had created "a musical structure that's both personal and universal." Black Sabbath was louder than Led Zeppelin and gave their listeners "a dark vision of society and human soul borrowed from black magic and Christian myth" (223). Black Sabbath addressed the darker side of humanity, the Jungian shadow, and they faced a world of oppression. Their lyrics are ambivalent: seeking hope against an evil world, recognizing that evil is not only a problem but a part of life. Masters of reality wrestle for hope in that world. In "The Children of the Grave" people are involved in revolution. They resist nuclear annihilation. "Symptom of the

2. Black Sabbath

Universe" seeks a love that will not be overcome. "Spiral Architect" from *Sabbath Bloody Sabbath* echoes like the sound of a prayer. Satan is a presence that winds through the songs in an allegory of society.

Black Sabbath's presentation of worldly evil, of heaven and hell, is not only a good/evil binary but a contestation, a deconstruction.[4] Heaven and hell are joined together, not merely in a Manichean opposition but more like an intersection, an interweaving, acknowledging the ambivalence of good/evil in this world. Their social critique is intimately connected with this perception of evil-darkness: with war, nuclear holocaust, and distortion. Social criticism and horror are connected. In Black Sabbath the heavy and the dark are not just tricks or publicity stunts. They are, at least initially, a world view, a criticism, and a transgressive challenge to conventional social order. They are a challenge to "the people of the lie," including the "war pigs" who conduct business as usual from behind their masks of respectability.

One enters the shadow, like the writer Nathaniel Hawthorne's characters in the age of the Salem witch trials. Young Goodman Brown enters the woods to face not only the devil but to face himself, the internal shadow, and to encounter the poseurs of society: Goody Cloyse and the upright reverend who belong to a witches' coven in the woods. In Hawthorne's "The Minister's Black Veil" the minister appears one day on the altar wearing a dark veil across his face. The people wonder what his sin must be. They neglect to see that the mysterious minister is calling them out to face their own darkness. Likewise, Black Sabbath, donning their black, points to the hellish.

Blatant and fearsome, Black Sabbath did not gain popular top forty radio airplay. They cultivated a loyal following—one that set forth the possibilities of heavy metal. Rock could be a quasi-religion, an identifier, a community. Black Sabbath dedicated itself to being heavy. Tony Iommi, in his autobiography, recalls that the members of Black Sabbath knew the members of Led Zeppelin. Bonham and Plant were from the Birmingham area. Bonham played fiercely and could be heavy. Black Sabbath would be heavier, Bill Ward asserted to Tony Iommi (Iommi, Chapter 19). Led Zeppelin visited them when they recorded *Sabbath Bloody Sabbath* and the bands jammed. It was the only time they played together.

In his foreword to *The Complete History of Black Sabbath: What Evil Lurks*, Robb Flynn of Machine Head recalls how a Black Sabbath lyric affected him when he was introduced to the band's music by a teenage friend. It was "depressing and dark." Then his friend played "Iron Man" and he was horrified and hooked. "Evil, sinister, otherworldly and impossibly heavy," he calls his first encounters with Black Sabbath (x). Black Sabbath scared him but the protest part of the band interested him the most. That protest is indissolubly linked with their haunted world-view.

Some forty years after the band bid farewell to Ozzy Osborne—and more than eight vocalists later—Black Sabbath produced their studio album *Black Sabbath 13* and followed it with a tour. "End of the Beginning" speaks of rewinding the future to the past and of releasing your mind. It insists that to find solutions there has to be a way to recast the system. Myth is a way of doing this. The song plunges along in the characteristic major 5ths that Tony Iommi has used in the past: F#5, C#5, D5, G5 chords repeat. "God Is Dead?" asks that question. The singer says that he is fading from the light of faith and he cries out that he needs assistance to make it through the darkness of the night. There is blood and murder and gloom and death on his mind and there are the questions of a searching soul: Is God alive or dead in our world? It is the same question that Black Sabbath asked decades ago when a black figure with fiery eyes approached on that first arresting song they called "Black Sabbath."

Images of the Demonic

In medieval literature the notion of demonic music is characterized by dissonance and cacophony. In legends and morality plays there is the idea of pandemonium as a realm of shrieks and groans, intense volume, thunder and shrill, blasphemous laughter. In Dante's *Inferno*, sound is discordant, in contrast with the harmonious music of *Paradiso*. In John Milton's *Paradise Lost*, written in the mid–1600s, Milton draws upon notions of the fallen angels and their pandemonium. In Hieronymous Bosch's paintings musical instruments resemble torture devices and symbols of torment.[5] In the modern period the idea of music as having a demonic aspect was regarded as a metaphor, rather than as part of a spiritual reality. All of these aspects are embodied in heavy metal's mythical turn toward darkness and the unknown.

The term "demon" in English refers to evil spirits and to more neutral ones (*daimons*). The Hebrew testament does not have terms that can be easily translated specifically as "demon." There is the influence of other

2. Black Sabbath

cultures—a wider context in which demons are referred to and discussed. However, there is a general view that demons are "evil spirits": *sedim* (demons) and *seirim* (satyrs). This is related to the idea of the worship of false gods (Deuteronomy 32:17, Psalms 106:37 [*sedim*], Leviticus 17:7, 2 Chronicles 11:15 [*seirim*], Isaiah 13:21, 34:14 [*seirim* after the judgment]). In the Old Testament, Lilith is mentioned in Isaiah 34:14 and associated with animals that are unclean. Rabbinic literature will suggest that Lilith is a succubus, a rebellious demon who steals children. Another demon is Azazel, mentioned in Leviticus 16: a goat, a place in the wilderness.

Destruction is found in pestilence and plague, in fire, in the terrible night (Psalm 91:5). There are beings connected with the Underworld: *mawet* (or death in Isaiah 28:15, Jeremiah 9:20, Job 18:13 and 28:22). A thing of Belial [*debar beliyaal*] Psalms 41:9 and *melek ballahot* or King of Terrors appears in Job 18:14. There is no clear connection in the Hebrew scripture between Satan and these demons mentioned here.

In the Christian testament the presence of demons is fairly clear. However, the broader context includes that Greek myth recognized the spirits of the dead and Egyptian myth and magical practice used incantations to ward off the evil spirits. Zoroastrians included Manichean views of a dualism of the spirit world and the dark Ahiriman warring against the light of Ahura Mazda. Jewish literature in the intertestamental period reflected on the demons. This contributed to the New Testament view of harmful spirits surrounding the human. The *daevas*, powers of evil, are called by the same name among the Persians as the gods of the Vedas. In Sanskrit (*deva*), in Persian (*div*), in Latin (*divus*). In Iranian regions Angra-Mainyu-Ahrman was prince of demons. The diabolical *daevas* were inclined toward trickery and falsehood and worked against efforts toward the good.

Demons are mentioned often in the New Testament. The word *daimon* appears in Matthew 8:31, Mark 5:12, Luke 8:29 and in Revelation 16:14 and 18:2. More common is the word *daimonion*, which appears sixty times in the synoptic gospels (Matthew, Mark, Luke). (Reese II: 140) Jesus casts out demons. We also see the phrase *penuma akartharton* in the Gospels of Mark and Luke. Demons promote tendencies to self-destruction (Matthew 17:15), cause blindness (Matthew 12:22), cause insanity Mark 5:1–5, Matthew 8:28) or cause convulsions (Luke 9:39).

In *The Exorcist* by William Peter Blatty there was a case of demonic possession. The protagonist Father Karras was a psychologist. Several modern explanations of presumed demonic possession follow the view that this represents a psychological problem. The diagnosis in these cases is that this is a matter of psychosis.[6] The demythologizing Rudolph Bultmann concluded that the appearance of demonic possession was a manifestation of an individual's existential crisis. It was an expression of an individual's deep desire to transcend evil in the world (Reese, 142). There are, however, those who believe in a spiritual realm in which demons actually exist and claim that this is not in contradiction with modern science. Exorcism breaks the power of the demon and possession by the forces of wickedness.[7]

The kingdom of God faces off against that of Satan (Matthew 10:8), or Beelzebub, and always overcomes Satan. The devil is a fallen angel who promotes evil, temptation, sickness. The Devil is a supernatural adversary of God and the good. He is described as a slanderer and a betrayer. He is spoken of as *diabolos* (Revelation 12:9). He is Beelzebub and Belial (2 Corinthians 6:15), the dragon in *Revelation* (Revelation 12:9, 20:2). The devil is a murderer and a liar (John 8:44, Revelation 12:9). He comes disguised (2 Corinthians 11:14) and oppresses all (Acts 10:38). The devil is the "prince of demons" (Matthew 12:24). He is the enemy (Matthew 13:39, Luke 10:19) and ruler of this world (Luke 4:6, John 12:31, 14:30), the bringer of sin into this world (2 Corinthians 11:3), the betrayer (John 13:2, 27; Luke 22:3). In this view, if one is "running with the devil" one is flirting with disaster.

The devil dwells with demons. Exorcism breaks the power of the demon and possession by the forces of wickedness. In Jesus' ministry he cast out demons (Matthew 12:25–29, Mark 3:23–27, Luke 11: 17–22). Some critics believe that the Manichean views in Zoroastrianism contributed to the notion of a cosmic conflict between good and evil. In the Bible, the kingdom of God faced off against that of Satan, or Beelzebub, and always overcame Satan (Matthew 12:26–27). Revelation 20:1–5 contends that the Great War between heaven and Satan will end with the fall of Babylon, Satan's city. From heaven an angel will descend and imprison Satan, the dragon, for one thousand years: the millennium. Then Satan will return, prompting Armageddon, and he will be vanquished to a lake of fire and the judgment day will come.

In heavy metal music the devil is "not simply conjured to be worshipped," Robert Walser points out (151). Satan often stands as a symbol for mystery, sublime awe, terror, or powers of the unknown. Rock critics,

2. Black Sabbath

sociologists, and other observers tend to agree that most heavy metal bands that refer to the devil are not themselves Satanists. They are repeating heavy metal horror tropes, critiquing society, or giving free rein to imagination and fantasy, rather than speaking literally.

The devil is figured as a force of freedom from restraint in Van Halen's song "Running with the Devil." Robert Walser has discussed the structure of the Van Halen song "Running with the Devil" in some detail (51–55). While David Lee Roth's vocal is out front, Eddie Van Halen's guitar work and the chorale vocals of the band are central features of the song. The song, Walser observes, presents running with the devil as "a trope for having freedom" (51). This fantasy of escape, he says, is questioned by the lead vocal amid "pained/ecstatic" screams and the group reasserts the fantasy in the choruses.

In his meticulous song analysis, Walser points out that the verses are in one key and the chorus is in another. The verses offer "syncopated, descending chords" and the chorus brings power chords and a busy, strong bass line. There are shifts in key and mode as we move into the chorus and also "dynamic, timbral, and rhythmic changes" notes Walser (51). The analysis highlights the musical moves that Van Halen makes: how the song moves through its harmonic and rhythmic changes and moves between tension and release. He mentions the unique four bar guitar solo and observes that this is unlike many other heavy metal guitar solos: "for metal guitar solos typically take the form of rhetorical outbursts" (Walser, 53). The typical heavy metal instrumental guitar solo wants to soar, to scream, to rise to transcendence and freedom.

The guitar solos of Jimmy Page take us there. So do some of the fast and intricate guitar leads of Randy Rhoads, who accompanied Ozzy Osborne on some of his solo efforts. Led Zeppelin, with musical variety, reaches for transcendence and to break through to musical bliss and mythical landscapes. The world of Black Sabbath, in contrast, is tainted with smoke and monsters, chaos and evil, lunacy and dread. Musically, Led Zeppelin stretches magnificently across hard rock blues and ethereal wonder, the exotic eastern rhythms of "Kashmir," and the heights of powerful, wailing guitar leads and soaring vocals. Black Sabbath sets the pattern for the myth of darkness and music constructed from modal structures, down-tuned strings, and heavy bass. The mythic aspects of both bands contributed to the consciousness of the heavy metal bands that followed.

3

Power, Noise and Rebellion

Heavy metal is about performance, power, and sound. Myth intersects with metal performance in the music, attitude, and visual iconography that is presented by a band as well as in the ideas that are expressed in their heavy metal song lyrics. Here we will trace an outline of some heavy metal bands that drew upon myth in their recordings and performances in the 1980s, the decade that gave rise to metal. In heavy metal these gestures toward the mythical are often accompanied by grandeur of sound, by the exhilarating guitar leads of power metal bands, or the deep ominous pulse of heavy bass and drums. Some thinkers have suggested that creative artists draw upon archetypes and a collective language deeply embedded in the human race. Heavy metal performers enlist myth in dramatic musical settings of legends. They call upon grotesque imagery and monstrous powers and sometimes create large scale works that audiences have called "epic."

Heavy metal's development has been traced to bands that were anchored in the blues, like Cream, to British invasion rock songs like The Kinks' "You Really Got Me," to the loudness of Blue Cheer and MC5, and to ominous vocals like Doug Ingle's heavy baritone on Iron Butterfly's 17 minute long "In-a-Gadda-Da Vida." As a performance art, heavy metal owes something to the makeup of Alice Cooper and Kiss and to glam-rock. The guitar-work of Jimi Hendrix was another predecessor, influencing a long line of dynamic heavy metal guitarists. The hard and fast energy of Motörhead, with Lemmy Kilmister, emerged from the space rock of Hawkwind. There was the appearance of a new wave of British power heavy metal with bands like Iron Maiden. With them came lyrics that drew upon myth and history. Images of heroism and

3. Power, Noise and Rebellion

mythical landscapes were conveyed in gestures and words, in songs that told stories.

Myth in metal is generally signaled to an audience by the stories and images that are expressed in song lyrics and conveyed visually in performances. Song lyrics are literate forms of expression but they are not the most important part of a metal song. The sound is what matters most. Musical meaning, if it is to be found at all, lies within the processes of the music itself. Music is melody, rhythm, harmony, timbre, pitch, key, mode, and volume. The voice of heavy metal is in its sheer loudness, its vocal lines, its harmonic progressions, its riffs, and its attitude. Bands develop their own signature sound, even as they subscribe to the metal code. Those high, streaming, piercing guitar leads and wailing vocals act as a counterpart to the heavy bottom of the bass and drums and big power chords. Music is a social practice. It is non-propositional and unlike language. Yet the music itself is central to the message and life of rock music; it is the breath and heartbeat of heavy metal. The sonic power and music of heavy metal comes first before lyrics, before imagery. It is the aural atmosphere and ground upon which any mythology proceeds.[1]

In his writing on the 1960s literary critic Morris Dickstein writes: "poetry has no intrinsic need to be read aloud, [but] music or choreography scarcely exists as a fulfilled performance." (*Gates of Eden*, 196). Dickstein makes the point that at high volumes the music may seem to come from within rather than from outside (190).[2] This music is experienced physically, emotionally, and music has a way of erasing words in sound. The mythical in metal emerges in the music—in performance, in theatrics, and in visual art, as well as in song concepts and lyrics. Metal draws upon the rich repository of mythic stories and imagery to entertain, to reach and stimulate the audience, and to address contemporary issues. It might also be said that heavy metal reflects a spiritual hunger: a desire to revive a vital sense of life and imagination and to encounter community in a postindustrial, postmodern age. Heavy metal is music, an attitude—and for some fans a lifestyle—that embraces motifs of chaos, death, or violence and it protests against repression, injustice, and soul-suffocation by mechanism, materialism, and modern anonymity.

Dionysian creativity in heavy metal is surely embedded in responses to situations in the modern world. Heavy metal re-enlists ancient myths to observe, protest, and reconfigure how we might live now. Encompassing a great diversity of styles today, heavy metal utilizes myth, madness, rebellion, and horror to critique and upend assumptions about contemporary reality. Focused on power, it empowers communities and enlivens imaginations. Metal explores mystery and otherness. It faces alienation and de-industrialization in the post-industrial society, rejecting systems of control, hypocrisy, or corruption: the "suicidal tendencies" that are not so much the dark pains of troubled adolescents as they are of the very civilization in which we live. This is a rock music medium that tries to make sense of the world. It has used powerful music and mythical narratives to compensate for disempowerment in limited socio-economic contexts, much like hip-hop /rap has responded to urban life, seeking vitality beyond deprived and stultifying environments. Deena Weinstein states that young people were re-claiming their lives through metal and revolting against an authoritarian culture (*Heavy Metal: The Music and Its Culture*, 48). Heavy metal has been commercialized, co-opted, applauded, dismissed and reviled. It continues in its varieties as one of the most popular music forms of our time. It asserts that the mythical mind (the metaphorical sense) is a necessary corrective to an over-rationalized environment.

Heavy metal is filled with constructed fantasy and so it draws liberally upon mythology. Metal recognizes what Robert Walser has called "the significance of mysticism, horror, and violence" (*Running with the Devil*, 137). Heavy metal exudes power. It builds upon the steady control of rhythm and pulse and the soaring freedom of guitars. The bass drives persistently, creating tonal rhythmic changes. Guitar solos are well-practiced but seem spontaneous and suggest energy and virtuosity. The distorted guitar signals power and power chords amplified with distortion flood us with overtones, adding bottom amid a driving beat. In performance the heavy metal band pumps out energy, aches for freedom, speaks to an audience with pleasure or dread. It claims a sense of urgency. It plays with violence, anarchy, and irresponsibility. Metal lives in fantasy. It evokes myth, regurgitates its hell, climbs toward fascination in what one critic has called "the semiotics of frantic but futile struggle" (Walser, 118). Metal explores the darkness, the occult, the esoteric. It usually does not speak of romantic love. Flamboyance and fantasy overtake it. The desire for a good time drives it. Put across with skill, complexity, and originality, with determination and attitude, it appeals to passion and force. It engages a heavy metal community that enters its pulse and spectacle. And they are on fire; they are alive in free movement; they are breaking out. They know that metal is a monster, a contrivance, an insult and an assault: brutal, unexpected, irrational, banging through the threshold of the mundane into a world of wonder.

Obviously, not all heavy metal performers are sitting around reading myth and literature, or watching horror movies. Steve Harris and Bruce Dickinson of Iron Maiden clearly have read some literature. They have watched films and they are familiar with myth and history. Geezer Butler of Black Sabbath has talked about his reading. So did Ronnie James Dio. Manowar's Joey De Maio has made informed allusions to myth in the classics. Rush and Dream Theater are familiar with science fiction and mythology. Other bands, like Guns n' Roses and Mötley Crüe, have been more attracted to hedonism and decadence than attracted to myth. However, the photography of Nikki Sixx of Mötley Crüe suggests a fascination with archetypes presented imaginatively in visual form. His visual sense shows the imagination of a creative artist at work. That curiosity and opening of the imagination is the root of heavy metal mythic exploration.

Heavy metal lyricists and composers are steeped in the mythical language and tropes that have come to them from their rock music predecessors. "The myths of heavy metal tend to emphasize power, conflict, violence, and death ... potency of the individual but also the power of imagined communities and ideals," Keith Kahn-Harris observes. He reminds us that metal explores ancient pasts and historical heroes (*Coming Out*, 26). While some heavy metal artists may explore those myths, several who apply themselves to the metal code repeat clichés about hell, evil, darkness, and violence for commercial purposes. Whatever the motivation may be for rock songwriters, the archetypes and cultural past live in those images in their songs.

The modern audience's need for myth and fantasy is answered by heavy metal. This creativity is paralleled by today's veritable explosion of myth, horror, and fantasy on television and in film. T.S. Eliot, writing "Ulysses, Order, and Myth" asserted that modern art has to offer the "mythical method" as a structure or "scaffolding" for a modern age that is seeking for meaning. Rock music, literature, and popular culture have responded. If a rationalized, secularized, scientifically reductionist, commercial culture has left a vacuum, heavy metal has reacted by providing myth and imagination. Heavy metal has offered a community in contemporary circumstances where there has been less of one.

The heavy metal community participates in a language of mythic power and rebellion, a counter-cultural declaration of uniqueness that draws upon ancient sources to reaffirm its place in the contemporary world. The philosopher Paul Ricouer suggests that as modern men and women we are not able to coordinate myth with history any longer and "mythical space can no longer be coordinated with our geography" (162). So, "we are tempted to give ourselves up to a radical demythologization of all our thinking." That is, we may tend to try to explain everything, to analyze and unravel every myth, to seek rational terms rather than just letting the myth live in our imaginations as myth. Mythical thinking, however, can bring us back into an experience of wonder. Myth can echo in our own subconscious minds, like a dream. In heavy metal we can rediscover that mythical imagination.

Iron Maiden, for example, explores history and mystery, power and horror, in song narratives where myth or ancient lives are embedded. In their songs the horror is not gratuitous; the drama that is constructed is artfully built and delivered with remarkable precision. From the 1980s on Iron Maiden has mastered the art of sounding spontaneous on record with music that upon close listening appears carefully, at times mathematically, crafted. Iron Maiden's song cycle *Seventh Son of a Seventh Son* (1988) gathers together songs with topics of fate and destiny, prognostication and visions. The liner art for the album includes mythological references and otherworldly signs: a crystal ball, candlesticks, an angel and a demon. The band presents symbols of mystery as sources of power and contact with an otherworld. On the song "Seventh Son" the harmonic structure of C-D-E sets a somber mood and pattern. Some vague *vox humana* chorale vocals emerge from synthesizer. Then comes a steady, persistent rhythm.[3] The song remains locked on that E and moves to a chorus with the C-D-E pattern on which rides a vocal with vibrato. We next move on to the song's instrumentals and then come back to the main harmonic pattern.

Across the years, Iron Maiden has provided many mythical landscapes. On *Powerslave* we meet with an Egyptian pharaoh. On other albums the esoteric lives alongside Biblical symbolism, or ancient mythical tales. These stories are sometimes given a twist, a retelling of the myth, as when Icarus falls from the sky and we learn that his father, the inventor Daedelus, was responsible for his doom. The band also turns toward the doomed in history. Iron Maiden's "Run for the Hills" holds criticism of the genocide of Native Americans.

3. Power, Noise and Rebellion

Several other bands have adopted a mythical framework across the years, drawing upon ancient stories, or upon horror and science fiction films. One of these bands, Blue Öyster Cult, was an important transitional band in the movement toward heavy metal. Their strong guitar riffs and horror and science fiction lyrics were innovations that fed into the guitar virtuosity and the signs and symbols of metal. Their relentless touring across some forty weeks of the year in the 1990s kept them visible and available for audiences into the twenty-first century.

Heavy metal began to emerge when the blues-based music of The Yardbirds and Cream, The Kinks and Steppenwolf, met with the loudness and forcefulness of bands like Blue Cheer and MC5. The virtuoso blues guitar playing of Eric Clapton and Jeff Beck and the powerful guitars of Jimmy Page, Leslie West, and Ritchie Blackmore led to further heights and were followed by the dazzling musicianship of Eddie Van Halen and Randy Rhoads. The fantasies of progressive bands in the late 1960s and early 1970s added another dimension to rock that was absorbed in heavy metal. UFO, with singer Phil Mogg and guitarist Michael Schenker, for example, moved from space rock to heavy metal. Meanwhile, as the mythical palette of the sixties generation drifted toward progressive rock, elaborately laced with keyboard sounds, heavy metal took another direction with a guitar sound. Punk reacted by stripping rock down to the minimalism of a few chords. Heavy metal distinguished itself by building upon a heavier sound characterized by weighty bass lines and drumming, complemented by fiery guitar work.

Judas Priest emerged in the mid–1970s with K.K. Downing's guitar and Rob Halford's vocals. With *Sad Wings of Destiny* (1976) themes of occultism became apparent in their recordings. With their black leather biker wardrobe they affected a fierceness, a determined heavy metal pose that drew fans and also drew the rancor of conservative groups that cringed at their lyrics.[4]

Motörhead merged metal and punk. Lemmy Kilmister had begun with the psychedelic space rock band Hawkwind. Beginning in 1976, Motörhead asserted a sound of heavy distortion and adopted an anti-respectable stance of working class subculture distaste. Their first song on their first album, "Motorhead," suggested an amphetamine high. The fourth song on that album, "Iron Horse/Born to Lose," projected the mythic image of the biker outlaw. By their albums *Overkill* (1979) and *Sacrifice* (1980) they were still too objectionable for top forty radio airplay, which is exactly how they wanted things to be. They gained a strong cult following in the 1980s and their work inspired other bands. Motörhead fitted well the term "proud pariahs" that Deena Weinstein has used to describe some working class metal performers. They looked askance at the modern world and expressed a class politics critique and a proud no-holds-barred authenticity. By Motörhead's 2006 *Kiss of Death* recording, their endurance and persistent creativity had made them one of the most influential of bands.

Part of heavy metal's growing popularity in the 1980s came from the airplay success of the "hair metal" bands like Dokken, Cinderella, Whitesnake, or Bon Jovi. With cable television came MTV, which caused songs to be read more through visuals than lyrics. Quiet Riot, Mötley Crüe, Scorpions, Twisted Sister and Dokken appeared on some of the first videos. Don Dokken produced high, clear vocals for the band's MTV power ballads. Whitesnake vocalist David Coverdale broke onto the pop charts with "Here I Go Again." Lite metal pop/rock bands like Bon Jovi from New Jersey and Def Leppard, with vocals by Joe Elliott, took to the radio airwaves and drew new audiences. Female fans flocked to metal—to power bands like Iron Maiden as well as to the lite metal acts that included gestures toward romance. Aerosmith, Alice Cooper, and other hard rock bands incorporated aspects of metal into their sound.

Mythical Lyricists

In February 2007 Manowar's Joey De Maio commented to an interviewer: "these days there's a real lack of big, epic metal that is drenched with crushing guitars and choirs and orchestras" (Harris, MTV Interview, February 2009). De Maio has consistently brought a mythical orientation to Manowar's recordings and the large canvases of some of his songs are reminiscent of grand opera. (He has even turned to Puccini in the past for "Nesum Dorma.") Ronnie James Dio was also a mythically minded lyricist: one with an operatic voice. Maybe it has something to do with a latent layover from a lapsed Catholicism, a trace of Dante's Inferno still in the blood of Italian American rock lyricists. Along with Iron Maiden's Steve Harris, Ronnie James Dio and Joey De Maio of Manowar, both Italian-Americans, were among the most mythically oriented song-creators in heavy metal. Amid the commercial rise of metal, myth persisted in the work of these creative metal lyricists. Vocalist Ronnie James Dio was a central figure, a powerful singer who wrote fantasy and drew upon myth. His operatic vocals for Ritchie Blackmore and Rainbow brought him to public attention and he later sang with Black Sabbath. (Blackmore was more interested in rock and blues guitar and drawing upon classical music than in Dio's fantasies. The band Dio followed.) His vocals, which are described by Deena Weinstein as "gritty-operatic," were an influence on other heavy metal singers (*Rock 'n' Roll America*, 26). Such vocals are known for their power, emotionality, and intensity.

Manowar

One of those powerful vocalists is Eric Adams of Manowar, one of the most mythically oriented heavy metal bands to emerge in the 1980s. The band was founded in Auburn, New York, by Joey De Maio and Adams, who were friends in school. Donnie Hamzik was their first drummer. Manowar continued into the new century with Karl Logan on bass and Scott Columbus on drums. The band has been performing since about 1980. They have frequently embraced ancient Greek myth, sword and sorcery fantasy, Norse myth, and bombastic loudness. Manowar insists upon loudness on "All Men Play on Ten" (the highest volume on an amplifier) and on "Blow Your Speakers."

Often Manowar lyrics call for a kind of heroism. "Dark Avenger," for example, urges listeners to fight the good fight against forces of darkness. "Call to Arms" is spoken by a warrior who speaks of defenders with steel, a brotherhood of warriors who will defend the kingdom. "Mountain" gestures to the heights and insists that life can be lived fully: it's right here for us to take. On "House of Death" there are blood and thunder that mix with rain and lightning and grotesque Dante-like images of bodies burning in flame. The lyrics provide a terrifying glimpse at the underworld that lies out ahead. De Maio knows about the many myths that indicate that there are seven gates to the underworld.

Manowar's tenth album *Gods of War* presented a lengthy musical suite based on *The Iliad*, featuring Achilles in the age of metal. The use of classical references, critic Iain Campbell has pointed out, is "a subset of a larger mythical reservoir" (122). Manowar taps into Greek mythology and moves into Norse mythology in songs like "Overture to the Immortal

Warriors," "The Ascension," "King of Kings," "Army of the Dead," "Sleipnir" (named after the stallion on which Odin rides), "Sons of Odin," "Gods of War," "Hymn of the Immortal Warriors," and "Die for Metal." With this album Manowar toured Europe and appeared on the Greek, Norwegian, German, Finnish, and Italian charts. During those years the band included guitarist Ross the Boss Funicello, who had been with the new wave-punk band the Dictators, which often played at CBGB in the mid to late 1970s. Eric Adams has remained the singer and Scott Columbus was their drummer across much of the band's history. When Scott Columbus died in April 2011, De Maio and the band turned to Donnie Hamzik for a drummer.

Manowar's *Into Glory Ride* on Megaforce Records centered upon heroic fantasy and mythology. The song "Defender" appeared on that album and songs like "Sign of the Hammer" set the tone for Viking metal. "Sign of the Hammer" immediately says that a spell has dissipated and in the black wind the gods have provided a sign. On the heels of the *Hail to England* album they toured with Merciful Fate. They appeared on Liberty Records in 1981 with a voice over by actor Orson Welles and they provided support for a tour by Ted Nugent. By 1988's *Heart of Steel* there was no more Ross the Boss in the band. David Shankle came in as the guitar player. *Triumph of Steel* in 1992 included the 28 minute "Achilles, Agony and Ecstasy in Eight Parts" and a world tour followed. They signed with Geffen Records but Shankle left Manowar at this time. That is when drummer Scott Columbus returned. In 1996 Manowar's *Louder Than Hell* anthology appeared and they recorded a live album: *Hell on Wheels* and then *Hell on Stage*. *Warriors of the World* emerged in 2002, including myth based songs like "House of Death" and "Call to Arms."

Sons of Odin (2005) clearly set out the Norse myth theme. In the lengthy lyric of the title song we meet with images of a blaze and black night, dreams of glory and recollections of instruments of war. The narrator is thinking ahead to Valhalla where he will one day go after a heroic death in battle. This idea of heroism also appears in *The Iliad* but it is here trained on images from Norse myth. The hammer of Thor is mentioned and we hear of the souls of thunder who await the doors of Valhalla. Odin will choose who will enter. *Gods of War*, their 2007 concept album which is focused on the Norse god Odin, repeats this Sons of Odin motif. The booklet was written in Runic script. The recording, with keyboards and choir, can be called symphonic metal. It is on this album that

De Maio draws heavily upon Wagner's Ring cycle. Manowar's enduring catalog is among the most myth and fantasy driven among heavy metal bands.

Thrash Metal: Metallica, Megadeth, Slayer, Anthrax, Exodus

In the early 1980s, at about the time that Manowar was beginning to assert their sense of myth and metal, other trends were starting to break. For, then came thrash. It came with Slayer, Anthrax, Megadeth, and Metallica, the so-called big four, and with the important early thrash band Exodus. The emergence of thrash coincided with the rise of heavy metal in the 1980s as metal became one of popular music's most widespread forms. It spoke to contemporary issues. "The heavy metal of Iron Maiden and Megadeth ... articulates the anxieties and discontinuities of the postmodern world," writes Robert Walser (159). Walser adds that these bands suggest that "survival in the modern world" is possible despite the disruptions (159). A confrontation with the modern world is clear in the lyrics of Megadeth's Dave Mustaine. His lyrics accompany fast rhythms and complex arrangements. The apocalyptic titled *Countdown to Extinction* faces the contemporary world, while drawing upon archetypes that have been with Western civilization for centuries.

Metallica

Metallica brought thrash metal to the airwaves. Tenaciously confronting the modern world, they too drew upon imaginative resources. The band's debut album *Kill 'Em All* (1983), on the Megaforce label, included a song based on the legend of the Four Horsemen. This was followed by the album *Ride the Lightning* (1984). *Master of Puppets* (1986) was their first gold album. *And Justice for All* (1988) followed. The early Metallica album titles suggest violence, high energy and power, a concern with social justice, and opposition to authoritarianism: "Kill 'Em All," "Ride the Lightning," "And Justice for All," "Master of Puppets." Metallica song titles gravitate around familiar metal themes. On their self-titled album we hear "Enter Sandman," "Holier Than Thou," "The Unforgiven," "Don't Tread on Me," "Through the Never," "Of Wolf and Man," "The God That Failed," "My Friend of Misery," "The Struggle Within."

The self-titled black album debuted at #1 in 1991. It brought new listeners and landed the band within mainstream radio airplay. Metallica was at the top of its game and *Load* and *Re-Load* followed across the next years.

The black album by Metallica broke upon the world with "Enter Sandman." The narrator seems to address a child, urging the child to keep an eye open, warning that something haunting and fierce may appear. In the nineteenth century the legendary figure of the Sandman was featured in a horror story by E.T.A. Hoffmann. (Hoffmann, who held a mystical regard for music, was a formidable music critic who also wrote the story *The Nutcracker.*) Metallica's self-titled 1991 album had twelve songs recorded between October 6, 1998, and June 16, 1999. It was released on August 12, 1991, as an album in a black sleeve, with a logo and a coiled snake. The record was produced by Bob Rock with James Hetfield and recorded by engineer Randy Staub with assistance from Mike Tucci. The production focused on a bass heavy sound on the first song which had a guitar picked introduction. We are in F sharp and soon drop to a half-time feel. Hetfield's vocal rides up on the F sharp as the chorus comes. On the word "hush" the vocal drops low, into the bass. An E-F pattern underscores the verse and a riff binds the song. Hetfield suggests nightmares and something that is hiding—maybe just outside the window or under the bed. What may come are not dreams of Snow White but of something darker.

The *Metallica* album continues to resonate powerfully. Following "Sad but True," with its sharp snare drum, Metallica gives us "Of Wolf and Man" and "Don't Tread on Me." The song "The God That Failed" addresses a religion that appears to fall short on its claims. "Holier Than Thou" builds upon a driving riff and takes aim at 'religious' people who are judgmental. The song lyric cautions listeners not to judge others. "Of Wolf and Man" is spoken by the wolf in the mist of a new day. In spoken words we hear of the speaker's change into a werewolf. The shape-shifting creature has a message: To preserve the wild is to preserve the world. "My Friend of Misery" has a first line that could recall the kind of angst we see in Edvard Munch's arresting painting "The Scream." "The Struggle Within" begins with tom-tom overdubs and tympani overdubs. The vocal begins in F sharp and rises to a high E.

3. Power, Noise and Rebellion

Slayer

Producing some of the darkest mythical lyrics in thrash metal, Slayer was formed in 1981 in Huntington Park, California. Slayer was soon considered one of the primary thrash bands. The band has included guitarist Kerry King, drummer Dave Lombardo, Gary Holt, Paul Bostaph, Jeff Hanneman on guitar. Across the years band members have included Tony Araya (bass/vocal), Jon Dette, and Tony Scaglione of Whiplash. Hanneman was their guitar player for more than 30 years until physical issues limited his playing. They toured with Exodus and Venom in 1985 with songs from their *Hell Awaits* album. That album with hell and Satan as its subject incited religious groups. Critics complained about Slayer's themes of Satanism, murder, torture, and anti-religion. With the criticisms the band became more visible. *The Reign of Blood* (1986) album with the single "Eyes of the Insane" earned five Grammy nominations. It was recorded for Def Jam Records, which is mostly a hip-hop label. In 1988 Kim Nelly of *Rolling Stone* identified their recording as having "offensive Satanic overdrive." Columbia Records refused to release their song "Angel of Death," which alluded to the Nazi experiments of Josef Mengele. The recording was distributed by Geffen Records. Slayer's *Season in the Abyss* (1990) included a reference to Egyptian mythology. Their video for the title track was filmed in front of the Gaza pyramids in Egypt. *Christ Illusion* was their 2006 album. From 1991 to 2013 they sold about 4.9 million albums.

Anthrax

Anthrax produced their first record *Howling Furies and Metal Hammer* (1981), which reflected myth. The band included Scott Ian (guitar), Dan Liker (bass), Dan Spitz (guitar), and Charlie Benante (drums). Emerging from New York City, their EP demo was produced by Ross the Boss of Manowar. *Fistful of Metal* (1984) was their first recording on the Megaforce label. (*Fistful of Metal* and the *Armed and Dangerous* [1985] album were released again in 2005.) They played a cover of Alice Cooper's "I'm Eighteen." Lilker was replaced. Matt Fallon contributed vocals and he was followed by Joey Belladonna and then Frank Bello. Thrash metal met with operatic vocals. Anthrax tended to repeat heavy metal figures that had become clichés. There was power and energy in the delivery.

Exodus

Exodus is a thrash band formed in Richmond, California, in 1979. *Bonded by Blood* was released in 1981. The band went through several changes, with two members making an exodus from life. When Exodus played in the heavy metal circuit in California, Paul Balford sang the vocals. He was followed by Steve Souza. Metallica's Kirk Hammett was also an original guitarist for Exodus. Greg Holt followed on guitar and became one of the band's central creative voices. Geoff Andrews on bass was followed by Rob McKillop. Tom Huntig was the drummer, then John Tempesta. For some time they were associated with San Francisco area thrash metal and held in regard alongside Metallica, Possessed, and Testament. *Bonded by Blood, Pleasures, and Flesh* (1987) was followed by *Fabulous Disaster* (1989), *Force of Habit* (1992), and *Tempo of the Damned* (2002). *Hellfest* appeared in 2012.

Playing It Loud

Metal is a medium that may be best appreciated live, in concerts. Some live albums from heavy metal's precursors are Deep Purple's *Made in Japan* (1973) and UFO's *Lights Out* (1979). Heavy metal band live albums began to appear in the late 1970s and early 1980s: Judas Priest, *Unleashed in the East* (1979), Scorpions, *Tokyo Tapes* (1978), Iron Maiden, *Japan* (1981), Ozzy Osborne, *Speak of the Devil* (1982), Black Sabbath, *Live Evil* (1983).

In the 1980s, heavy metal began to diversify into a rich myriad of styles, sounds, and subgenres. There was thrash and speed and metalcore, black metal and white metal, death metal and progressive metal. Heavy metal's diversity includes Motörhead, combining aspects of punk and metal, and Limp Bizkit's synthesis of styles. It includes the death metal of Venom and the power metal of Iron Maiden. Some listeners with an expansive sense of heavy metal might include the pop/rock of Bon Jovi or the progressive music of Rush.[5]

3. Power, Noise and Rebellion

Heavy metal bands increasingly expressed psychological issues, inner turbulence, and existential issues like dread, emptiness, and despair. Titles reflected the troubled mind: Edge of Sanity's *Spectral Sorrows* (1994), Morbid Angel's *Altars of Madness* (1989), Black Sabbath's *Paranoid* (1970). Bands celebrated chaos and death, as in *Haunted*, by Six Feet Under (1995), *Osculum Obscenum* (1993) by Hypocrisy. References to the devil appeared often. A few examples are: *Shout at the Devil*, Mötley Crüe, 1989. *The Number of the Beast*, Iron Maiden, 1980. *When Satan Lives*, Deicide, 1998. *La Masquerade Infernale*, Arturus, 1997, *Reign in Blood*, Slayer, 1986. Other bands have taken names associated with religion. Ministry, for example, was founded in 1981 by Al Jourgensen as an industrial metal band with Paul Barker and Mike Scaccia. They incorporated synth-pop in the mid 1980s. Along the way, they drew upon Aleister Crowley, *The Book of Lies*. They broke up after 27 years. Yet, there have been studio albums since 2011, like *Relapse* and *From Beer to Eternity*.

AC/DC

AC/DC will assert that they are not specifically a metal band. Their music—loud, hard, and guitar driven—may best be described as hard rock. However, there are people who will say that they are indisputably metal. Therein lies the ongoing problem of categorization. While AC/DC has referenced the underworld and they have given their listeners "Highway to Hell" and "Hell's Bells," their songs are constructed on straightforward major and minor power chords. They are not modally developed as are a good deal of heavy metal compositions. Their sound is loud and crisp, not muddy or down-tuned.

AC/DC emerged from Australia, from a Scottish working class background. Malcolm Young and Angus Young led a band with Dave Evans, vocals, Larry Van Kneef on bass guitar, and Colin Burgess on drums.[6] Their blues and punk origins do not scream "heavy metal." The brothers were interested in the Velvet Underground, the guitar playing of Eric Clapton and Jimi Hendrix, and the sounds of Mountain and the band Cactus. After Malcolm and Angus Young started the band, Margaret, their sister, is said to have named it after looking at directions on her sewing machine. She also suggested a uniform. The band replaced Evans with Bon Scott. He was from Kirriemoir, the same Scottish town as Peter Pan author James M. Barrie. After Bon Scott died, AC/DC enlisted Brian Johnson to replace him.

The AC/DC sound is characterized by heavy rock guitar (Angus Young played a Gibson SG, 1968 model, Malcolm often plays Gretsch guitars), layered power chords, and strong vocals. Well after attaining wide recognition, AC/DC appeared on the *Rolling Stone* cover November 13, 2008. By then, few bands outside of black metal and death metal had referred to "Hell's Bells" and the "Highway to Hell" as often as AC/DC.

While Mötley Crüe would "Shout at the Devil," Van Halen would run with him, as a sign of liberating freedom. While David Lee Roth's vocal is out front, Eddie Van Halen's guitar work is a central feature of the band. The song, observes Walser, presents running with the devil as "a trope for having freedom" (Walser, 51). This fantasy of escape is questioned by the vocalist amid his "pained/ecstatic screams," as Robert Walser points out, and the group reasserts the fantasy in the chorus. The verses are in one key and the chorus is in another key. There are shifts in key and mode as we move into the chorus. In the verses there are the "syncopated, descending chords" that Walser points out. The chorus brings power chords and a busy bass. Walser's careful analysis highlights the musical moves that Van Halen makes: how the song changes and moves between tension and release. He notes the unique four bar blast from Eddie Van Halen's guitar and observes that it is unlike other heavy metal guitar solos: "for metal guitar solos typically take the form of rhetorical outbursts" (53). The typical heavy metal solo wants to soar, to scream, to rise to transcendence and freedom.

4

Mythical Roots

Myth is that out of which literature emerged. The mythopoeic is the root of literary creation. Modern critical interest in myth was launched by the symbolist movement, which looked to mystery and hermetic meanings, as in the work of Charles Baudelaire, Stephen Mallarme, or William Butler Yeats. It intensified with the development of anthropology and psychology in the work of intellectual figures like Emile Durkheim, Lucien Levy-Bruhl, Henri Bergson, Jane Harrison, and Carl Jung.

Mythology is perplexing to modern common sense. If it is not "real", if cannot be measured or put to use, what good is it? Yet, we continually tell stories to say where we have been, what we have done, what experience has shown us. Myths remind us of enchantment. They were for primitive people a way of explaining the world and its natural phenomena. Around the fire they told elaborate stories. The shamans described their visions. The parents told bedtime stories—or warned of nightmare figures, like Metallica does in "Enter Sandman." The archetypal psychologist James Hillman reminds us that there are three "bridges" for "transporting the unseen into the seen": mathematics, music, and myths (*The Soul's Code*, 94). We tend to associated myth with storytelling and *fabulae*, or fictional stories. We may overlook the function of myth for 'primitive' cultures in explaining phenomena, or for us, in establishing and binding communities, inspiring awe, fear, and wonder, or conveying meaning. The close connection of myth with ritual can be seen in the heavy metal concert: a communal event.

Many centuries ago music was closely connected with astronomy and mathematics. In the view of Pythagoras, a strange and mysterious figure in Greek antiquity, the universe was formed in mathematical ratios. Pythagoras is said to be responsible for the geometrical theorem named after him. He also suggested that the length of strings were reflected in the music of the spheres. The ratios of 2:1, 3:2, 4:3 corresponding to the octave, the fifth, and the fourth were fundamentally present among the planets and the stars. In a symbol, the *tetractys*, this could be presented in an equilateral triangle of ten dots. (We can see the triangle on cover artwork for the band Rush.) Plato was influenced by Pythagoras in his assessment of myths and in his view of the universe. Pythagorean cosmology found its way into Plato's dialogues the *Phaedo* and the *Timaeus*, which include reflections on the transmigration of souls.

Heavy metal plays with dissonance. Musical thought in the West is still in many ways influenced by notions of balance and order. The warning label legislation proposed in the Parents Music Resource Center in the 1980s reveals a dim recognition of the Platonic idea that music influences the ethical life. Rock music, from its beginnings, seized upon and reveled in the notion that the passionate qualities of music were a threat to social stability, an older generation, and the established order. Heavy metal follows boisterously and gleefully in this spirit of rebellion.

While warnings about the Siren song of music abounded in ancient texts, classical literature also discussed the positive values of music. Philosophers believed that an understanding of music would lead to a fundamental understanding of the principles of the universe. The tonal intervals of music could be submitted to mathematical analysis and displayed ratios and sequences. It was believed that the universe had a consistent order: one based upon these mathematical correspondences. The Greek word *harmonia* meant a fitting together of parts. The ancient Greek notion of harmony had to do with relative proportion, an order in the ratio of quantities to each other. This derives from the Pythagorean interest in music and mathematics which became the foundation of their cosmology. The medieval Quadrivium, the basis of studies in higher education, linked music with geometry, arithmetic and astronomy. The neo-Platonic ideas of Plotinus, Boethius, and Augustine prevailed for a time. However, in the age of Copernicus it became evident that the planets did not form a harmony but numerological and rationalistic concepts lingered. During the Renaissance these ideas were still circulating and Shakespeare referred to the music of the spheres in his play *The Merchant of Venice*. Lorenzo speaks with his beloved Jessica and says of the beautiful night around them:

> There's not the small orb which thou beholdest
> But in his motion like an angel sings

4. Mythical Roots

> Still quiring to the young eyed cherubims
> Such harmony is in immortal souls
> But whist this muddy vesture of decay
> Doth grossly close us in, we cannot hear it.

The mythical mind is today nurtured by music from heavy metal bands, rap/hip-hop groups, some forms of advertising, and television shows and films that deal with supernatural characters. The medieval battles, dragons, white-walkers, evil queen, and King of the North of *Game of Thrones* and the mysteries to be unraveled by a symbologist in *The Da Vinci Code* are other examples of this contemporary craving for the mythical.

Investigating Mythology

Heavy metal participates in an ancient dialogue with symbols and stories. Mythology appears in humanity's earliest experience and across all cultures. Myth, expressed in music, in story, and in visual art, has brought together communities and aided the understanding of life for millennia. There are a variety of perspectives from which we can begin to think about mythology and its impact on the imagination and expression of rock music. The importance and value of myth has been affirmed from the perspectives of psychology, anthropology, sociology, religious inquiry, and literary practice. Myth is a way of speaking about what matters: a means of using story, images, symbols, and sound to entertain, question, and communicate. In heavy metal, myth celebrates life, energy, primal emotions like fear and wonder, and the power of imagination.

As explorers of the human mind uncovered what they called the unconscious they offered interpretations of the dreams and symbolic representations that arose in the minds of their clients. In Sigmund Freud's psychoanalytic view, myths were fantasies that expressed primal urges and drives. He explored dreams as desire or realizations of repressed desire and he pursued the question: what were the origins of culture? For Freud, myths are substitute gratifications through fantasy (Eliade, *The Sacred and the Profane*, 312). After working with Freud, psychologist Carl Jung broke away from Freud's conclusions about repression. He proposed a different model of the unconscious. Jung proposed that there the human mind is embedded in a collective unconscious which extends across time and place. Jung observed similarities in myths and symbols across cultures. These primordial archetypes, representations in symbols, were expressed in myths and in dreams. They are the language of the unconscious. Jung did not see this as expressions of repressed libido or wish fulfillment, as Freud did. Rather, myths and dreams are grounded in archetypes which exist deep in the mind prior to culture. "The primitive mentality does not invent myths; it experiences them," he wrote (Jung and Kerenyi, 101).

Jung's view suggests that the mythical comes from a place beyond conscious, ordinary daily reality. In this view, myths are archaic structures in the psychic life of people. The archetypes are fundamentally unconscious and they appear in symbolic expression in dreams and stories, in human constructions, including works of art. Jung worked closely on a study of myth and imagination with the scholar Karl Kerenyi. In Kerenyi's view, myths lay the groundwork for a meaningful world. He wrote that the teller of myths steps backs into the primordial in order to tell us what originally was (Jung and Kerenyi, 10).

Following in the path of inquiry opened by Jung, Joseph Campbell discussed mythic patterns in *The Hero with a Thousand Faces*. From culture to culture Campbell saw the monomyth at work. This is a story pattern in which the hero is called to adventure, faces initiation, rises to the occasion and has to address conflicts. The hero is aided by helper figures, or wisdom figures, while facing great adversity, then returns home with a gift (Campbell called it "a boon") to bestow upon his or her society. In *Masks of Gods*, Campbell explicitly referred to depth psychology and "early cultures."[1] Jungian psychologists continue to investigate the symbolic formulations of the people who come to see them for therapy and dialogue with them about their dreams, stories, and experiences.

Joseph Campbell focused on comparative mythology and the archetypal hero's journey. He identified four functions of myth: the metaphysical; the cosmological, which explained the universe; the sociological, which addressed social order; and the pedagogical, in which the myth provides teaching and guidance for life. In his symbolic interpretation of myths he partially drew upon the thought of Carl Jung. For Campbell, mythic narratives are variants of a single story and basic story patterns lie beneath these myths. The term monomyth was one he borrowed from *Finnegans Wake* by James Joyce, an author whose work he was much attracted to. Campbell drew upon Adoph Bastian's distinction between folk ideas and elementary ideas which he believed are fundamental and

4. Mythical Roots

archetypal. Campbell also believed that there is a psychic unity among people across various cultures. Myths emerge from these common depths of the human psyche.

In a different approach, a sociologist like Deena Weinstein examines heavy metal by considering social behavior, the symbolic interaction of heavy metal fans, the front-stage and backstage patterns of heavy metal music acts, and the dynamic ritual of the concert. Sociologist Emile Durkheim and philosopher Ernst Cassirer each held the view that one can only understand myth by understanding social ritual. Ritual is dramatic and expressive and we see that manifested in heavy metal concerts. Myth is the "epic element" in this collective process. Cassirer, in *An Essay on Man* (1956) asserted that "in mythical imagination is always implied an act of belief" (101). Cassirer saw myth as following ritual. Myth was a practice that created connection and solidarity in a group. "To mythical and religious feeling nature becomes one great society, the society of life" (101). His protégé Susanne Langer viewed myth an expression of fantasy, as a dream narrative that became a story. Myths concern the human "quest for an understanding of nature and the meaning of life," she suggested (Weiner, 315). In myth, dream narratives are transformed into stories. Myths suggest a search for understanding of the phenomena of the material world and a quest for the meaning of life. Myths arise in fantasy but they also express the human condition through language, symbol, and other expressions of imagination. The thinker Gilbert Durand once commented that mythical thought is primordial and "precedes any other type of thinking."

The anthropological approach to myth has been particularly significant. Studies in cultural anthropology in the twentieth century became closely linked with theories about language and the use of signs in human communication. Myth was central to Ferdinand de Saussure's linguistics and to Claude Levi-Straus' attention to signs and language structures, or what he called mythemes. Claude Levi-Straus did not look for the meaning of myth on the level of consciousness. He asserted that "a kind of logic which is used in mythical thought is as rigorous as that of modern science, and that difference lies not in the quality of the intellectual process but in the nature of the things to which it is applied" (Sebeok, 66).

In *La pensee sauvage* (*The Savage Mind*, 1962) and in *Du miel aux cendres* (1966), Levi-Straus suggests that myth is more like music than language. Myth works on the mind and the senses and generates ideas and emotion (Eliade, 317). The investigations of music and communication in indigenous cultures by anthropologists presented twentieth century thinkers with many interesting views. Nearly one hundred years before Levi-Straus, in *Primitive Culture* (1871), Edward Burnett Tylor offered a perspective that reflected some of the thinking of the Victorian era. Tylor believed that the people in the cultures that he studied were still in a myth-making stage of the mind. "Myth arose as the savage condition prevalent in remote ages among the whole race," he wrote. However, although Tylor recognized that later societies retain aspects of mythical traditions, he did not say a great deal about his own society's myth and its myth-making capacity. Like August Comte, Burnett Tylor regarded earlier stages as primitive and tended to consider mythical thinking as pertaining to human thinking in its childlike state. So, one looks to what he called "the less civilized peoples." Of course, we might ask what made Burnett Tylor so assured that his own society was more civilized. In his work he sought "the nearest representatives of primeval culture" (I, 287). He did realize the power of myth for these societies. For Tylor "the basis on which such ideas are built is not to be narrowed down to poetic fancy and transformed metaphor" (I, 299).

The Victorian Andrew Lang saw myth as different from religion. For Lang myth was irrational and it had more to do with animistic practices than the "rational" religion of "earnest contemplation and submission" that he believed in. Myth had to do with "playful and erratic fantasy," whereas Victorian religion—well, that was an altogether serious matter. Lang looked at mythopoeic processes but it seems that this earnest Victorian had forgotten how to play. Toward the end of the century, the British scholar W. Robertson-Smith regarded myth as connected with ritual. Myths likely all had ritual origins, he concluded. In his discussions of myth and ritual, mythologist Mircea Eliade observes that "myth has been seen whether as a sacred story, model, or justification of a meaningful and creative human time" (317).

Anthropologists have pointed to ritual as preceding myth. Jane Harrison wrote in *Themis* (1912): "Indeed, a myth is not merely a word spoken; it is a re-utterance recited collectively—or at least with collective sanction. When it is related to the ritual, myth becomes a narrative charged with magical intent and potency" (330). Mythos was for the Greeks "just a thing spoken, uttered by the mouth. There was also "the thing done, enacted, the ergon or work" (328).[2] Following the Second World War mythologists,

4. Mythical Roots

historians, and phenomenologists of religion emphasized the value of mythical thinking.

Musicology, which also provides us with another approach to heavy metal, can be combined with the study of heavy metal codes, practices, and fan behavior. One can develop what anthropologist Clifford Geertz once called a "thick description" of heavy metal culture. The narratives, dreams, symbolizing practices, and music of indigenous cultures have been investigated by ethnomusicologists. In the ethnographic approach of the participant-observer the musical anthropologist inserts himself or herself into a culture. What makes the work of musicologist Robert Walser, or sociologist Deena Weinstein, so valuable in their studies of heavy metal is their knowledgeable participation in rock music criticism and their interaction with the heavy metal community. Weinstein is as much a don in the school of rock as she is a trained sociologist and Walser is a guitar player who has as much of an authoritative grasp of musicology and theory as of the variety of chords and melodic runs one can make across the guitar fretboard. They are, in this sense, well-prepared investigators of the subculture of heavy metal and their now classic studies (Walser's *Running with the Devil* and Weinstein's *Heavy Metal: The Music and Its Culture*) are crucial reference points for this book.

Another perspective on the relation of myth to heavy metal is the literary one, which is central to this study. Myth may be compared to a kind of folktale. Tales are told to entertain and as recollections of history. They are part of an oral literary tradition. From the German writers Goethe and Herder to the Russian folklorist Vladimir Propp's morphological study of folk tales, a literary approach to myths has offered clues to their origins and practice. In the twentieth century, the literary critic Northrop Frye developed an archetypal criticism in which he characterized stories within the categories of tragedy, comedy, romance, and irony: a model that referred to the four seasons. More recently, Christopher Booker has taken an archetypal approach in his masterful study *The Seven Basic Plots: Why We Tell Stories* (2008), in which he considers a wide variety of stories and how they express themes like overcoming the monster, the quest, and the voyage and return.

In ancient myths we see gods and goddesses, ritual combat, confrontations with the gods or with monsters, heroes in battle and clashes with Satan. Monsters personify chaos. In their search for wisdom in philosophy the ancient Greeks turned to reason for explanation. Plato's Forms suggested ideal realities which are not visible. This world is a shadow of those Ideas or Forms. Myth can help a person to glimpse into this but one cannot see the higher truths. Plato used myth to describe the idea of life after death, including images of a chariot and winged horses (*Phaedo*, *Laws* X, *The Republic* X). Aristotle in his *Metaphysics*, early on in his text, says that the lover of myths offer societies suggestions and ideas of how to live.

The Elizabethan period of the late sixteenth century was fully alive to the power of myth. Shakespeare's use of myth in his plays, Spenser's poetry in *The Faerie Queen*, and the mythopoeic imagination of Renaissance poets and artists strongly attest to this. They knew that ancient cultures had created fantastic myths like the Sumerian Gilgamesh. Myths existed throughout the ancient world from India to Babylonia to Egypt and among the Assyrians, the Chaldeans, and the Hebrews. The Miletans suggested that thunder was caused by the wind blowing free from the clouds. The Pythagoreans reflected that the universe was a system of proportions, geometries, and coordinates and that behind it lay a music of the spheres. Looking back in time, men and women of the Renaissance recognized that the ancient Greeks had developed an organized mythology of gods and goddesses which had a deep impact upon Athenian drama in the 400s BC. Mythology added energy to the arts and literature. Medieval story making relied upon the mythic mind to produce tales like Beowulf, the Song of Roland (which Elizabethans did not yet know of), and the Arthurian legends. The Italian Renaissance is filled with the creations of brilliant artists like Michelangelo, Botticelli, Leonardo da Vinci and others who drew upon the myths and Biblical sources in their assertion of humanity. The esoteric traditions of the Renaissance period explored magic, cosmology, witchcraft, alchemy, and the occult.

Renaissance poets and audiences were receptive to allegorical and cosmological interpretations of myth. Myths encompassed meanings that were collectively understood by these audiences. This is because they were "related to rooted habits of thought," observed literary critic Rosemary Tuve in *Elizabethan and Metaphysical Imagery* (1947). William Shakespeare employed mythology often in his plays. Edmund Spenser's *The Faerie Queen* connected myth with the allegorical method. Francis Bacon in *De sapienta veterum* (1608) developed allegorical interpretations of thirty-one myths from classical mythology. While this shows evidence of how alive the mythical tradition was in English writing during the

4. Mythical Roots

Renaissance perhaps the more interesting thing is the context. The audience, familiar with this tradition, was well-prepared for mythical-allegorical devices and stories. The heavy metal audience is much like this: they are a collective body that knows and responds to the classic songs and codes of the genre. Heavy metal now engages in a variety of codes and signs: an interpretive experience in which images, songs, and musical passages are linked with others that the listener has previously heard. Familiarity with bands, sounds, song lyrics and images invigorates communication and the energy of an interpretive dialogue. Heavy metal audiences interpret the songs and participate in the images and the energy and life of the bands that they love.

Perhaps it was Puritanism, the rise of modern science, rationalism, a church's denigration of the esoteric and Gnostic that curtailed this great wave of interest in myth. The eighteenth century rationalist or empiricist was critical of mythology. Christians, deists, and rationalists disparage myth and esoterica. That position reflects a movement in Western culture, the Enlightenment, which called metaphorical and religious thought irrational and superstitious and privileged a particular notion of reason. The view that myth is superstition was reductive and dismissive of myth. The philosopher David Hume recognized the problem that myth poses to rationality. He approached the claims of myth skeptically. In France, Condorcet assumed stages of progress: that modern man had gone beyond the primitive stages. In the nineteenth century Auguste Comte insisted upon three rational stages of human progress. Myth was a fetishistic feature of primitive society that proudly modern people had begun to overcome. However, while Enlightenment reason and early positivism securely mocked myth as primitive and superstitious, a pre-romantic approach to myth arose in Germany with Johann von Herder. Myth was central in Herder's thought and his emphasis upon the folk and their mythic tales and folk traditions was directed toward a sense of nationalism. Goethe, one Germany's greatest artists, made a study of story and myth. Elsewhere in Europe, Paul Henri Mallet translated the Eddas, in 1755–56, including the myths of Odin, and ancient Norse figures. The British colonial enterprise in India brought them the ancient myths of that region of the world.

Herder was a precursor to Romanticism, which embraced myth as a valuable and mysterious mode of human expression. Herder would not separate reason and imagination, or sensuous symbolic communication. He held that myth is creative and communal and there is a mythic wisdom in the people. Herder's thought affected Goethe, whose uses of mythology include his master work *Faust*. Nineteenth century German Romanticism, which followed, merged mythology, music, literary criticism and philosophy. The composer Richard Wagner wished to recall a mythic past in which music, voice, and dance were reconnected. In his music drama Wagner brought together poetry, theater, and music in ways that anticipate the bombastic theatricality and mythical imagery of heavy metal.

German poets like Novalis, E.T.A. Hoffmann, Friedrich Holderlin, and the Schlegel brothers sought "to recover the primordial mythic form" (Eliade, 320). The idea arose that poets may create new myths. European Romantic music drew heavily upon mythological subjects and utilized myth in its program music. The British Romantic poets were intensely involved with myth. The poet and visual artist William Blake developed his own system of mythic figures (Urizen, Loas) that represented concepts. William Wordsworth's poem about the world being too much with us concludes with the hopeful affirmation that the speaker would embrace an outworn creed if he could just hear the mythical figure of Triton blow his horn and reanimate life. Samuel Taylor Coleridge, in the *Lyrical Ballads* written with Wordsworth, turned to the supernatural: dark images of the witch Christabel, the phantasmagoric landscapes of "Kublai Kahn," and the eerie haunting mysteries of "The Rime of the Ancient Mariner." John Keats and Percy Bysshe Shelley repeatedly returned to the subjects and figures of mythology in their poetry. The sublime and the Gothic in Romanticism remain at the root of heavy metal mythology.

Perspectives from Psychology: Jung's Collective Unconscious

Psychologists have long been fascinated by myth. Psyche, from which the study of human behavior takes its name, is a figure in mythology. The Greek word "psyche" is often correlated with the word "soul." Psyche, or mind-soul, is connected with all of life. To have this psyche, this mind-soul, is to be alive, to be animated. Psyche is a principle of life and individuality. Embracing this ancient view was a distinguished explorer of the mind, the psychologist Carl Gustav Jung, who Sigmund Freud thought would become his psychoanalytic successor.

C.G. Jung's psychology of archetypes has much to offer us in our

4. Mythical Roots

inquiry into the myths behind heavy metal. Jung's thought provides a path for analysis and discovery and it offers much to literary and cultural criticism. Jung is an investigator of depth psychology where the unconscious is the most significant focus. What is one to make of this psychologist who might be described as a modern Gnostic? Jung was brilliant and imperfect. Jung studied parapsychology, followed the *volkisch* movement in Germany, thought about ancient symbols, questioned UFOs, alchemy, and the occult. He criticized positivism, drew the interest of theosophists and presaged the New Age movement, insisting that psychology should consider the spiritual. Jung asserted that archetypes reach back "into the mists of time," the ways that we form meaning "make use of certain linguistic matrices that are themselves derived from primordial images." We find ourselves "confronted with the history of language, with images and motifs that lead straight back to the primitive wonder-world" (*Collected Works* 9: 1:32–33).

Jung de-centers the ego. He offers a theory of personality types: the introvert, who is inwardly directed, and the extrovert, who is outwardly directed. Human development is a process of increasing individuation. The individuated person is one who has developed into a unique person. Jung offers the idea of the collective unconscious. He suggests that at the depths of the human mind the unconscious taps into a reservoir of archetypes: common images and symbols. Jung also asserts that there is a shadow side to consciousness. Projections of hostility toward 'the other' are reflections of one's unresolved self: one's own shadow. The shadow is the other within. The cultural shadow represents those that one has been conditioned to make abject. The shadow passed in families from generation to generation is a common theme in Gothic literature. In Jung's theory of the person there is the anima (the female other within the male) and the animus (the male other within a female), which can lead us to cultural reflection about gender. (Anima may be within males the idealized woman, a spirit or guide, or perhaps an evil force.) The persona is a psychological mask: an individual's image or role as presented to the world (*Collected Works* 9:1, 40–41). The person becomes engaged and constructed in a social role. Jung also wrote about the persona: the image or mask the individual presents to the world. Heavy metal bands and rock bands have used masks: Slipknot, Marilyn Manson, and Kiss are among them.

"Archetypes have their own force but they are also reinterpreted" (Jensen, 11; Jung, *Collected Works*, 9: 1:40–41). Our cultural creations in stories, drama, songs, films, and television broadcast imagery are culturally specific signs. Archetypes presumably lie deeper within and are reflected in popular culture. Following Jung, we may ask if the human mind taps into the consciousness of the race. Or, is it the case, rather, as some cognitive psychologists and behaviorists believe, that there is no collective unconscious? If Jung's model is correct, the mind is a vehicle for dreams and archetypal patterns. Songs and the literature of the fantastic reflect the archetypes in myth and narrative. The monomyth that is addressed by Jungian thinkers like Joseph Campbell structures some of our stories: The hero responds to a calling, faces initiation, goes on a journey amid adversity, and returns. The archetypes appear within popular songs.

If Jung's psychological theory has any validity, the creativity of the rock composer is a "visionary" art. In the Jungian view, the heavy metal artist is a vessel for creative forces: an expositor of dreams and symbols. Something forces itself upon the musician (*Collected Works*, 15:72). The artist is a "vessel, the site in which archetypal patterns express themselves" (Oliver Davis, 62). Jung writes: "The work brings with it its own form ... while his conscious mind stands amazed before this phenomenon, he is overwhelmed by a flood of thoughts and images which he never intended to create and which his own will could never have brought into being" (*Collected Works*, 15:72). Of course, the creator of a song may work consciously in shaping images, or work rationally with music theory. However, often enough a song will emerge from playing an instrument and finding a new pattern, or from a lyrical idea that prompts one to explore that idea and let go into it. More is at work in creativity than conscious rationality. Sometimes a sense of surprise or wonder moves the musician. Something that may seem at times mysterious may be involved.

That something mysterious may also echo in the listener. Songs can trigger memories and recall a personal occasion or cultural moment, as the novelist E.L. Doctorow once pointed out. People say: "That's our song they're playing." Doctorow writes: "When people say 'our song' ... The song names them, it rescues them from the accident of a historical, genetic existence. They are located in cultural time" (177).

James Hillman writes that myth is "the inflow of another sort of remembrance" (*Dream of the Underworld*, 55). Hillman's Jungian Orphic psychotherapy "encourages creative, artistic image work" (Meachem, 211). Hillman wrote: "If our society suffers from failures of imagination,

4. Mythical Roots

of leadership, of far-sighted perspectives, then we must attend to the places and moments where these interior faculties of the human mind begin" (*Blue Fire*, 111).

Heavy metal may be threatening to some because it dares to kick up what Jung called the dark half of the psyche. Jung writes: "And indeed it is a frightening thought that man also has a shadow-side to him, consisting not just of a little weakness but of a positively demonic dynamism" (*Collected Works*, 7:29). As if that notion was not terrifying enough, Jung adds that the shadow contains all of the faults which we "obviously have ourselves" (*Collected Works*, 12:29). These are things which do not fit with "normal daily life," he says (*Collected Works*, 11:198). The shadow is an internal rebel (Elkins, 243).[3] Heavy metal externalizes personal and cultural shadows.

Freud and the Uncanny

In heavy metal the posture and the style is bold, the images are wild and visionary. Heavy metal expresses a Gothic intensity that revises the idea of the sublime. In Edmund Burke's classic account the sublime was prompted by a sense of awe, intense emotion or horror. It was a power that seized the individual. The Gothic writers offered something else: a landscape of terror, one of violent storms, and treacherous places, precarious precipices and high towers, ghosts, madmen, moans and whispers and cries in the night. Terror comes from whatever shocks or moves us to "an apprehension of pain or death" (Burke, 131). However, David B. Morris points out that Burke's theory "deliberately ignores the tangled psychological and cultural dimensions of terror" (301). "Gothic explorations of terror" and Freud's essay "The Uncanny" (1919) offer other perspectives. The grotesque, exaggeration, and excess in speech and image characterize both heavy metal and the Gothic. "Gothic sublimity demonstrates the possibilities of terror in opening the mind to its own hidden and irrational powers" (Morris, 306).

In his explorations of the unconscious, Sigmund Freud, the founder of psychoanalytic method, was deeply interested in myth and in dreams. *The Interpretation of Dreams* (1900) was his first major book to explore the dynamics of the mind. With it Freud affirmed that the seemingly random, chaotic mental activity of dreams conveyed meaning. In his psychoanalytical investigations he recalled the myth of Oedipus. Freud was a Viennese neurologist whose fundamental ideas were formed during a time of positivist reaction to Romanticism. He was well aware of Gothicism in the German Romantic tradition and he offered his own perspectives and analysis of dread.

Freud provides a theory of terror and fear. The uncanny brings the terrible from something that is 'strangely familiar'. Repression is at the center of Freud's psychoanalytic theory and it is central to the way he looks at terror and horror. The uncanny confronts us with the unhomelike, the return of the repressed, the disguised images of repressed desire, the aspects of self and society that we have neglected or disowned. In supernaturalism the uncanny returns. In the images of death and the supernatural in heavy metal, as in the Gothic novel, new terrors await. "Death and supernaturalism are closely linked for Freud because they both derive their ultimate terror from a return of the repressed," writes Morris (310). The heavy metal song that trades in Gothic horror is like the Gothic novel of which Morris says: "in its preoccupation with death shocks us with the return of something familiar and old-established in the mind but also estranged and unknowable" (310). Fear is rooted in our biology, in our psychology, in our response to alarms, in our fight and flight mechanisms.

Consider Edvard Munch's Expressionist painting *The Scream* (1893). Its lone figure expresses terror with his hands to the side of his head and the wide O of his mouth. He crosses a bridge, horrified, with two vague shadows of people behind him and a swirl of light and color beyond. The scream is "the ultimate Gothic reduction of language," says David B. Morris. It is "the point of excess" almost unable to name what it fears (313).

Heavy Metal and the Classics

The turn of heavy metal bands to classical resources parallels a practice that goes back hundreds of years. The artists of the Renaissance were alive to classical models and asserted human power. Neo-classicism in art was dominant at the end of the eighteenth century and in the early decades of the nineteenth century. Heavy metal gets hold of this in novel fashion. Its artists make use of those symbols and stories in contemporary ways

4. Mythical Roots

that would be barely recognizable to the Greeks, the Romans, or to the Egyptians. They employ themes of heroism, the clash of titans, the encounter with primordial terror. Stories are re-written. Fragments are brought together in the varied assemblage of a postmodern puzzle.

In ancient antiquity, Homer held that the poet is an entertainer who produces entertainment. That is what the lyricist is today. There may be a message, an emotion, an expression of concern that accompanies this but the role of song as entertainment has those ancient origins. Homer also believed that he was inspired by the Muses. That is not to say that he was not actively involved in constructing his epic poems. Of course, he was. Plato, in his dialogues the *Phaedrus* and the *Ion*, claimed that the poet is passive: that some spirit works through him and he is susceptible to *furor poeticus*, or a kind of madness. There may be moments of what might be called inspiration and even a sense of feeling like one is the vehicle for what is written. However, there is no question that composers have studied and learned their craft and the particular language of their musical genre. Through much listening, the styles and techniques of his or her predecessors are absorbed. The genre has its own code, the unwritten rules of the trade, a back catalog of works with which the songwriter is involved. Simply put: heavy metal musicians listen to heavy metal musicians. Images are absorbed and appropriated, symbols and figures are repeated, and the creative mind digs down into myth, contemporary experience, and musical resources for novelty.

This turn toward the mythical is nothing new. In *Care of the Soul* (1992), where Thomas Moore probes myth and the mind, he observes the arresting, grotesque imagery in the history of art. He speaks of the visual images of Medieval, Renaissance, and Modern painting with their "blood, twisted crucifixions" and "surrealistic landscapes." He considers physical symptoms as a voice of the soul and looks at the family and child, narcissism, depression, and creativity, among other subjects. What he means by soul he describes as "a quality or dimension of experiencing life and ourselves" (5). The entire study is steeped in Greek mythology but it is intended to speak to our contemporary lives, to our souls *now*. It is this use of ancient myth to address the contemporary world that is at the heart of heavy metal.

Metal may turn toward elaborate myths but in creating these mythical-musical dramas it points to the contemporary world. Beneath a pose of respectability may live irrational issues. "The façade of normality can hide a wealth of deviance," writes Thomas Moore in *Care of the Soul*. This care of soul "is interested in the not so normal," he adds. (18).[4]

The Greek Myths

Within popular culture, heavy metal makes a contribution to the literature of the fantastic. Bands exploit the resources of mythology. One can, of course, say that in a band like Iron Maiden or Manowar the entire sphere of the universe in referring to Greek myth is repeating a familiar trope. They have heard Led Zeppelin play "Achilles Last Stand" and they too will turn to Greek mythology for a theme. Yet, something deeper may be going on. When Metallica creates "Atlas, Rise" they recall a burdened heroic figure who holds the weight of the world—indeed the entire sphere of the universe—on his shoulders. His fate is seen as a punishment as James Hetford sings of the bitterness and the burden he bears. The ancient figure of Atlas has become a figure of modern man as well. Holding that tortured pose for all eternity, he is a sign of the weight of things, as much as is the heavy bass that pulses through Metallica's music.

The word myth can be traced to the Greek word *mythos*. Once upon a time this word meant message or speech, a story that was spoken. Around the 5th century BC the notion of an entertaining tale began to emerge. The Roman word *fabula* tends to cast myth as just a fantastic story. However, we can consider the importance of the inner truth of myth for a people and their transmission of their values across generations.

Myth has always been connected with entertainment. Stories entertained groups of people, who listened to them for hours. Homer recognized that songs brought wonder and delight to audiences. The spectacle of theater, dance, and song drew visitors to the Athenian tragedies. Myth shared in oral traditions, conveyed lessons: how to live the good life, how to avoid or overcome difficulties. Myth spoke of the distance between the gods and mortals and the limitations of humanity. For the ancient Greeks, myth helped to define and explain the world around them and their place in the universe. Stories, some writers and critics have suggested, continue to serve the same function for us.

That sense of entertainment, drama, and social function appears in heavy metal songs. For example, Manowar performs the suite "Achilles:

4. Mythical Roots

The Agony and the Ecstasy in Eight Parts" from their 1992 album *The Triumph of Steel*. These songs foreground masculinity and warrior spirit. The overt allusions to *The Iliad* include "Hector Storms a Wall." Hephaestus creating new armor and a new shield for Achilles in Book 18 of *The Iliad* is Manowar's occasion for a drum solo. Themes in the lengthy song include the acceptance of Fate. In contrast with *The Iliad*, Achilles expects to meet Patroclus in the sky rather than in the Underworld. There is no clear reference to coming to Troy for gold in *The Iliad*. Hecuba in *The Trojan Women* suggests that Helen had her eyes on her son Paris and the wealth of Troy. The Greek argument is that Helen was stolen away from Menelaus by Paris. Hecuba's argument is that Helen had designs on the city and a lust for Paris. Her position emerges clearly in Michael Caccoyanis' film with Katherine Hepburn as Hecuba.

Greek mythology has ancient roots. The Ancient Greeks told fantastic stories of travel into imaginary lands, entertaining tales of adventure beyond the known-boundaries of the world. Their fantastic stories told of the supernatural. Many of these stories appear to go back to the Mycaenean Age, or to have emerged sometime between 1200 BC and 800 BC. The stories of Hercules, Jason and the Argonauts, and the cycle that later became the Theban plays (the stories of Oedipus and of his daughter Antigone) are pre-Homeric.

Myth existed throughout the ancient world. Myth was present in India and Persia, in Egypt and Crete and Greece, and among the Hebrews. Myths served people who did not have science as they attempted to explain physical phenomena. The Miletans suggested that thunder was caused because the wind blew free from the clouds. There was, for them, a kind of mechanism. Greek cosmology appears to have drawn upon Akkadian myths of Mesopotamia and this contact with Babylonians and Phoenicians of the east likely took place during the Iron Age. However, Greek mythology is uniquely anthropomorphic.

The Greeks structured and organized mythology and it would add energy to the arts and literature. The common myths and values of Greece contributed to a sense of community, or "Greekness." People migrated and so did the stories. Greeks knew the stories of *The Iliad* and *The Odyssey* and the story of Narcissus, so proud of himself that he fell face-first into a pool and drowned. They knew the story of Hades abduction of Persephone and their residence in the Underworld. They were familiar with Ariadne who assisted Theseus who was guided by a thread through the labyrinth constructed by Daedelus to kill the Minotaur and then escape. They knew the story of Icarus, the son of the inventor Daedelus, who flew too close to the sun: a story that is repeated in a song by Iron Maiden.

Myths created and bound together communities. Contacts between the Greek colonies brought the common legacy of these great myths to people. These myths offered them a way to connect their lives with a pan-Hellenic sense of what it meant to be Greek. The Greek poets embellished upon ancient myths and produced new ones. They performed at festivals. In the Homeric period of the 8th century BC they created epic, as in Homer's *Iliad* and *Odyssey*. References to *The Iliad* in heavy metal include Manowar's 28 minute suite on Achilles and Blind Guardian's fourteen minute song about *The Iliad* for *A Night at the Opera*. Bands that have made use of *The Iliad* also include Virgin Steele's "The House of Atreus," Warlord's "Achilles' Revenge," Manila Road's "The Fall of Ilium," and "War Trophy" by Stormwind. References to Achilles occur on Hades' 1987 album *Resting Success* in their song "On to Iliad."

What has this modern imagination to do with the imagination of ancient poets and storytellers? The ancient poets created the choral lyrics of the 6th century BC and the tragic dramas in the 5th century. The earlier period of Archaic myth, like some metal lyricists, told dramatic stories of heroes. In the Periclean age of the 400s BC the polis society centered on democracy and issues of society and family. Many of the myths of heroes begin as myths of initiation, including the venture to the Trojan War, the journey of Telemachus in *The Odyssey* to seek his father, and the story of Jason and the Argonauts. There is also the initiation and growth to womanhood of Europa, Io, and Iphigenia.

Homer and Hesiod declared that the poet is inspired by the Muses and thus poetry is a gift from this divine source. (See Hesiod, *Theogony*, 1–114.) In Greek mythology the Muses were the goddesses of inspiration. The names of the nine Muses come to us from Hesiod (*Theogony*, 76). They represent the arts: Calliope (epic poetry), Clio (history), Euterpe (flute playing), Terpsichore (lyric poetry and choral dancing), Erato (lyric poetry), Melpomene (tragedy), Thalia (comedy), Polyhymnia (hymns and pantomime) and Urania (astronomy). Homer addresses the Muse at the start of his epic, *The Iliad*. So does Virgil at the start of the *Aeneid*. This became a trope repeated by any poet who would write an epic.

The poets drew upon mythical sources. However, they sometimes

4. Mythical Roots

told stories that seemed scandalous. They spoke of immoral gods, aggressive and violent heroes. The philosopher Plato opposed this inspiration that was claimed by the poets. In his dialogue *The Republic* he would throw the poets out of the republic. Meanwhile, only the modes of music that would lend order were acceptable to Plato. Paradoxically, Plato who wrote dialogues that were like poetic plays was critical of poets who neglected to promote moral values and preserve society. From this perspective, as critic Allan Bloom was to argue in *The Closing of the American Mind* (1987), the rockers should be banished. As Deena Weinstein reminds us: "Those familiar with Rush's epic *2112* will recognize that Plato's arguments are the same as those offered by the priests of the Temple of Syrinx" (*Heavy Metal: The Music and Its Culture,* 263).

Plato developed a theory of art as imitation, or mimesis. In his philosophy, our world is at a remove from the higher Forms or Ideas. We can only see shadows, distant reflections. Plato held that rhetoric was a form of evasion of the truth, a kind of pretense, rather than an expression of the truth. Aristotle, whose *Poetics* became important to literary criticism, tended to separate poetry and rhetoric. In the *Poetics*, he considers poetry as mimetic art and he provides an analysis of tragic theater. Central to his analysis is the idea of *katharis*: that audiences of theater respond with pity or fear to the difficulties of tragic characters and are thereby liberated from their own deep emotions.

In the *Poetics* Aristotle says that the action of a tragedy inspires and moves the audience with a sense of pity or fear. We have pity for the hero who is suffering and fear perhaps that we ourselves are as vulnerable. Following this view, the song, like the dramatic play, causes recognition (*anagnorisis*) and learning. In the audience the emotional experience of watching the misfortunes of the characters, like participating feelingly in a song, helps us to see the vulnerabilities of our own lives.

The modern study of the Greek myths by European scholars began in France in the 18th century. However, the practice of philology in Germany led to a more intense focus on Greek myth. The Germans explored myth as culture and as history, as a root of language and communication, and as an ancient society's way of attempting to explain phenomena in nature: the lightning and thunder and ocean storms, fertility and the change of seasons, earthquake and the warmth of the sun and the canopy of the stars. Toward the end of the nineteenth century there was more of an emphasis on ritual in anthropological and sociological studies.

Myth and Magic in Heavy Metal Music

The Dionysian Spirit

The heavy metal concert is a communal affair that reflects the Dionysian, or bacchanalian, festival. The Bacchic cult was of Greek origin but also spread across southern Italy. It may have included a protest against Roman authority. Mythologically, heavy metal is of the Dionysian spirit. Dionysius was the twice born son of Zeus and Semele, the god of wine and intoxication. In some circles, Dionysius was regarded as hermaphroditic—both male and female, young and old, and forever on the move. The mythic cults regarded Dionysius as sometimes eccentric or violent. He represents art, enchantment, and a challenge to social order. While he is creative he can also be destructive. In *The Closing of the American Mind* (1987), Allan Bloom directed his criticism of rock music, which he did not understand very well, against Dionysius and the Dionysian spirit. He called Mick Jagger of the Rolling Stones "Nietzsche's nihiline."

Heavy metal is Dionysian. The god of wine and intoxication is creative and destructive. He is the god of the mask and impersonation and spirit of ritual madness. This ritual madness had nothing to do with drugs or alcohol. Rather, it had to do with ecstasy and being seized by the energy in the Bacchic rites. That wildness was viewed as mad by the uninitiated ones. Clearly, we might draw a parallel with the communal aspect of the initiated heavy metal audience.

From the Dionysian, claimed Friedrich Nietzsche, emerged the birth of tragedy from the spirit of music. He is a perplexing god who can cross boundaries and transcend the earthly. Dionysius is the master of epiphanic moments, illusion, and change: a god of exuberance. In Euripides' *Bacchae* he is the inventor of wine (274–283). Between Athens and Delphi, the place of the oracle, lies Thebes. In Sophocles' Theban plays he is the patron god of Thebes (*Antigone*, 1122). The dithyramb is a chorale song sung in honor of Dionysius.

The scholar E.R. Dodds and Niezsche's friend Erwin Rohde studied the maenadic ritual from an anthropological perspective. Rohde conjectured that a wild Thracian Dionysius was tamed by Greece: he was a barbarian who was Hellenized (Rohde's *Psyche*, 1894). Dionysian festivals occurred across the entire landscape of ancient Greece. Festivals dedicated to Dionysius were often fertility festivals, some signaling the coming of spring. These festivals involved myth, cross-dressing,

4. Mythical Roots

drunkenness, obscene gestures, phallic monuments, and group procession. The wild dark side of Dionysius is frenzy, madness, violence, and bloodshed.

There is a wry dark humor in some heavy metal material. Comedy for the Greeks usually expressed the light and frivolous. Yet, the chorale dance of Greek dramas may include play as well as madness. Tragedy may be connected with Dionysus or Pan or the darker destructive traits. Strangely perhaps, the Dionysian god of vital energy and life is also related to death and to Hades in the Underworld. Nietzsche regarded art as an interplay of the Dionysian and the Apollonian. We may see Dionysius as a psychological principle, or other to the orderly Apollonian in society.

Prometheus and the Greek Gods

Prometheus was a vigorous and rebellious spirit, a figure of revolt who gave fire to mankind. Hephaestus grabbed and bound Prometheus with chains to Mount Caucasus where an eagle flew to pick at his liver, which was restored by night. Hercules rescued Prometheus. Mount Olympus was home of the gods and there the gods presided. Geographically, on the edge of Thessaly and Macedonia, on the shores of the Aegean Sea is a mountain range where Olympus is said to be situated. The greatest of the gods were twelve: Zeus, (the great overlord), and Hera (wife of Zeus), Poseidon (fierce god of the sea), Hermes (the messenger), Hephaestes (god of fire), Ares (god of war), Apollo, Athena, Artemis, Hestia, Aprhrodite (the goddess of love), and Demeter. Further down in rank were Selene, Leto, Helios, Dionysius, Thamis, Eos. Hades was in the Underworld with Persephone and Hecate. There were goddesses of inspiration, the Muses, and the forces of Nemesis.

Hesiod's *Theogony* (8th century BC) classifies Greek mythology, recalling stories of the origin of the gods and providing a cosmology of how the universe was designed. Hesiod tells us that in the beginning there was chaos and darkness upon the universe. From this emerged Gaia, the Earth, and the love of Eros: the principle of attraction. There came into this world day and night. The sky filled with stars. Gaia and Uranus, her son, created the Titans, the Cyclops, and three other monsters. The Titans were the male figures Oceanus, Coeus, Hyperion, Crius, Iapetus, Cronus and the female figures Theia, Rhea, Mnemosyne, Phoebe, Thetys, and Themis.

Cronus was time (chronology). From the Titans came Prometheus and Atlas and Menoetius. From Hyperion there were Helios, Selene (the Moon), Eos (Dawn). From Cronus and Rhea came Hestia (of the Sun), Demeter, Hera, Hades, Poseidon, and Zeus.

Orpheus, the mythical Thracian musician (or Orfeo), has been celebrated in many operas. In myth he seeks his wife Euridyce in Hades. He is warned that he cannot look back at her until he reaches the River Styx. Unfortunately, he does look and Eurydice must stay locked away in the Underworld. In one telling of the myth of Orpheus, he is torn to shreds by the maenads. On the opera stage we have Peri's *Eurydice* (1600), Cacconi's *Eurydice* (1602), Monteverdi's *Orfeo* (1607), Joseph Haydn's *Orefeo y Euridyce* (1637) and Gluck's opera which also focuses on the mythical couple. In a later century we see Offenbach's satire, *Orpheus in the Underworld*, with a book by Hector Cremieux, which had its Paris premiere October 21, 1858. Orpheus is the subject of many other works that project themselves dramatically and theatrically.

Celtic Myth and Metal

Heavy metal bands have dipped into the world of Celtic mythology. Iron Maiden draws "The Wicker Man" from Celtic lore. The black metal band Celtic Frost brings a reference to the Celtic world into its name. Cruachan, begun by Keith Fay in 1992, the black metal Primordial, and Waylander are Irish bands focusing on Celtic material in their heavy metal music. Scholars at the University of Leeds have explored how four bands that draw upon British or Celtic roots (Winterfelleth, Wodensthrone, Old Corpse Road, and Oakenshield) construct mythologies, heritage narratives, and a sense of identity. Stonehenge has been referenced by Ten Years After, Hawkwind, Spinal Tap, and Black Sabbath. Led Zeppelin also turned their gaze upon Celtic myth.

Led Zeppelin's tours took them across the globe. Page and Plant traveled widely and gained exposure to mythical ideas and to sounds like those heard on "Kashmir." They trekked through Europe, Arab North Africa, India and the Far East. Page and Plant read mythology and Page explored occult and esoteric traditions. The imagination that Robert Plant brings to his Led Zeppelin lyrics appears to be primarily informed by Celtic and British sources, like J.R.R. Tolkien's mythical world, Arthurian myth, and

4. Mythical Roots

vague recollections or dreams of Avalon and of Albion: England's green and pleasant land.

Albion is a name for Britain. The name appears as Alba in Scots, Albain in Gaelic, Alban in Welsh. There is a legend of giants—that an exiled individual learned of the place from the goddess Diana. There is the Albina story in which a woman named Albina and her sister encounter a race of giants. Geoffrey's tale appears in Edmund Spenser's *The Faerie Queene*. Legend says that Avalon is where King Arthur drew forth the sword Excalibur. Avalon is where the king went after the Battle of Camlann. It was his final destination. There is mention of the legend in Geoffrey of Monmouth's *Historia Regnem Brittaniae*.

The Celtic Druids clearly loved music and poetry. Diodorus Siculus wrote: "They have lyric poets whom they call bards. They sing to the accompaniment of instruments resembling lyres" (207). In Welsh literature the Druids were poets and musicians. They may also have been an intellectual caste. They used lyres, pipes, drums, the trumpet, and chanted verse forms. The Druids pointed toward the otherworld and are said to have been practiced in keening (*caoine*): a piercing lament for the dead. (Scholars have suggested that their Celtic music parallels Hindu musical culture [Green, 212].) Native Celtic music confronted Latin Church music and Ireland maintained the pentatonic scale.

In Celtic myth, Bran MacFebal is "tempted by a goddess" into joining her in the otherworld. "There is nothing rough nor harsh but only sweet music striking the ear," she says. A warrior comes to Cormac at Tara with a branch on which there are three apples. Once shaken, the branch makes music and this lets the wounded fall asleep. There are references to the harpers of Cainbile in the Tain Bo Cualnge. There are the men of prophecy and magic.[5]

"The Druids are a priestly caste. They regulate public and private sacrifices and decide religious questions. The people hold them in great respects," wrote Julius Caesar (Caesar, 154). "It is said that these young men have to memorize endless verses, and that some of them spend as long as twenty years at their books" (155). Caesar criticizes their "unwillingness to publicize their teaching" (155). There is a rumor that the Druids officiate at "human sacrifices" (155). Caesar says, "The Gallic tribes as a whole are slaves to superstition.... Their central dogma is the immortality and transmigration of the soul" (155). Caesar conflates the Roman gods with the Celtic ones that remind him of their Roman parallels: "Their principal god is Mercury, of whom there are numerous images up and down Gaul" (156) (VI, 16).

Polybius saw courage in the Celts: a warrior spirit. The Roman historian Tacitus records a massacre of the Druids in AD 60 (*Annales* XI, v.29). For Cicero the Celts were wild men. He recalls their attack on Delphi and Rome and their aggression (Cicero, *Pro Fontex*). Livy tells his readers that the Celts are ferocious warriors. They are unpredictable and make a tactical use of noise with shouts and horns and beating of their shields. "The fine order and the noise of the Celtic host terrified the Romans," writes Polybius (Histories, II: 29). "In their usual custom they raised their shout of triumph," writes Caesar (*De Bello Gallico,* V: 37). "They had trumpets peculiar to them and barbaric in sound," writes Diodorus Siculus (*History,* V: 30.3).

A search for the pre-Christian in Celtic-Irish literature, a world apart from the ecclesiastical-Christological heritage of Ireland, seeks its ideal in the mythic-heroic, in lyrical, dramatic prose and verse. It draws upon secular tendencies and inclines toward tales of the otherworld. An oral tradition lies behind the written texts which refer to myth and legend. The Ulster Cycle of Tain Bo Cualnge presents a story of heroism beginning with the boyhood deeds of Cu Chulainu. (Modern scholars have classified this into four cycles: the mythological cycle, the Ulster cycle, the Finn cycle and the king cycle.) Oral tradition tended to be controlled by an elite and privileged class of poet-savants, or by the Druids and then the *filidh.*

The medieval literature of Wales reflects this oral tradition. Sioned Davies remarks that "certain mythological themes and characters in the 11th and 12th centuries are recognizably Celtic in origin." They are creations that passed through oral transmission. Literature in Wales had been mostly found in monastic circles. Native learning was maintained in legends and lore. The Cyfarwyddyd was about guidance direction and instruction (785). The Cyfarwyddyd was also a story, or referred to a storyteller. The Welsh collections include the *White Book of Rhydderch* (c. 1350) and *The Red Book of Hergest* (c. 1400). There are also fragments of tales from one hundred years or more earlier. These are known as the Mabinoglon. Lady Charlotte Guest translated and named this. They include an Arthurian prose tale "Calwwchae Olevae" and three more tales.

These mythical frameworks involve a search for vital and vigorous primordial culture and romanticize primitivism. Heavy metal may turn

4. Mythical Roots

to them, in part, because heavy metal bears the legacy of European Romanticism's responses to Jean-Jacques Rousseau's claims for the noble savage. The noble savage was the unaffected natural youth who was free in a primitive way before social institutions put him in chains. He was the wild and passionate man, the rebel who broke free from rationalist Enlightenment confinement. Musical art would likewise break through rules of harmony or measure into terrible violent storms of sonic thunder, nightmare, apocalypse, and revelation. Heavy metal would shatter the tame and shake up the prosaic common world. It would howl the wild howl of a primitive and rediscover primal force.

5

Shadow Dreams
The Legacy of Gothic Romanticism

Rock music's spirit of rebellion and creativity has at times been linked with the Romantic movement in Europe in the late eighteenth century and in the nineteenth century. Given heavy metal's attraction to myth this perspective is a useful one. Romanticism's emphasis on individualism, authenticity, creative genius, and folk culture, its attention to irony, nostalgia for the past, and concern with the sublime can all be found in heavy metal music and performance. Metal and Romanticism share an appreciation of the capacity of symbolism and myth to address the ineffable. Metal, of course, bears aspects of postmodernism but it is also filled with fierce imagination, including Romanticism's interest in the shadowy areas of horror and madness.[1] This is, of course, not the popular understanding of the word "romantic." Romanticism, instead, points to independence of thought, vivid imagination, and—in some strands of metal, like black metal—to some very dark and supernatural regions of myth.

The British Romantic poets were intensely involved with myth. William Blake developed his own mythic system of contraries and mythic figures that represented concepts. William Wordsworth's poem "The World Is Too Much with Us" concludes with the hope that if only he could hear Triton blow his horn or see Proteus rise from the sea again the myth would arise that would renew his life. Samuel Taylor Coleridge in his contributions to the *Lyrical Ballads* with Wordsworth turned toward the supernatural: dark images of the witch in "Cristabel," the phantasmagoric landscape of "Kublai Kahn," and the eerie, haunting mysteries of "The Rime of the Ancient Mariner." John Keats and Percy Bysshe Shelley returned repeatedly to subjects and figures drawn from mythology. We see Queen Mab and Prometheus in Shelley's poetry. The sublime, the Gothic, and Romanticism and its appeal to myth lie at the root of some heavy metal imagery and song narratives.

Myth and Monstrosity

Gothic Romanticism brings us the rhetoric of monstrosity. From Mary Shelley's *Frankenstein* and the strange figures of Ann Radcliffe's *The Mysteries of Udolpho* and Matthew Lewis's *The Monk* to the madwoman in the attic of Charlotte Brontë's *Jane Eyre* and the vampire of Bram Stoker's *Dracula*, monstrosity haunts the Romantic and Victorian public. Franco Moretti reads the monster Frankenstein, Mary Shelley's "hideous progeny," through a Marxist lens as being the working class. The creature is the collective patchwork of dead bodies and expresses "the terror of a split society" (Moretti, 83). These disruptive social forces appear in the rebellious Luddites who break machines and are depicted in Brontë's novel *Shirley*. They are the heavy metal anarchists of the proletariat.

Heavy metal began similarly: with proud, strong voices that questioned a limiting modern environment and called for rebellion and renewal. The themes of "disorder, conflict, opposition and contradiction" that Deena Weinstein sees in heavy metal are all present in the "monster" figure of Frankenstein. They are "the other" or, as Weinstein says, the "proud pariah" (*Heavy Metal: The Music and Its Culture*, 39). Their stance becomes one of resistance against injustice. Alien, not wanted, and not nurtured, Mary Shelley's creature becomes a troubling shadow for the community. Examples of the monster abound in Gothic fiction: Ambrosio in *The Monk* (1796), Falkland in William Godwin's *Caleb Williams* (1794), Schedoni in Ann Radcliff's *The Italian* (1797). In response to the Gothic tale *The Monk* by Matthew Lewis, a critic for *The British Critic* (June 7, 1796) wrote: "We are sorry to observe that good talents have been applied in the production of this monster" (Brantlinger, 677). A modern Parents Music Resource Center critic could have written that statement about Ozzy Osborne. From the time of the French Revolution of 1789 the Gothic meant revolutionary terror. Viewing the French Revolution as monstrous Edmund Burke writes: "You are terrifying yourself with ghosts and apparitions, whilst your house is haunted with robbers." (5:248). He called the French Revolution "orgies of destruction, massacre, and rapine" (*Works*, 5:237).

Myth and Magic in Heavy Metal Music

A World Too Much with Us

The poet Wordsworth laments that the world is too much with us. Getting and spending we lay waste our cares and little we see in nature that is ours. We have given away our power. We are caught up in things. The narrator in his poem says that he could be suckled in a creed outworn—he could turn to a pagan, mythological, pre-Christian world that has faded away—if only he could feel the power of myth again. If he could see the shape-shifting god Proteus or hear Triton, a god of the sea, blow his horn he would be renewed in his spirit. He would feel vital and alive again.

Such a vision was not a matter of escapism. The poet was searching for that spirit that could reanimate life in a contemporary scene. He was nostalgic for a purer time. Once the child played and lived in a remarkable world of energy and fascination. There were moments where he could almost see something profound. Now that vision rarely returns and the glory of that time is gone. He lives in a pained nostalgia in a broken world. Myth and song, some dramatic art, might revive the spontaneous wide-eyed child and bring back playfulness, wonder, and awe. Our world is too much with us. Rock responds with the blues, with something visceral. It responds with heavy metal fantasy. Rock music is commercial—getting and spending—but its heavy metal fantasies and its hard-edged blues speak of life. In its fantastic forms it has put myth to use in performance and on recordings to stir, entertain, and re-enliven audiences.

So rock is the progeny of the Romantic spirit, the soul that wrestles with modernity. As a young man, Wordsworth, who lived in the Lake District in England, witnessed the unfolding of the French Revolution and the first waves of industrialism. He listened for the voices of the common people of that region and he sought something visionary in the midst of the ordinary. Wordsworth lived in a setting more in tune with the natural world than the grit and grime of the industrial landscape of Birmingham. It was amid working class communities, industrial walls, and machinery that rock bands would arise two hundred years later. Like Wordsworth, they would react to the encroachments of the industrial age on the human spirit. They would look for myth—morbid or fantastic—and music and theatrics to inject new life into a prosaic, vacuous world.

That same quest was central to the poetic work of John Keats, a poet who often turned to mythology for his subjects. Keats was a writer of lyric poetry and odes, including "Ode to Psyche," "Ode on a Grecian Urn," "Ode to Melancholy," and "Ode to a Nightingale." His themes include reflection on dream and vision and reality, or the ideal and the real, contrasts of joy and melancholy, and meditations on life and death and being mortal or perhaps immortal. Keats lived a mythical quest to re-enliven language and thought and he saw life as a vale of soul-making. He kept a journal in which he charted vowel sounds for the emotional impact they would have in poetry. Keats knew that those high a and e sounds conveyed something quite different from the low moaning o's and the "uh" of short u's.[2]

Myth, Metal and William Blake

Myth has to do with metaphorical thinking. "Literature is a conscious mythology," literary critic Northrop Frye once said. Frye was an archetypal critic whose careful attention to poetry included what we call intertextuality: that is, the way that texts intersect and refer to each other in a variety of allusions and mutual influences. In *Fearful Symmetry* he says that he hopes that readers will recover a lost art of reading poetry (11). In that book Frye looked specifically at the poetry of William Blake, a poet whose mystical and rebellious stance critiqued the British society of his day as sharply as do any heavy metal lyricists. Blake was a visual artist as well as a poet; he was an unorthodox Christian who attacked the poisonous conformity he saw in the church of his day and the poverty and suppression of the human spirit he witnessed in industrial England. Blake created his own mythological poetic territory in poems filled with figures like the heroic Albion and the distressing Urizen. To approach his art a reader has to develop an understanding of metaphors and the language of symbols.

When the literary critic explored Blake he recalled the Elizabethan sense of sound and symbol, the contrapuntal symbolism that had been lost in the eighteenth century period of rationalism. In the eighteenth century, Enlightenment reason and order were emphasized. With the Romantic poets, who began writing late in that century, myth and symbolism were rediscovered and emphasized. William Blake requires us to read symbolically. Likewise, we can say that heavy metal music—its lyrics, its imagery, its aggressive sounds and calls into the depths—urges us to listen and to "read" symbolically. A listener to this genre, like the reader of Romantic poetry, will consider how the song relates to other works in the genre. The listener will understand the narrative and images of a song through this familiarity with these reference points. Like the medieval or Renaissance reader of poetry, or listener to poetry, the well-versed heavy metal listener understands the figures of fantasy and responds to the archetypes that are in play.

Blake portrays the dusty ruins of industrial darkness: the kind of landscape that Black Sabbath arose from in Birmingham. In his poems we see the London of slums that would later be stuffed behind the railroad tracks and the factories. We meet the chimney sweep, the little black boy, a garden so tightly managed by clerics that, impoverished of all redeeming light, it has gone to seed. The sick rose withers. In Blake, as in some heavy metal, we see a fallen world, an apocalyptic landscape, a demonic frame in which individuals are isolated. This is Blake's mythos. His hero of Albion in *The Four Zoas* ventures through chaos. In the work of Romantic poets like Blake—or certain heavy metal lyricists like Iron Maiden's Steve Harris—mythology shifts our attention to the creations of the imagination. The narrative quest becomes one to remake the world.

Blake's mythology appears in a striking way in his poem "Milton." The writer of *Paradise Lost*, John Milton, is viewed as something of a spiritual father by Blake, although Blake seeks to revise his Puritan rebellion into something more contemporary. Throughout his poetry, Blake is continually meditating on contraries, or oppositions. In this case, it appears that he is wrestling with his own journey through conflict to find a point at which reason, instinct, and passion may be reconciled by imagination. Milton wrote of angels and demons, temptation and the fallen state of Adam. In Blake's poem Milton returns to justify the ways of God to man. However, the very spirit of poetic genius that connects Blake to Milton argues that Milton has to revise his sense of Natural Religion: one informed by the world-view of Isaac Newton, John Locke, and the Enlightenment. This worldview takes him away from his true self, away from Albion the archetypal figure. There must be a new journey: a visionary quest. Along his way the poet meets with Urizen (Reason) who represents too much rationality. Milton is tempted by Luvah, or Passion, in the form a child. He meets with Tharmas, or Instinct, and with Urthona, or Imagination. These are the Four Zoas that stand alongside Albion, who is the archetypal man. In the fall of mankind, the Four Zoas tumble to the depths with Albion into "the pale and cold." Milton lies in the Satan space where reason, passion, and instinct are at war. Milton recognizes that Satan is not "other" from this world but is part of its reason and instinct. Satan is Milton's own self shut against the world which creates outer conflict and war by neglecting to deal with its own inner conflict. Reason and Passion are unreconciled. The creative person is incomplete until he can break out of this prison and see the Infinite through the powers of Imagination. Milton comes naked and empty to the space where the world of Adam and Satan intersect and he looks through those contending forces. He returns to the archetypal man. He recognizes that the contraries are positive and suddenly sees everything from within in a new light aided by the imagination. Heavy metal attempts to reopen the gates. Some might claim it opens the gates of hell, while others may say it opens what Aldous Huxley once called "the doors of perception."

Coleridge's Imagination

Rush has set to music the phantasmagoric poem "Kublai Kahn" by Samuel Taylor Coleridge, a mythical verse that the poet reported had emerged from his reading of an exotic place and from slumber and an opium dream. "Kublai Kahn" is called a fragment. It is mysterious, a poem in which the literary critic John Frederick Lowes finds "the unconscious playing its game alone" (Lowes, *Road to Xanadu*, 104). The process of creative invention appears to be referred to in the poem. Coleridge suggests spontaneous creation from within a dream. Coleridge offers his poem to the world as a psychological curiosity. The reading is supported by Coleridge's preface in which he accounts for the creation of his poem:

"In the summer of the year 1787, the author, then in ill health, had retired to a lonely farmhouse between Porlock and Linton, on the Exmoor confines of Somerset and Devonshire. In consequence of a slight indisposition, an anodyne had been prescribed, from the effects of which he fell asleep in his chair at the moment that he was reading the following sentence, or words of the same substance, in *Purchas, His Pilgrimes*: 'Here the Khan Kubla commanded a palace to be built, and a stately garden thereunto. And thus ten miles of fertile ground were enclosed with a wall.' The author continued for about three hours in a profound sleep, at least of the external senses, during which time he has the most vivid confidence, that he could not have composed less than from two to three hundred lines, if that indeed can be called composition in which all the images rose up before him as things, with a parallel production of the correspondent expressions, without any sensation or consciousness of effort. On awakening he appeared to himself to have a distinct recollection of the whole, and taking his pen, ink, and paper, instantly and eagerly wrote down the lines that are here preserved. At this moment he was unfortunately called out by a person on business from Porlock, and detained by him above an hour, and on his return to his room, found, to his no small surprise and mortification, that, though he still retained some vague and dim recollection of the general purport of the vision, yet, with the exception of some eight or ten scattered lines and images, all the rest had passed away like images on the surface of a stream into which a stone had been cast, but, alas, without the after restoration of the latter" (Coleridge, Preface to "Kublai Kahn").

Some critics have questioned how Coleridge would have found a rare book like *Purchas, His Pilgrimes* in a "lonely farmhouse" (Fruman, 337). However, few would question Coleridge's deep interest in the workings of the imagination. Coleridge wrote in his *Biographia Literaria* of his view that imagination was not only receptive but also constructive of reality. Fascinated with metal imagery he drew upon the thought of the philosopher Immanuel Kant and on the empiricism and epistemology of John Locke and the early psychologist David Hartley, after whom he named one of his children.

When the time came for Coleridge to collaborate with William Wordsworth on what became the *Lyrical Ballads*, the poets decided that Wordsworth would seek the common language and folk stories of the rural people of England and Coleridge would write of the fantastic and the supernatural. With his remarkable imagination Coleridge wrote the mythical "Christabel," about a witch, "Kublai Kahn," about a stately pleasure dome, a sacred river, and a tumbling avalanche, and the haunting tale of an ancient mariner destined to forever sail and encounter the ghosts of his doomed crew.

Poe's Tales of Mystery and Imagination

Edgar Allan Poe, the creator of mysteries, detective fiction, and horror stories, recognized art as a rational construct. His use of horror critiques the presumptions of rationality and is related to his critical discourse. Poe, an American Romantic, interrogated Enlightenment reason. A common

5. Shadow Dreams

mistake is to conflate Poe with his narrators, his invented fictional voices. This misrepresentation of Poe was fostered by the jealous editor and executor of his estate, Rufus Griswold, who disparaged Poe after his death with fabrications. In that critic's vicious scenario, Poe's alcoholism and drug use was exaggerated and linked to charges of instability. In actuality, Poe, while having those habits, was an influential and clever story writer, poet, and one of the finest literary critics of his time. Poe's work had deep resonance for the French symbolists Baudelaire, Mallarme, and Valery. His craft, his uses of horror, and his suggestions of irrationality beneath the surfaces of conventional society are distant precursors to the challenges posed by heavy metal. (Poe has been viewed as a precursor to post-modern thought by Jacques Lacan in his seminar on "The Purloined Letter" and in Jacques Derrida's response to this.)

Poe was a master of wordplay and parody. He was a theorist of the short story and his theory of seeking the "single effect" in a story is relevant for the composition of a song also. Poe's account of literary production in "The Philosophy of Composition" seems to rule out artistic inspiration and "ecstatic intuition" (Poe, *Essays,* 14). He emphasizes close analysis, planning, ratiocination, and procedure. He asserts that his "The Raven" was consciously constructed. Yet, Poe also said that poetry can transport the reader or listener to "an elevating excitement" and an experience of the sublime and that music can enhance this. Like heavy metal creators, Poe seeks to create atmosphere and emotional effects. His story themes and poetry have been set to music by Lou Reed, Blondie, the Alan Parsons Project, and Iron Maiden.

Night

Night is a realm of uncertainty in dark Romanticism, as it is in heavy metal lyrics. *Night Thoughts* was the title of Edward Young's book which contributed to the tone of the Romantic Age. For Novalis, the coming of night is a crossing into another world. He wrote his night poetry in *Hymnen*. The French poet Alfred de Musset wrote four *Nuits* between 1835 and 1837. Night provided a mysterious atmosphere for the dark romanticism of Poe, which influenced Charles Baudelaire's *Fluers de Mal* and the writings of the symbolists. Dark Romanticism took an interest in melancholia, the irrational, and the grotesque, as well as the night. Night is the time of the moon that wanders over lunatics and lovers, a time when John Polidori's vampire and Bram Stoker's Dracula will arise.

Writing on heavy metal, Deena Weinstein points to the frequent use of the word "night" in songs to connote "a time of danger, obscurity, and mystery" (42). In heavy metal it is the time when "the forces of chaos are strongest," notes Weinstein (43). The notion itself has a mythical quality. Night is a time for party and revelry, as well as for mystery. In pop rock the word "night" is used often to punctuate melodies. It is a time of sexuality and a time of adventure. The word "night" is pervasive not only in metal but across many rock songs. We hear the word at the end of lyrics where the vocal falls on the word "night" to accent it or to provide a punch, like the hit of a cymbal.

The Mask

The mask, the persona, is an expression of anonymity and ambiguity. Carl Jung speaks of the mask as the persona that one must shed to achieve individuation. The persona is "a kind of mask, designed on the one hand to make a definite impression upon others, but on the other, to conceal the true nature of the individual" (Jung, *Two Essays on Analytical Psychology*, 190). The danger is that they "become identified with their persona" (Jung, *Memories, Dreams, Reflections*, 416). In the Greek theater masks were worn by characters onstage. The word *prosopon* means face. Masks were used in Dionysian worship ceremonies. The playwright Aeschylus identified masks as a creation of the Greek theatre. For Nietzsche passions lay underneath the masks of the actors. The masks were used to create a sense of dread in the audience. They appear in the Furies in Aeschylus' *Eumenides* and in Euripedes' *The Bacchae*.

Masks were once used by the Greek Chorus to represent unity, loyalty, and uniformity. This is the purpose of Slipknot's masks, Corey Taylor of Slipknot has said: to indicate their mutual loyalty. The purpose is "to become unconscious of who we are," Taylor told his interviewer (Soghomanian, *N.Y. Rock*, 2002). Slipknot is a metal band from Des Moines that emerged between 1995 and 1999, when their album appeared. (They have been called nu metal, although they reject the category.) Themes of nihilism, anger, and psychosis find a way into their lyrics. They wear individual masks and jumpsuits.[3]

5. Shadow Dreams

In the view of philosopher-poet Friedrich Nietzsche a mask, in the context of ancient theater, was an outward symbol beneath which lay the passions, the central emotion of each figure on stage. The Greek tragedy was born from the spirit of music, he contended in his first major work, *The Birth of Tragedy*. While as a philologist he looked back in time at ancient Greece, Nietzsche's reflections on drama and music were also directed at his own time. He was intrigued by the philosophy of Arthur Schopenhauer for whom music was an ineffable art through which the very will of the world expressed itself. Nietzsche also became fascinated by the mythic music-dramas of Richard Wagner.

Drama is all around us: on stage, on screen, in everyday life. Heavy metal is a form of drama; it is a performance art in which singing, musicianship, imagery, and story come together. While heavy metal can be frozen in time on a recording, heavy metal is a live medium with a vital immediacy that is enhanced by the reactions of a concert audience. Like the early Greek theater, heavy metal is engaged in a ritual that depends upon collective responses. Like that ancient drama, it enlists myths and strengthens a sense of communal identity.

Heavy metal, like theater, is not meant for the printed page. It is a Dionysian expression. Like those ancient mythical plays, heavy metal is meant for public occasions: for festivals and concerts. It is an ecstatic kind of drama in which one is taken out of oneself. It is drama in the sense of Wagner's music-drama: a space where action, music, iconography, and human energy all join in an arresting and interactive way.

Nietzsche's Zarathustra

While heavy metal recognizes darkness in the world it is not fundamentally nihilistic. Beyond its dark imagery, it aims to challenge the status quo, to deconstruct in order to reconstruct life. In his strange modern myth *Thus Spake Zarathustra* the philosopher/poet Friedrich Nietzsche set forth an enterprise that seems similar to the hard edge and pointed lyrics of Metallica or Megadeth. It is a story that is darkly mythical. In Zarathustra's descent into what Nietzsche finds to be the abyss of a godless world, he brings the gift of a search for meaning within a tragic perspective.

In fashioning his story, Nietzsche was an original and creative thinker who offered thoughts in mythical form which sounded several steps ahead of his culture. Nietzsche wrote like an oracle; he was a poet who hurled thunderbolts down at church steeples and against the decaying cultural edifices of Europe. He viewed European society in his day as complacent and saw its church as empty and impotent. Men and women were acting as mass minded conformists and not as fully realized persons. He sought to reinstall the unbounded forcefulness of the Dionysian spirit into humanity. The spirits of men and women had been leveled out; they had become fragments of men and women. Nietzsche urged that men and women must learn to live tragically, to recall the great resources of irrational energy and power within them. Nietzsche insists that God is dead for such a society. God has been relegated to meaningless rituals in the tomb of empty churches. But the death of God is an opportunity for humanity to reassert itself. When there is a God over and against humanity this God inhibits human creativity and men and women abdicate their responsibility. The old idols must be discarded. They needed a living myth. So, he reached back into Zoroastrian mythology for a character and he invented his myth.

Nietzsche's *Zarathustra* represents the artist as radical and prophetic, as someone who can engage in "down going" and in celebrating the irrationality in this type of existence. The heavy metal performer is such an artist: one who, in his or her action of creation reflects the mythical figure of Zarathustra. *Thus Spake Zarathustra*, Nietzsche's myth, is the work that he identified as his "symphony" (Janz, 97). The musicologist John Daverio writes that the inner divisions of *Thus Spake Zarathustra* group themselves into an introductory invocation and four movements (218). In *Ecce Homo* in 1888, Nietzsche wrote: "Perhaps the whole of Zarathustra can be reckoned as music: certainly a rebirth of hearing was among its preconditions" (295). Years of rock music set up a "rebirth of hearing" that made the auditory challenges of heavy metal overdrive, dissonance, and distortion possible. The heavy metal performer, making himself or herself mythical, risked the down going into the underground. Zarathustra chants or sings: "Like you, I must go down—as men, to whom I want to descend call it.... Behold! This cup wants to be empty again and Zarathustra wants to be man again!" (*Zarathustra*, 39).

Zarathustra goes down the mountain alone. In the forest he meets an old man who recognizes him. "How changed Zarathustra is!" the old man says. "Zarathustra has become a child, an awakened one." Zarathustra asks

5. Shadow Dreams

the man what he does in the forest and the old man replies, "I make songs and sing them." When the old man tells Zarathustra that his songs praise his god Zarathustra leaves the forest bewildered, saying: "Could it be possible that this old saint has not yet heard in his forest that God is dead?"

Zarathustra then begins his teaching."Man is a rope, fastened between animal and Superman—a rope over an abyss" (Zarathustra, 43). Humanity must have the tenacity and fortitude to cross over that abyss. "What is great in man is that he is a bridge, not a goal; what can be loved in man is that going across and down-going." As he finishes his prologue a tightrope walker falls into the market square. Zarathustra is sent away. "Whom do they hate most?" he declares. "Him who smashed their tables of values, the breaker, the lawbreaker—but he is the creator" (Zarathustra, 51) This creator seeks "those who inscribe new values on new tables.... They will be called destroyers and despisers of good and evil. But they are harvesters and rejoicers." He says: "I shall sing my song to the lone hermit" (Zarathustra, 52).

Zarathustra is like the heavy metal singer who dares to be different and to sing an unpopular song. In Nietzsche's myth, Zarathustra now sings "The Night Song." We might again remember rock music's many references to "night." Zarathustra says: "It is night: only now do all songs of lovers awaken. And my soul too is the song of a lover" (Zarathustra, 129). This song, he says, springs from "something unquenchable ... that wants to speak out." There is some inner imperative for expression here: it is the impulse of an artist, likened to the yearning of a lover. It is music searching for a language. "The Dance Song" and "The Funeral Song" follow, both ending with "Thus sang Zarathustra" (Zarathustra, 130, 133, 136). In "The Funeral Song" Zarathustra questions "a murderous singer." He says, "Yes, something invulnerable, unburiable is within me, something that rends rocks: it is called my Will" (Zarathustra, 135). Zarathustra is creator and destroyer: "Shatter, O my brothers, shatter this new law table too" (Zarathustra, 223). Zarathustra the creator speaks: "If ever a breath of the creative has come to me ... if ever I have laughed with the laugh of creative lightning" (Zarathustra, 245).

In "The Sorcerer" a man wails, voicing a song to the unknown God. The Sorcerer says of Zarathustra: "he often seems to me like the beautiful mask of a saint" (Zarathustra, 307). The Sorcerer seizes his harp and sings, calling Zarathustra a poet and a fool (Zarathustra, 308–11). Nietzsche's myth concludes with "The Intoxicated Song" in twelve sections.

Popularly, we know the opening phrases of Richard Strauss's symphony

Myth and Magic in Heavy Metal Music

Thus Spake Zarathustra from the Stanley Kubrick film *2001: A Space Odyssey*. The symphony begins with an invocation to the sun. It ends with a "Song of Intoxication" (Das Nachtwanderlied). Strauss sets out eight sections from Nietzsche's work, reordering them. The pious religion that Nietzsche detests is represented in a chorale for strings and organ (Von den Hinterweltern). The midnight tolling bell (Zarathustra, 327) sounds before the intoxicated song, like Black Sabbath's introduction to their first album on the song "Black Sabbath." Daverio conjectures that Strauss's intention was to suggest that traditional musical form was something that needed to be overcome. This theme connects the plan of the symphony with Nietzsche's objective: to challenge the form of the culture.

It is a strange myth that Nietzsche gives us but his meaning soon becomes clear. Zarathustra preaches that with courage a person can reinvent himself or herself. Life's meaning can come from within. For, in Nietzsche's view, no longer can people accept the moral tradition in a passive way. A person must make meaning. Like Zarathustra an individual must go into the abyss of modern life and be an autonomous creator of his or her own destiny.

This is the down-going. Humanity has come out of the clouds and has recognized its earthiness. Formerly, a grand moral order, one calling him a sinner, has been set against him. Now man is crossing the chasm, inching out on a tightrope over the abyss in a newfound freedom. He is finally becoming fully human.

From this perspective the heavy metal rock artist is an architect of a new phase in human life. That is, he or she is a maker, a creator, a will to power. The contemporary individual is a bridge, a rope reaching out toward the possibility of the higher man or woman. This individual is self-determined. He bows before no altar. He confesses no sins. Nor does he inhale and cough on any incense shaken at him ritualistically from a round container that swings back and forth on a chain, endlessly and hypnotically. He has broken through the hypnotism of that sort of ritual and has awakened, with a new song and new symbols, to a sense of power.

Myth and Nationalism

"The world must be romanticized," wrote Novalis, a German Romantic poet and storyteller. "Only in this will we rediscover its original

5. Shadow Dreams

meaning.... If I give a higher meaning to the everyday, the dignity of the unfamiliar to the familiar, the appearance of infinity to the finite, then I am romanticizing it" (KS II, 545).[4]

The importance that German Romantics found in myth and culture is displayed fully in the works of Achim von Arnim, Clemens Brentano, and the Brothers Grimm who collected folk tales, folk songs, and native customs. They believed that in these tales resided the natural voice and the national spirit of the people. Arnim believed that the connection of medieval myth and present reality would release the spiritual forces of the past (Hughes, 93). Preaching liberation for the people, the German Romantics patterned their lyrics on old folk song forms. In ballads and romances they sought to reawaken the Middle Ages, a more glorious time of German or Nordic antiquity. "There was called into poetic life a long gone age of German integrity," writes Oskar Walzel. "It was the age of German emperors, benevolent and mighty, of brave German knights, and of high-minded German women" (Walzel, 164).

Romantic medievalism has been viewed by critics as one of the regressive myths called upon by those who are uncomfortable with modernity. The Romantic project of searching for the pure and unadulterated language and myths of the German or the Nordic folk has been linked with nationalism by political scientists and historians like Louis Snyder, Gordon Craig, Hans Kohn, and Abraham Ashkenasi. Snyder regards the Brothers Grimm as ardent nationalists. Craig and Kohn make numerous connections between the Romantic project and nationalism.

The relation of Romanticism with a nationalistic atavism, or backward looking revolution, has been called problematical by these scholars. This type of Romantic nationalism appears in the case of German Romanticism, which appears "messianic but past oriented, a search for a millennium that never was" (Ashkenasi, 24). One can suggest a connection between this kind of Romanticism and a form of nationalism which is socially and politically conservative.

Critics have leveled several charges against this populist Romanticism. Historians have claimed the following:

1. Romanticism is an escape. It is running away from rational reality into a world of illusion, irrationality, and unreality.
2. Romanticism is founded upon myths.

3. Romanticism can be linked with nationalism and with the ills of nationalism.
4. Romanticism is regressive because it seeks a utopia in medievalism, or the voice of a people in the primordial.
5. Romanticism's emphasis on the folk, folkways, and organic community is inherently flawed.

The assumption behind these charges is that all of this is bad, if not disastrous, for a society. The critique pulls out the nastiness of the Third Reich to solidify the argument. However, it neglects to fully acknowledge the positive contributions of Romanticism: emancipator nationalism, renewal through literature, poetry, song, and a religious sense of life, and the value of every-day people and the integrity of their life-stories. This Romanticism sought to add a fully human dimension of emotion, intuition, and instinctual life to create beauty, honor, imagination, and spur along human creativity. Of course, it was not without its urgency of rebellion or its criticism of a supposedly rational society and its dark shadow. That is heavy metal's inheritance. Heavy metal can be quite overt in its anger, its rebellion, its exploration of darkest night, and its desire to realize Promethean power and break free.

The Faust Myth

Heavy metal likewise seeks musical power, one that is coded masculine. This too is Promethean: a daring willingness to seize the fire. Critics may argue about how this assertion is liberating, or about the things which may be potential entrapments for the soul. This dilemma is captured in the Faust myth.

In Johann von Goethe's work we read the powerful myth of Faust which tells the story of a man who wanted power and all knowledge and sold his soul to the devil to obtain it. In Faust we see the figure of Mephistopheles, a demon who makes the offer to Faust. Goethe's *Faust*, one of the most important works of German literature, is concerned with power and with humanity's place in the chain of being. Faust is not content with the limitation of his place in the world. He wishes to exceed these limits. His intent is to do godlike things. Faust is restless and seeks the power of knowledge. He requests the presence of Mephistopheles, a

5. Shadow Dreams

diabolical force who becomes a vivid presence in the story. He seeks to surpass the limits of human knowledge. In Faust we have the Promethean enterprise. Faust seeks for a means of transcendence and substitutes a search for power for the search for meaning.

French composer Hector Berlioz, whose work had some influence on Wagner, explored the Faust myth and the quest for power in his opera *La damnation de Faust* (1846). Opium taken for nervousness contributed to his *Symphonie Fantastique* (1830). Berlioz sought a colorful sonic power throughout his work.

Goethe was another of the many influences on Wagner. Indeed he was an influence upon all of German literary culture. In Goethe's writings on art and aesthetics we read that the symbolic can create the universal in the particular: "as the seed germinates in the plant or the poem such interpretations as we make of it" (Adams, 19).[5]

Goethe writes that: "true symbolism is where the particular represents the more universal, not as dream and shadow, but rather as a living-fleeting revelation of the inscrutable" (Goethe, *Werke*, 12:471 [1799]). This notion affected many German thinkers, from Schelling to August and Wilhelm Schlegel. It was also known by Coleridge, who read German and borrowed from Schelling and the Schlegels. The years between 1814 and 1832 brought Goethe's more fully developed critical thoughts about symbol and allegory. Goethe recognizes that allegory comes from seeking the particular for the universal. He says that to see the universal in the particular "is really the nature of poetry" (*Werke*, 12:471).

One hundred years later, the novelist Thomas Mann, in his "Appeal to Reason" (1930), warned the German people: "against alliances with the unknown, the dynamic, the darkly creative ... the obscurity of the soul, the sacredly fertile underworld" (qtd. by Craig, 209). In his essay, Mann writes: We find here ... a romanticism of professional Germanists, a superstitious faith in the Nordic." Mann publicly warned the German people against subsuming composer Richard Wagner's nationalism under National Socialist ideology. For Mann, this was an abuse against Wagner and "the innocence of the artist" (Mann, *Wagner*, 346).

Mann's brilliant novel *Doctor Faustus* treats at length the theme of a virulent strain. The striving of the modern Faust, Leverkuhn, for creative breakthrough by this dark means suggests the culture that he sees around him. The barbarism of the Nazi regime is the subtext of this work which makes use of the Faust myth. Mann suggests that while explorations of the irrational and the Dionysian work effectively in the arts, they are dangerous and detrimental when applied to the social and political sphere. In this retelling of the Faust legend, Mann centers his novel upon the efforts of Adrian Leverkuhn, a composer. In seeking to break through the rational intellect to a creative rationality Leverkuhn intentionally acquires a syphilitic infection. The striving of the modern Faust for a creative breakthrough by this dark means suggests an infection of culture. In the novel music represents an entire culture.

In Mann's novel, Leverkuhn's development of the 12-tone system by which he writes his compositions suggests a rigidity in this system. Mann studied the 12-tone system of Arthur Schoenberg. Schoenberg was incensed by Mann's use of this model. Leverkuhn, however, appears to be Nietzsche, who did contract a syphyllic infection which led to his ultimate insanity and death. The novel reflects the importance of music in the German cultural experience. Mann was appalled that the music of Wagner, which he loved, could inspire dark purposes. The shock of this prompted him to probe the dark side of art through this novel. (Zeitblom, who narrates Leverkuhn's story, makes several comments about the rise of National Socialism.)

Wagner's Music-Drama

Richard Wagner's attention to myth and leitmotif and his development of music-drama as a synthesis of music and dramatic performance could be viewed as a precursor to heavy metal. (Another modern composer we might consider is Igor Stravinsky, who explored atonality, myth, and primitivism. Several composers incorporated industrial machine sounds.) Wagner believed in the power of myth. He emphasized volume and power and he tested the limits of harmony. "The power of the composer is nought else than that of the magician," he wrote. "It is really in a state of enchantment that we listen to Beethoven's symphonies" (*Artwork*, 105–06).

Richard Wagner has been criticized for his Romanticism. It has been claimed that Wagner's histrionics, his massive ego, and his emphasis on grandeur in a bold artistic medium had a troublesome impact on the myth, war songs, and parades of the Nazis. He is censured for his anti-Semitism and for his resurrection of medieval Germanic myths because these myths purportedly fueled German patriotism and ideas of separateness and racial

5. Shadow Dreams

superiority. Wagner made of art a religion, an art that esteemed itself as salvific. It has been suggested that Nazi propaganda used Wagnerian music-drama within a seductive array of myths which served as a substitute religion. All of these factors weigh heavily against our seeing the positive contributions of Wagner's art.

In 1848, upon the failed revolution in Dresden, Richard Wagner fled to Switzerland. For several years he did not compose any music. However, Wagner, who always wrote the libretto before composing music for his music-dramas, was incubating a massive work, the Ring cycle, which was to be his masterpiece. Wagner was now at pains to justify himself and his art. With this goal, Wagner embarked upon a series of theoretical writings. *Art and Revolution*, *The Artwork of the Future*, and *Opera and Drama* would tell the world where he stood aesthetically and through these works he would assert his role as an artist.

The Artwork of the Future reflects Richard Wagner's rebellion against what he felt was a sterile social order and his championing of a new artistic vision. Wagner's objective was to renew the drama and thus the society from the *Volkgeist*: the spirit of the people. Toward this end, Wagner resurrected the legends and romances of the Middle Ages and the Nordic myths whose roots lie deep in prehistoric times.

The Artwork of the Future proclaims an art of the Folk and a rebirth of Greek tragedy in modern terms. Wagner sought to express in music-drama an image of the elemental force, a notion which parallels the emphasis on the will in the philosophy of Arthur Schopenhauer. Wagner sought a new art form in which the artist, through myth and by merging the arts, represented the roots and soil of society. Wagner sought a new sociopolitical world through the music drama, in which the arts of dance, tone, and poetry would be reunited. For Wagner, in isolation each art form is "unfree." But in love, embrace, and absorption into each other the barriers fall and there are "no more boundaries but only Art, universal, undivided." (Wagner, *Artwork*, 98).

It is questionable whether any of these theoretical writings may mean anything to heavy metal artists. However, they underscore Manowar's Joey De Mario's recognition that Wagner "invented heavy metal." Wagner's thoughts about the unity of myth, song, and performance in *The Artwork of the Future* and his subsequent resurrection of myth in his music-drama prefigure heavy metal's embrace of mythology and its bombastic performativity.

Myth and Magic in Heavy Metal Music

Wagner sought for Germany a musical language connected with the spirit of the Folk. The artistic project of Richard Wagner parallels the work of the brothers Grimm who sought to find a voice in the folk tales of the rural German people. Wagner looked back to the Middle Ages at the minnesingers and to the legends collected by German writers like Wolfram von Eschenbach (*Parcival*) and Gottfried von Strassberg (*Tristan*). In the *Ring de Nibelungen* Wagner found a more purely Germanic story which became the basis of his famed operatic cycle.

The composer's goals were essentially artistic. Art was his religion: an art springing from the Folk that would be vital and create a new future. He concerned himself with innovations in musical composition, principally the leitmotif, and with techniques in the correspondence between the word and the tone that was to be sung. His creative harmony prepared the way for atonal music. His theory of music-drama was a holistic one: the singer-performer embodied and became the song; the artist's voice and the people were one. There is a clear parallel with heavy metal in this.

Wagner could not have forecast the future developments in Germany in the 1930s. His aesthetics, his individualism, and his liberal socialism would have stood in opposition to the statism and conformity of Nazi culture. Wagner's music and sense of mythology evokes pride in German ancestry and his project could be called nationalistic. However, despite his participation in the 1848 revolution, he was not a notably political man. The only economics he was ever concerned with was the patronage which enabled him to do his art. He was an egotist, an anti-Semite, a powerful composer steeped in myth. He was also one of the consummate Romantic artists of the nineteenth century. Wagner gave to the world the mythical, the grand, and the dramatic. Manowar's Joey De Maio, in the *Kingdom of Steel* liner notes, says of Richard Wagner: "He invented heavy metal."

6

Iron Maiden
Mythology and the Ancient Mariner

It is one of the goals of the heavy metal band Iron Maiden to animate people's imaginations. So vocalist Bruce Dickinson and drummer Nikko McBrain have said. To that end, the band's primary songwriter, Steve Harris, has turned for song concepts to science fiction and to Greek mythology, as well as to war stories, dystopias, and the eerie reflections on death that are typical of many heavy metal bands. *Book of Souls* (2015) is a double album with provocative song titles like the "If Eternity Should Fail" and "Empire of the Clouds." Behind all of this is a fascination with myth. When bassist Steve Harris and guitarist Dave Murray formed the band they named it after Alexandre Dumas' *The Man in the Iron Mask* and a medieval torture device. They quickly moved from their *Soundhouse Tapes* EP toward mythological subjects. Harris turned to science fiction novels and films, history, and occult fantasy. This imaginative embrace of myth, history, and science fiction would extend across multiple gold or platinum albums.

Formed through the dreams and ambitions of Steve Harris, Iron Maiden's adventure began when they were offered a record contract in 1976, if they were willing to "go punk."[1] However, in the early days of the band, with vocalist Paul Di Anno, there was an innovative sound that broke with British punk and Iron Maiden went their own way. They adopted the Faustian heavy metal attitude that Philip Basche began to document in *Heavy Metal Thunder*. Iron Maiden, with *Sanctuary* (1980), *Killers* (1981), and *The Number of the Beast* (1982), took a turn toward power chords, lyrical leads, motivic development, Gothic mysticism, and horror.

Mythical references were worked into Iron Maiden's songs. For example,

Myth and Magic in Heavy Metal Music

Iron Maiden's song on the flight of Icarus retells the ancient story of flight. In the myth, wings were made by Daedelus so that he and Icarus, his son, could escape from King Minos. Daedelus warned Icarus not to fly too close to the sun and the wings lifting Icarus upward melted and he fell into the sea. In Iron Maiden's song, Daedelus watches from the ground after urging his son to "fly and touch the sun." He has sent Icarus toward disaster. On the cover of the album on which the song appears wings are torched by the band's mascot, Eddie.

Iron Maiden's songs were initially sung by vocalist Bruce Dickinson. They are arguably the most literate or literary of heavy metal bands and their lyrics and concepts continue to draw enthusiastically upon fantastic literature. In many Iron Maiden songs Steve Harris turns the bass guitar into a lead instrument, while dual guitar leads meet Dickinson's signature wailing vocals. Their first album, *Iron Maiden* (1978), offers a musical version of Bram Stoker's *Dracula* (1897). "Murders of the Rue Morgue," on *Killers* (1981), adapts Edgar Allan Poe. "Children of the Damned" on *The Number of the Beast* (1982) adapts a John Windham story title.

The mythological tendency persists throughout the band's creative work. "Total Eclipse" describes an environmental disaster and the end of the world. The song "To Tame a Land," on *Peace of Mind* (1983), makes use of terms from science fiction writer Frank Herbert's *Dune* (1965). Reportedly, they wanted to call the song "Dune" but Herbert, disliking heavy metal, did not grant permission. While the title of one of Robert A. Heinlein's best known works, *Stranger in a Strange Land*, appears on Iron Maiden's *Somewhere in Time* (1986) the song does not adapt the concepts in Heinlein's novel. Iron Maiden uses the title but they move in their own direction with the song. A frozen arctic explorer is discovered after a century locked in the ice. "Out of the Silent Planet," likewise, makes use of a familiar science fiction title: one by C.S. Lewis. The record does not work with the C.S. Lewis story, however. The Iron Maiden song "Childhood's End" on *Fear the Dark* only uses the Arthur C. Clarke title and none of the ideas or content. *Seventh Son of a Seventh Son* draws directly upon a novel by Orson Scott Card and themes from Aleister Crowley. Iron Maiden offers *Brave New World* (2000), recalling Aldous Huxley's title of that name. They offer a thirteen minute retelling of Samuel Taylor Coleridge's "The Rime of the Ancient Mariner." By focusing on Iron Maiden's use of mythology and science fiction, we can see how this well-known heavy metal band weaves together the themes of myth.

6. Iron Maiden

In 2008, for their stage shows Iron Maiden turned toward Egyptian imagery. They used figures from Egyptian mythology on their 1984 album *Powerslave*. The myth of a king who wondered why he was not a god runs deep. Osiris was worshipped by the Egyptians as a god of the dead. His legend comes to us through Plutarch. Osiris was said to have been born in upper-Egypt when a mysterious voice called out: "Behold the universal lord." Iron Maiden's character would have this godlike figure as a reference point. The story of this royal family is intriguing. In Egyptian mythology Ra celebrated the birth of Osiris, for Osiris would one day be an heir to the throne. After Geb retired from earth to the heavens, Osiris would become the Egyptian king and Isis would become queen. Osiris was an enemy of violence and he sought to extend a regime of peace to the world through music and song. Unfortunately, Set, an evil brother, was jealous of his reign and conspired to do away with Osiris. Isis, through her powers of sorcery, returned the body of Osiris to life. However, Osiris chose to leave the earth and disappear into Elysian Fields, where he would await the arrival of the just and become the god of the dead. He would forever provide the promise of a just rule in an afterlife.

The Egyptian Book of the Dead accounts for Osiris in about one hundred songs and poems. Osiris is a transformative god who appears in the guises of animals and other incarnations. Isis remains closely connected with Osiris, with whom she had borne a son, Horus. Isis reconstituted the body of Osiris. She represents the restoration of life: the fertile plains of the Nile region and the annual flooding which brings life. The opposite of this is the desert: the emptiness and aridity of Set. The cult of Isis was celebrated with festivals in spring and prospered until the Emperor Justinian closed the temple of Philae in the southern region of Egypt, making of it a church. In the temple of Ramses III at Karnak the pharaoh wears the double crown. Statues within the interior court of the temple date from the twentieth dynasty of 1200–1100 BC and show Orisis statues, arms folded, hands holding the scepter in the image of power. So, Iron Maiden hearkens back to the mysteries of the truly ancient when they cast their work in Egypt. They evoke the power of exotic deities of the desert and divinities of birth and death. The imagery reflects a world that is to us strange and mysterious and the music combines this with a sense of power and magic.

For Iron Maiden, that magic all begins with the music. Developing as a bass player, Steve Harris listened to Chris Squire of Yes and John

Entwistle of The Who. He listened to Martin Turner of Wishbone Ash and Rinus Gerritson of Golden Earring. He listened to the bands Free and Black Sabbath. Harris has commented that his ideas for songs emerge from watching movies, reading books about natural history and science, or reading science fiction or horror. He told an interviewer that he reads *New Scientist* and *Scientific American*. Music, science, horror, myth and science fiction coalesce into imaginative song narratives performed with great energy.

The imagination of Steve Harris and the instrumental skills of Iron Maiden may be described by exploring their thirteen and a half-minute setting of Samuel Taylor Coleridge's mythical poem "The Rime of the Ancient Mariner." The song, driven by Harris's basslines and featuring Dickinson's soaring vocals, concludes *Powerslave*, an album that offers us history, myth, presence and power. With this song, the kind that is often dubbed "epic," Iron Maiden infused listeners with musical and lyrical nostalgia for wonder. If "The World Is Too Much with Us" in its scope and ambition, as Wordsworth's poem of that title claimed, Steve Harris's reworking of Coleridge's poem was a modernist metal *tour de force* that renewed modern life in driving rhythms and mythical imagination.

Iron Maiden compresses Coleridge's haunting poem. Shifting into new keys and tempos, they de-center the narrative, placing the song after the title cut about an ancient Egyptian king. We listeners are invited into other times and places, into a region of wonder that collapses history and replaces it with an overlapping bricolage in which all times are one. History is no longer linear but cyclical, as in "The Rime of the Ancient Mariner" itself. This panoply of affective changes, images, and sounds mirrors the displacement or dislocation of history, as Robert Walser has observed.[2] Yet, in its resistance to this de-centeredness, the Ancient Mariner enacts the quest for unitive mystical experience in which, as the mystics say, all times are one and all history is now. This quest reflects Deena Weinstein's assertion that metal's "core audience really seeks a true ecstatic experience," one that "removes the everyday-life world."[3] The weaving of sound and myth in Iron Maiden's song, reflecting that bricolage that Robert Walser has viewed as postmodern, is akin to this quest for unitive vision, in which all time is present in the mystical moment.

To listen to Iron Maiden's "The Rime of the Ancient Mariner" is to be entranced. The listener is absorbed in the guitar lines played by Dave Murray and Adrian Smith, Bruce Dickinson's vocals and theatricality, Steve

6. Iron Maiden

Harris's forceful and extraordinary bass lines, and Nikko McBrain's driving rhythms. Like Coleridge, Iron Maiden's members give themselves up to visions and offer dreams and gesture toward extraordinary consciousness. They explore "tensions between reality and dream," as Robert Walser has pointed out (*Running with the Devil*, 152). The stories of an ancient Egyptian king, or that of an Ancient Mariner, draw listeners toward unusual and mythical realms of thought. With Iron Maiden's songs on *Powerslave*, listeners are invited both into narratives and into other times and spaces, into a region of wonder. To listen is to be caught by a spell as Iron Maiden's *Powerslave* enacts the romance of metal.

In their songs, Iron Maiden embraces the power of mystery that is found in mythology, astrology, alchemy, esoterica, war, dueling, or the Biblical book of *Revelation*. Heroism and mishap clash as Iron Maiden's music powers through songs, in tension and release, echoing a sense of a struggle for survival. The band reaches for the breakthrough vitality conveyed in technically precise octave leads, or dual guitar lines. Throughout *Powerslave* there is a battle for vision and life, an appropriation of symbols of power, and a quest for what Robert Walser has identified as the "experience of power and transcendent freedom" that can overcome the anxieties and discontinuities of the post-modern world."[4] Songs represent what Deena Weinstein has seen in metal as "challenges to the sources of disorder, fighting the good fight."[5] There is a call to the heroic journey, a summons to adventure and wonder.

On *Powerslave*, repeatedly, the band's musical arrangements echo their songs' lyrical content. Amid darkness and combat, songs seek vitality, action, transcendent flight, and heroism. For example, there is sword and sorcery in Dickinson's "The Duelists" and an overcoming of duality, as music, lyrics, and sound are woven into one, in the duel of guitars. "Aces High" and "Two Minutes to Midnight," both of which were hits on the U.K. charts, recall with fierce energy the Battle of Britain and a fight with impending doom. Iron Maiden brings their audience images from literature, history, and myth to reflect human aspiration. "The Rime" also bears one line from Tennyson ("water, water everywhere / nor any drop to drink"). Tennyson's poetry also appears in the 1983 hit "The Trooper," a version of "The Charge of the Light Brigade," a poem referring to heroism and mishap. In 1986, Iron Maiden pointed to Alexander the Great, paraphrasing Plutarch in their opening lines: "My son, ask for thyself another kingdom, for that which I leave is too small for thee" (Plutarch, *Alexander,*

6.8). Such an appeal to the heroic and to the attempt at flight is found in "The Flight of Icarus," and, perhaps more successfully in "Aces High."

Listeners were fascinated by Iron Maiden's *Powerslave* (1984). Rich in energy and drive, this record signals the band's awakening tendency toward progressive metal. On *Powerslave*, producer Martin Birch and the band create an atmosphere of energy and mystery. From the striking beginning of "Aces High," launched by the fierce guitars of Adrian Smith and Dave Murray, the record dwells in narrative and mythology. Steve Harris's lyrics tell stories and touch upon themes that recall myth, heroism, science fiction, and ancient worlds. The lyrics suggest struggles: a duel for life in the 1984 world. The ancient mariner suggests a kind of mental and spiritual entrapment. On the title song "Powerslave," the Egyptian Pharoah wonders why he has to die when everyone around him is telling him that he is a god. There is a Romantic nostalgia for ancient worlds and a yearning for more vital prospects.

The Music

It is significant that Harris, a bassist, a musician from the rhythm section of the band, was the composer who adapted and set Coleridge's poem to music. Harris's bass emerges as a lead instrument and sets rhythmic patterns in novel ways. His experiments with rhythm correspond with the experimentation that lies at the heart of the romantic poetic enterprise. Harris, who Iron Maiden biographer Mick Wall identifies as the creator of "the songs, the idea and attitude" of the band (14), plays an instrument that anchors many bands and establishes rhythmic figures within a song. His development of Iron Maiden's "Rime of the Ancient Mariner" attends to themes of growth, decay, change, and dynamism. This song-poem is a narrative ballad that captures a movement in time through varying time signatures. Chords, guitar hooks, rhythms and melodies engage listeners with energy, or evoke haunting atmosphere. Iron Maiden and producer Martin Birch create an atmosphere that is by turns energetic and haunting.

Iron Maiden's song is washed in sound, driven forward by Steve Harris's bass lines, much like the Mariner's boat has been driven by the sound made by spirits. As in Coleridge's poem, the band's version emerges with spell-like, incantatory patterns. The song is filled with highly coordinated

6. Iron Maiden

transitions and carefully timed tempo changes that maintain interest across more than thirteen minutes. The motifs demand change. They push, like the Mariner, toward horizons and vary from a dynamic and energetic pulse to a haunting middle.

There is order in the crashing guitars, just as there are patterns in waves breaking. We are held spellbound by Iron Maiden's music much in the same way that Coleridge's wedding guest is held spellbound by the Ancient Mariner's story. With rhythmic shifts we move between tension and release. Tonal relations organize the piece and riffs supply melodic figures, motifs that push the song from one tonal area to another.

The song moves in a manner consistent with Romantic form. The establishment of a dominant tonal center and mood is followed by a departure. The song comes back home, recalling an earlier musical theme, and then moves with a difference. It recalls the past but explodes into new exploration. Iron Maiden takes us on a journey. The spell comes over us as motifs build, diminish, and then return.

Musically, the song is carefully structured. The song opens explosively with a guitar run of five sixteenth notes landing on an E. Immediately, it begins to travel on a driving pulse in E that is established by Steve Harris's bass. Several measures into the song, at nine to ten seconds, the opening guitar riff returns, punctuating the driving march pattern in a circular phrase of quick eighth notes repeating the first four notes over and over, then resolving at the end of the phrase on E. Here the rhythmic pattern is doubled by bass and by drums, as McBrain rolls across several tom-toms. Dickinson's vocal follows, beginning the lyric with words like "mesmerizes," "trance," "spell," "nightmare," that suggest a haunted oceanic consciousness. "Hear," he says in the first line. "See," he says in the second. We are called to be witnesses by opening ourselves to listen and to see the vision of the mariner. The song rocks into tightly executed riffs about three minutes in. As Dickinson continues the story, the dominant harmonic and rhythmic pattern breaks up and the bass begins doubling notes in cut time in rapid sixteenth notes. This hugely energetic bass-driven movement continues until 4:58, where the bass stops.

It is somewhere after five minutes has passed that the eerie interlude begins and the song dips down into an atmosphere propelled by Harris's bass. The "spacey" interlude begins with guitar-like bass arpeggios, a creaking deck, and the narrative voice-over. Dickinson's singing/speaking is gentle and an entranced hush appears to have settled over the song.

This is the mariner's moment of repentance: music and character change together. At 7:30 a melodic bass functions again much like a guitar and the singing resumes. Then at 8:40, a scream erupts from Dickinson-mariner for about ten seconds, ending in a grisly laugh. The band breaks out with a return of the bass pattern followed by a burst of lead guitar. The bass begins to accelerate and the singing resumes, accompanied by guitar riffs.

Some listeners have found the middle of the song to sag. However, the spacey interlude provides musical contrast and suggests alternative consciousness. As a movement, it dwells in the uncertainty of the musical journey before it recapitulates and returns home. From the quiet bursts a fitting climax: a guitar leads breaks into life; with a powerful soloing, it sails across a stormy sea.

There is a build up into the crescendo in this final third of this song. Some nine minutes into the song, the tempo increases, a lascivious laugh issues forth, and the band pulses into blistering solos. From this exuberance comes the return to a motif from early on in the song. At ten minutes, as if carefully timed for 10:00, the guitars move into lyrical octave leads that are anchored by bass and drums. Thirty seconds later (at 10:30) they join the bass pattern. At 11:00, we return to the original bass pattern, announcing musically the return of the mariner, breaking from his nightmare, coming home to a newfound wholeness. This is indeed a musical return and there is a rejoicing of intertwining guitar leads. The story is told and brought to a culmination, rising to climax and we breathe again. The song ends after 13:20, as its final line drifts: "And the tale goes on and on and on," suggesting that it never ends. This story has an enduring quality because the recounting of it perpetually is the mariner's penance. Likewise, Iron Maiden concludes with the suggestion that neither will the echo of this album or its legacy end.

The Lyric

Steve Harris's reworking of "The Rime of the Ancient Mariner" is a *tour de force.* Harris's lyrical compression, summary, and careful selection of elements from Coleridge's poem organizes the way in which Dickinson's vocal works within Iron Maiden's sound. The listener is invited to listen to the story, entranced by music that complements the words Dickinson

6. Iron Maiden

sings: "mesmerises," "nightmares of the sea," "caught by his spell." Dickinson becomes the conjurer of the spell. Incantatory patterns emerge.

The poem is told by a haunted sailor who has been cursed for his crimes against nature: the shooting of the albatross. From its opening riff, the song demands attention. Harris deftly weaves Coleridge's poem into a song lyric with summary and quotation, and supports it with ambitious composition, filled with rhythmic changes. The changing time signatures themselves remind us that music dwells in time and that the fortunes of the mariner hang suspended in changing time.

The tale of the mariner is a lengthy story told by the mariner to wedding guests. He has shot down the albatross for sport and has doomed his crew to die at sea of thirst. The mariner repents and is spared but must tell his story over and over, wherever he goes. His theme is that one must be reverent and appreciative of the natural world and all creatures. Dickinson's voice matches this voice of repentance in the haunting interlude and ultimately breaks into a blood-curdling scream.

Many have called Iron Maiden's song "an epic" because it lasts for more than 13:20. However, it is also epic-like because it tells a tale and proceeds as a recollection of a mythical journey. Iron Maiden's musical creativity provides a temporal unfolding. The lyrics set forth imagery and use sound to organize time.

Bruce Dickinson sings that the Mariner must tell his story. The Mariner's story, like the tale of Odysseus, is a recollection. The romantic lyric poet is a singer and Dickinson projects a theatricality that makes this song work as a live performance. Dickinson's vocal renders this narration dramatically, projecting the sense of Dionysian ecstasy in performing of which he has spoken of with Weinstein.[6] On the World Slavery Tour, Iron Maiden could unleash their virtuoso guitar playing, and Harris's bass alongside Bruce Dickinson's soaring vocals. The theatricality of Dickinson's stage presence reflects the image of a Romantic virtuoso, such as Franz Lizst, of whom Eduard Hanslick once said, "Not only does one listen with breathless attention to his playing, one also observes it in the fine lines of his face [...] all this has the utmost fascination for his listeners."[7]

Steve Harris's lyrics and music record an experience and perform a reenactment of it. Iron Maiden's rendering of Coleridge's poem is quite consistent with Coleridge's poetics. Meter and rhyme, says Coleridge, support recollection and a song or poem is memorable partly because of its sound devices and repetitions. There is "a rapturous or singing tone" in much of Romantic poetry, as Thomas MacFarland observes.[8] Dickinson's vocal emphasizes this sense of rapture. Iron Maiden thus performs the work that Coleridge himself saw in the best poetry. Their song is one in which sound excites attention and meter and rhyme lift us from ordinary emotions and meaning.

From the opening riffs, we are beckoned to listen. Dickinson launches into the lyric with a call: "Hear the rime of the ancient mariner." "Hear" begins the first line, "see" begins the second. Dickinson has a great deal of story to tell. However, the song is structured to allow for a good deal of instrumental space apart from the singing of lyric. Following most passages of the narrative, guitar leads respond to the lyric.

The mariner and Dickinson as vocalist are conflated: he will sing the story. "Stay here and listen to the nightmares of the sea." As we accept the invitation, we are enrapt in the story, caught like the mariner in a spell. "And the music plays on" comes the chorus and we are propelled into the tale.

As the voyage begins, we are set upon a musical journey "to a place that nobody's been." In imagery of snow-fog we enter the chill of a land of snow and ice and we see the figure of the albatross, bird of good omen: The chorus resumes and the ship sails on—underscoring the interminable voyage. Then disaster strikes and the mariner kills the bird of good omen. His shipmates protest. The crew joins with him, however, and the spirit of the albatross exacts its vengeance upon them: a terrible curse has now begun. Blaming the mariner for their ill fate, the sailors hang the dead bird like a weight, or talisman of ill will, around his neck. And the curse, a thirst, persists at sea, on and on everlastingly.

The lyric personalizes this thirst, as Dickinson, the story's narrator, sings for the lost sailors and for himself. As in Alfred Tennyson's well-known poem, the speaker finds no means to slake the thirst. There is "water, water everywhere/ nor any drop to drink." It is at this moment that the ghost ship appears. The narrator wonders at the sight: But how can she sail with no wind in her sails and no tide? In sighting the ghost ship, the narrator again beckons to us: "See." He asks for vision, pointing toward the ghostly ship of the doomed in the distance.

The song is taken up in a living death, a liminal suspension. It is entirely appropriate that now a ghostly passage of musical change comes upon the listener. As the sailors drop down dead, so too does the music, into a haunted reverie. This is the quiet center of a tornado, the "eye" of

6. Iron Maiden

the storm in which the mariner is held in abeyance, in an apophatic darkness before his awakening. Here music drops out of the vocal and the narrator tells us the tale starkly. As the deck creaks, fragile tilting wood upon a vast open sea, we are buoyed up into the misty atmosphere of the music. Dickinson sings of the dogged moon and the ghosts who each curse him with a ghostly look their eyes. The gaze of the dead mesmerizes him, as did the wedding guest in the opening lines of this song. The gaze challenges the speaker with dread. It is now a collective stare, charging the mariner with profound guilt.

Sound is frozen here in a recollection of moments when the stunning hypnotism of this gaze cursed him too quick for groan or sigh. Music—and the human groan or sigh of emotion—has vanished and the soul once moved by music is paralyzed, suspended by this cursing challenge to "see."

Then we hear the heavy thump of bodies falling: life arrested, the vitality of music itself arrested. The mariner too wishes to die but the life force within, the natural world of the sea creatures and within himself lives on. And now, so does musical energy. It reappears, like the animation at the heart of creation. The mariner, now centered in a prayer for the natural world "blesses them/ God's creatures all of them too." The music revives: Then the spell starts to break. The weight of death eases and the bird around his neck drops away. Now comes sound and music again: We hear the groans of sailors long dead. Their resurrection is accomplished along with musical rebirth. Again we are cast into a trance and hear that the nightmare will continue.

The musical return comes with the transformation of the mariner. As in nineteenth century Romantic composition, Iron Maiden has orchestrated a series of movements away from the tonic and the motifs that the song opened with. There has been a difficult passage through musical tensions, changes in time signatures, and a modulation to a new key. Now the music comes home again with a difference. Strikingly, this return is very much in the mode of the mythical heroic journey, as outlined by Joseph Campbell and others. Such heroic myth echoes the flight of "Aces High" at the beginning of the album, bringing this recording full circle.

The mariner is released from the prison of spirits, who gather in their own light. A familiar boat sails toward him: an unexpected joy. Ship and sin sink with the past into the sea. The hermit shrieves the Mariner of his sins. The word "shrieve" is an archaic form of the Middle English word "shrive," meaning to impose penance and grant absolution. Dickinson sings that the Mariner is compelled to tell of his story wherever he travels. It is a tale that will go on and on. Iron Maiden closes this album with the open-ended notion that what we have just heard also will go on and on.

Iron Maiden's Musical Adaptation

Myth and fantasy, Iron Maiden affirms, is at the center of their heavy metal project. Are we to read Iron Maiden's transposition of Coleridge's dark poem as a paean to wonder and imagination, or as a fearful warning of spellbound disillusion? How might Coleridge himself have heard Iron Maiden's version? Likely, Coleridge would have appreciated Iron Maiden's celebration of imagination. In the thirteenth chapter of Coleridge's *Biographia Literaria* critics see one of the most profound reflections on imagination in all of English literature. Perhaps with this in mind, the poet Robert Penn Warren, in 1946, called Coleridge's "Rime" "a poem of pure imagination."[9] He argued that in the poem imagination itself is redemptive. Nineteenth century readers were often simply baffled, finding Coleridge's poem ambiguous and weirdly mysterious. Heavy metal fans have responded in a variety of ways to Iron Maiden's version. Steve Harris, however, appears to have found something in Coleridge's poem that spoke to his time and expressed the image and role of Iron Maiden.

The parallel between Coleridge's mysterious poem and heavy metal culture is striking. In Iron Maiden's song, imagination and sonic intensity seek peak experience, the pleasures of transcendence and awe. This however, comes with subjection to peril, to the grotesque, and the potential for anarchy. As Deena Weinstein puts it, "ideal metal concerts can be described as hierophanies in which something sacred is revealed."[10] In Iron Maiden's song we encounter hypnotic dread, and recognize, as Weinstein has indicated, that "the focus on vulnerability to the horrors of chaos is a very significant feature of traditional heavy metal."[11]

Mariner and singer welcome the listener into a state of vulnerability, an occult encounter with dread. The spell one is caught in is central to the band's musical exploration. As Robert Walser notes, "Iron Maiden is among the most mystical and philosophical of heavy metal bands."[12] With the song's musical spell, Iron Maiden makes an appeal to something other-worldly. Clearly, Iron Maiden appeals to elements of the supernatural that pervade the poem. The poem's journey through a kind of altered

6. Iron Maiden

consciousness may also have encouraged Harris's musical exploration. Harris likely saw the occult philosophy at work in Coleridge's poem, as John Livingston Lowes observed in his influential *The Road to Xanadu*.

Symbolic readings of Coleridge's mariner are an important aspect of the poem's critical tradition. They emerged with Maud Bodkin in *Archetypal Patterns in Poetry* (1934) and her view that the poem expressed the Jungian archetypes of rebirth. G. Wilson Knight in *The Starlit Dome* (1941) brought together psychoanalytic theory and Christian mysticism to expound upon the poem's imagery. In Kenneth Burke's and Richard Haven's readings the mariner is a psychological projection by Coleridge of his own relationships and issues. There is something similarly psychological and symbolic in Iron Maiden's treatment: an appeal to haunted consciousness and transformation. In the imagery of their lyrics and in the graphics on their album covers that feature their mascot "Eddie," Iron Maiden frequently appeals to symbolic imagery. This symbolic imagery is very present in "The Rime" and throughout the *Powerslave* album.

The poet W.H. Auden's socio-political approach to Coleridge's poem may suggest something else beyond these psychological approaches. Auden observed that the ship is a symbol of society. Following Auden, we might suggest that in Coleridge's poem—and perhaps in Iron Maiden's treatment—the state and society is creaking through an uncomfortable political and moral condition. Such a socio-political lens may provide us with another way of looking at Iron Maiden's voice in 1984, as an indirect comment on life in the Thatcher government's Britain. This is particularly relevant when one considers that the image of a decapitated Margaret Thatcher lies beneath the figure of Eddie on the cover of Iron Maiden's *Seventh Son of a Seventh Son*.

The political edge of Iron Maiden's work is barely touched in *Run to the Hills*, the anecdotal biography by Mick Wall, or in *Iron Maiden: Thirty Years of the Beast*, the unauthorized biography by Paul Stenning. Neither author makes mention of the political context that Coleridge's supernatural poem emerged from. As a young man Coleridge had been a pantisocratic admirer of the French Revolution. Coleridge biographer Richard Holmes describes this as "a turning point" for all of Coleridge's generation.[13] With *Powerslave,* Iron Maiden, likewise, may have been expressing romantic ideals within what they experienced as a generally stifling social and political environment.

Heavy metal is Dionysian and rebellious, as Deena Weinstein points out. It provides a "transvaluation of the values of respectable society" and, in her view, offers "a cultural coping mechanism." It is "inherently vitalizing, to tweak a devitalizing, bureaucratic, inauthentic, iron-caged, and unfair world."[14] Iron Maiden's appeal to heroism and the heroic journey is as fundamental to tweaking the world in our times as it was in the age of the Greek classics. It is an enduring aspect of that mythic core that Joseph Campbell identified in *The Hero with A Thousand Faces*. Yet, as in Campbell's model, the hero setting forth faces initiation and encounters adversity, darkness, and peril. Could charismatic metal gods duel with chaos and disaster with sonic power and rhythmic innovation?

We may wonder what goes "on and on" at the end of Iron Maiden's last song on the *Powerslave* album. Is their rendition of "The Rime of the Ancient Mariner" an affirmation of redemptive potential for society? Or are they suggesting that the story that goes "on and on" is less promising? Critics have been divided about the message of Coleridge's poem. John Beer, in *Coleridge the Visionary*, like Robert Penn Warren, emphasized the redemptive aspects of the poem. He also found sources behind it in the mysticism of Jacob Boehme, the allegory of Odysseus's homecoming, and the ballad collections of Walter Scott. However, other critics suggest there is only interminable retelling and a radical disjunction. Does Iron Maiden, with its adaptation, hold out a concern about alienation with a hope for the possibility of a new coherence? It appears that they achieve what Warren, referring to Coleridge's poem, once called "expressive integration."

It has often been said that artists are among the first to articulate what is "in the air" in a society. If this is true in Iron Maiden's case, what was the band saying through this album about consciousness in 1984 Britain? What cultural memory of heroism were they attempting to evoke in "Aces High" or with the odyssey of the Ancient Mariner?

In what sense was Iron Maiden positioning itself as "romantic" and "heroic?" Does Iron Maiden reflect "the romantic ideology" that literary critic Jerome McGann was writing about at the same time? McGann reaffirmed that Coleridge's poem dwells within romantic ideology and is Christian-redemptive in its theme, as well as Hegelian. In Harris's compression of Coleridge we can in fact see this Hegelian three part structure of thesis-antithesis-synthesis, or musical statement, drift to another key and time signature, and return to a new synthesis. All of this reflects the Romantic tendency in musical form. As Weinstein notes, British new wave

6. Iron Maiden

metal, bands like Iron Maiden, "famous for spiritual themes and strong tenor vocalists, often borrow from nineteenth century symphonic music."[15]

As in many of Beethoven's works, beginning with his Third Symphony, "Eroica," one experiences in Iron Maiden's songs on *Powerslave* a contest with chaos. The poem and Iron Maiden's musical adaptation appear to gather up the minstrel tradition, themes of imagination, the role of the Gothic, the fated hero, nostalgia and the melodrama that are all at work in English Romanticism. Gothic terror, the reality of death, a sense of the natural world, and nightmare are all figured in poem and song. So, in our "willing suspension of disbelief" as listeners, are we meant to hope for resolution? Does this journey through the "archaic, inhuman, uncanny" liminal world of the mariner bring us to a point of hope in the end? Or, does it interminably dance with chaos—on and on, forever?

As Odysseus once recalled, there is ambiguity in a heroic journey. Iron Maiden made use of the archaic, the symbolic, and the imaginative reach of mythology. "The Rime of the Ancient Mariner" fit well with the "heroic" motifs throughout their album, as well as with the notion of being enslaved to powers, as is the ancient Egyptian who speaks on the title track. Further, the Coleridge poem provided the band with a vehicle for instrumental virtuosity. Their song, like this poem, makes a journey across the boundaries of speech. Music is brought to bear upon the difficulty with language that critics have noted in the poem and this music underscores the poem's theme of transformation.[16]

"The Rime" is truly a performance piece. Dickinson's vocal invites a listener-response approach in which we experience the song as being in a dialogue with us. "The Rime" also gives the band an opportunity to shine as soloists. Dickinson, in particular, becomes the "ventriloquist" that critic Max F. Schultz saw in Coleridge. Dickinson adopts this alien voice of the mariner and makes it his own, projecting it toward us. It is a song of mesmeric power. Each time one listens to it, in memory, Iron Maiden takes the stage again and the story goes on and on and on.

7

Thor's Thunder
Norse Myth and the Gods of Valhalla

Metal bands of Scandinavia like Bathory, Einherjer, and Enslaved recall the heroic age of the Norse gods. This recollection has been transmitted through sagas and skaldic poems, Icelandic tales, and myths circulating in Norway and Denmark. There is a blend of history with these legends that has drawn interest from bands as different as Manowar, Emperor, and Darkthrone. Popular films have drawn upon the legendary tales of Thor and other Norse gods, such as Loki and Odin (*Thor*, 2011 *Ragnarok*, 2017). In the mythic creations of heavy metal, film, comics and graphic novels, Vikings continue to be popular as well. Black metal bands that hail from Scandinavia have made a distinctive creative claim with growling vocals, heavy bass pulse, myth, orchestration, and attitude.

Viking Metal: Myth, Power and Nostalgia

Vikings are sturdy, masculine warriors who characterize heavy metal by being loud, fast, in-your-face, dirty, obnoxious attackers. They are described as sailors, fighters, explorers with blond or reddish hair who carry swords and axes. Like heavy metal, they are direct, not subtle, often wild and barbaric, not submitting to authority.[1] Einherjer and Enslaved picture the Vikings more nobly, emphasizing strength, pride, and ancestry. In their work, a heathen soul gives homage to the past and celebrates life. There is no black metal semiology. The Viking is more heroic than marauder. These bands explore myth and raise their glasses to tradition and to the Viking image of one who is resilient, free, fit, and capable.

7. Thor's Thunder

Consider Bathory who made one of the first principal moves toward Viking metal. Bathory's *Blood, Fire, Death* sported a cover image of *The Wild Hunt of Odin*, a painting by the nineteenth century Norwegian artist Peter Nicolai Arbo. *Hammerheart*, the band's Viking concept album and *Twilight of the Gods* (1991) immediately followed. On the liner notes for *Blood and Ice* (1996) Quorthon called himself an "avid fan of history" and said that he was looking for the light in the darkness and finding it in "the Viking era." This, he said, was "great material for metal lyrics." It was his goal to restore a more vital pagan past: one that lived before "the Christian circus" came around in the 11th century (qtd. in Trafford and Pluskowski, 62).

Bathory was Quorthon (Thomas Borje Forsberg), Jonas Akerlund, Vvornth, Kothaar, and Frederick Melander. They were formed in Vallingly, Sweden, around 1983 and were active until Quorthon died in 2004. The first few albums were fundamental for Scandinavian black metal. There were provocative references to evil and Satan but the band members were not Satanists. With *Hammerheart* (1990) came their break away album into Viking metal and further Nordic mythical imagery and songs like "One Rode to Asa Bay." They turned to thrash metal on *Requiem* (1994) and *Octagon* (1995). *The Return* (1985) was the last album for which they performed live shows. *Under the Sign on the Black Mark* (1987) followed. *Blood Fire Death* (1988) continued the raw, distorted sound of the band. *Destroyer of Worlds* (2001) led back to Viking metal and Nordic myth on the band's final albums, *Nordham I* and *Nordham II*.

Viking metal has sometimes been seen as a subgenre of thrash metal. Bathory's recording *Hammerheart* has been described as a Viking metal album, while it includes Celtic and Norse myth (Weinstein, *Heavy Metal: The Music and Its Culture,* 4). The Viking motif has come in for parody in the versatile Todd Rundgren's "Song of the Viking" on his *Something/Anything?* album. Even so, since that time the Viking motif has made its mark. Some Viking metal bands believe that Christianity was imposed upon their society. However, they are not ready to embrace black metal and Satanism. Enslaved and Einherjer have shown an interest in the Vikings but reject Satanism and black metal. Einherjer drew upon Norse myth when they recorded *Odin Owns All* (1998). The album was laced with Gothic mystery and horror, occultism, and Norse legends.

Enslaved formed in Norway in 1991. The recording that is arguably their strongest, *Monumension* (2001) came ten years later. With Ivo Bjornson (vocals/guitar), Kronheim (guitar), Grutte Kgellson (bass), Dirge Rep (drums) they gravitated from black metal to Viking metal. There was a movement from black metal clichés and toward the exploration of Norse myth and Viking images. Ironically, Norway's ministry of culture and church affairs later sponsored the band. It was a strange turn of events to have government sponsorship of a band that once played death metal, which is notoriously anti-church and anti-Christian. Yet, metal had come a long way in popularity and the band had embraced of a Viking past that intrigued a large audience. Bjornson and Kgellson have been with the band since its origin. In 2014, Enslaved was called upon by Norway's government to create a piece to honor Norway's Viking past. They followed this with their recording *In Time* (2015).

The Enslaved band logo has Thor's hammer at the center, amid knotwork and images drawn from Viking art. The imagery drawn upon by bands with a Norse myth focus is often martial, or focused upon the heroic gods like Thor. References to Wotan appear on "Frost" (1994). On the cover for Enslaved's *Eld* (1997) vocalist Kgellson poses, wearing Thor's hammer pendant. They followed that album with *Blodhem* (1998) and *Mardraun: Beyond the Within* (2000) and *Monumension* (2001). The album cover for *Odin Owns Ye All* displays what appears like a carving of a one-eyed god, two ravens, and spirals that appear like those that might be carved into a church.

Einherjer, from Haugesund, Norway, were formed in 1993 by guitarist and vocalist Frode Glesnes and drummer Gerhard Storesund. Askel Herloe also plays guitar for Einherjer, which means "one who fights alone." Their sound is laced with folk sources and symphonic metal. In 2016 they re-recorded their first album, *Dragons of the North* (1996). The lyrics of Einherjer offer a clear narrative voice, a well-crafted poetry, and colorful images of northern landscapes and Viking warriors.

The title song "Dragons of the North" begins with blood, wolves, riches, a warrior march with hammers, and burning villages. Odin is watching from the distance. The vocalist builds a deadly picture of battle and asserts that no prayer will bring help against the dragons. "Dreamstorm" follows, with a clear narration by one who has drifted across many centuries in solitude with visions and dreams. He reflects upon death and destiny and the gate that lies before him. In "The Forever Empire" the speaker declares that he is his own eternity. The song begins with a dream of paradise and a longing for the sunrise from within a condition of bitterness, emptiness, lunacy, and fear. He will set sail for forever. "The

7. Thor's Thunder

Conqueror" follows, with the singer waiting for dawn. His ship is on the shore and the wind and the waves blow steadily as the snow falls. The quest is over and the winds call. He lifts his sword, knowing that the storms of the north will soon come. He will be a Viking conqueror in this land of the vast north and endless sky. In "The Fimbol Winter" the otherworld is to be encountered. The lyric is filled with colorful adjectives and speaks of storm, wind, and sea and a fight on the other side, facing Ragnarok. "Storms of the Elder" follows and the singer calls upon a monstrous one-eyed god to awaken and he offers a prayer for courage. He seeks an understanding of the ancient beliefs and Gnostic knowledge that come from inner chambers. He will set out on a quest, a journey on the path through a valley that is now forgotten in a treacherous place. In the last verse Odin is described as looking out over the world and calling to the other gods. As Einjerjer plays their next song, "Slagel Ved Hatsjord" (The Battle of Hafsfjord), the lyric is entirely in Norse. The album concludes with "The Battle of the Swords." Norsemen cross the ice and hear skalds sung about glory. We hear them too. The ravens speak to the narrator and he dwells upon mortality and the fight and dreams of glory.

Amon Amarth created their recording *Twilight of the Thunder God* based in Norse mythology. They were a death metal band that transmogrified into a Viking metal band performing Viking epics. The band formed in Stockholm in 1992 with the bearded Johan Hegg as the vocalist-front man. Olavvi Mikkonenen was the guitarist and with Johan Soderberg. Ted Lomdstrom played bass and he was followed in the band by Frederik Andersson. Martin Lopez was the drummer. They created the albums *Versus the World* (2002), *Fate of Norns* (2004), and *With Odin on Our Side* (2006). "The Pursuit of Vikings" was a video that highlighted their move into Viking metal and a slower, heavier sound.

Rock critic and sociologist Deena Weinstein notes that Viking music uses keyboards with "local cultural flourishes" and "a swift galloping pace" (4). She points out that Viking metal often focuses on the Norse mythical figure of Odin, god of war, or Thor, the hammer of the gods. Ross Hagen defines Viking metal as a subgenre of black metal without Satanic imagery (13). Imke Van Helden simply says that Viking metal is difficult to define (7). Ashley Anne Walsh sees a Nordic metal mythology that "plays with nostalgic images," romanticized the primordial, and works "as a means of criticizing the modern Christian world they perceive as being weaker than the ancient one" (www.duo.uio.no, University of Oslo Library).

Myth and Magic in Heavy Metal Music

The Eddas

In the Eddas, which are Nordic-Teutonic poems, we hear of the twilight of the gods (*Gotterdammerung*). The Icelandic term for this was *magna rok*, or the fatal destiny, the end of the gods. The word *rockr* meant shadows and obscurity, or twilight. The Scandinavian poets imagined their gods in palaces in Asgard. The age of peacefulness ended when in Valhalla the messenger from Vanir Gullveig was tormented in an effort to take gold from her. The wars broke out. A giant was deceived by Loki and with that deception all oaths lost their meaning. War and lying and the violence of battle occurred. Then on came the Vakyries, flying above the battles. Odin, the great god of war, looked on at the disruption. Then the murder of Balder brought on the great calamity. Loki, the evil trickster had persuaded the murderer and so they trapped him, making him more malevolent. Heimdall, watchman of the gods, emerged as the great adversary of Loki. His sword had been stolen by Loki, who was with the wolf Fenrir.

The field of battle at Vigridlag lay stretched out in front of Valhalla. There the gods and the warriors would fight an apocalyptic contest. Odin, with his Valkyries, flew above them, but even the great Odin was destroyed in battle. His son Vidar responded with fierce energy against the wolf Fenrir, tearing the wolf's heart with his sword. Thor then faced a monster, the serpent, and he smashed it with his hammer. But Thor had breathed the serpent's poison and he too fell. Heimdall forced Loki to return a stolen necklace to Freyja. In revenge, Loki sought and killed Heimdall and he died in the process. This was the death of the gods. Now humanity was lost and left alone without their protectors. The earth was collapsing and the stars fell from the sky. All fell into a void and the rivers rose and overflowed their banks. In a great deluge, the earth sank under the sea. Yet, from this devastation a new world would be born.

Thor is referenced often in Nordic heavy metal for his power and heroism. However, Loki, the trickster, has appeal also. Loki is inventive and immoral. He is characterized by fire and creative energy. He brings both provisions and deadly weapons and he conjures monstrous spirits. Archetypal critic Christopher Booker suggests that Loki represents ego-consciousness. He is unpredictability: the human capacity to be a maker and potentially to be a destroyer. Humanity has shown its ingenuity in developing technological marvels. Yet, for "one sided consciousness" there is "a price to be paid." Booker observes that humanity has gained an "unprecedented command over the forces of nature which has the potential to destroy the earth and all the life it contains a thousand times over" (648).

The apocalyptic Eddic poetry comes to us from the Codex Regius, from about 1270. There are ten poems of gods and 19 poems of heroes. Volupsa (the prophecy of the Sybal) begins the collection. In Volupsa the soothsayer-sibyl Volva tells the story. It continues to the end of the gods (*Ragnorok*). The pre-Christian world is expressed in the writings of Snorri Sturlson, who composed skaldic poetry and compiled sagas in the 13th century at about AD 1220. The deeds of the Danes was created by Saxo Grammaticus as a Latin translation of Danish poems from the pagan pre-Christian world which were mingled with legends. The Finnish Kalevala is Finland's national epic and is a source for a kind of mythic pride and for some heavy metal mythic creations in that country.

Mythologizing and Romanticizing History

To "romanticize" the Viking is problematic. Viking is a discursive construct: one focused on national identity and themes of resistance and power. There were no "better" primordial times. In history, life in the Viking era was nasty, brutish, and short and Norse fantasies do not clearly convey that reality. In AD 1000 life expectancy for men was 42 to 43 years old and 43.6 for women. In the highest, most well taken care of class life expectancy was 48.7 years. One third of all infants and young children died before the age of five. A Scandinavian faced the hardship of climate and topography. Most of the men and women of Scandinavia were illiterate.

The Viking Age (800–1200) shows an increase in population in Scandinavia. This was one factor prompting coastal raids to seek resources. "Changes in social organization contributed to an internal conflict in Norse society," writes John C. Sharpe (11). In AD 950 King Hakon made some of the first attempts to Christianize Norway. There was conflict about this from 950 to 1000. Varg Virkenes points back to a vibrant pre-Christian era: a time of civil war and cultural tensions and emigration to Scotland, Ireland and Iceland and rejection of the establishment of stave churches (barzum.org). This is the period of resistance to Charlemagne's

France in the 700s and 800s which corresponded with the rise of the Viking era.

In Norway, in the Viking era, Danish power was restored in the early 900s by the overlord Harald Finehair, who died in the 930s and was succeeded by Erik Bloodaxe, who tried to rule all of Norway from Trondelag. He faced Hakon the Good, who came to Norway via England and the court of King Athelstan (924–939). Erik Bloodaxe was removed from Norway by Hakon and was killed sometime between 952 and 954. His sons rebelled against Hakon the Good and Harold Graycloak gained some power but fell in the Battle of Limfjord. When Harald Bluetooth became overlord his son Sven Forkbeard rebelled.

The *Islendingabok* by Ari is a collection that tells of laws, history, and conversion. Ari was an Icelandic historian. In the *Islendingabok* Olaf Tryggvason is considered central to the conversion of Norway and Iceland to Christianity. Olaf Tryggvason is considered a founder of Norway. He instituted a partial reform of paganism when he returned to Norway in AD 995. Olaf Tryggvason was a raider. Legend says that he was injured when attacked by mutineers and he was visited by a seer near Sicily in 986. He experienced a conversion, was baptized, and returned to Norway in 995. Olaf Haraldsson was another instrumental figure who is spoken of in the great sagas. He is called "the fat"—*hinndigri*—in the great sagas (130). The sagas of the two Olafs recall political and ecclesiastical disputes.

In 1053 there was papal recognition by Pope Leo IX of the church in Scandinavian. Lund became an archdiocese in 1104. A cathedral was built there in 1145. In 1153 Trondheim became an archbishopric. Archdioceses were established in Denmark in 1104, in Norway 1153–54, and in Sweden in 1164. These regions became nominally Christian.

The Nordic Renaissance movement recalled and reinterpreted the poetry and myths of the Eddas and the Icelandic sagas. This was the root of Coleridge's "The Rime of the Ancient Mariner" that would be transformed into that powerful thirteen-plus minute epic by Iron Maiden. The mythical romantics recalled the folk ballad, the supposed Celtic songs of Ossian. Paul-Henri Mallet (1730–1807) of Geneva wrote an *Introduction to the History of Denmark*, while he was teaching French in Copenhagen. This featured an appropriation of Old Norse poetry. "The soaring flights of fancy may possibly more peculiarly belong to a rude and uncultivated than to a civilized people," writes Lannroth. "The great objects of nature strike more forcibly on rude imaginations" (Lannroth, 235). What

7. Thor's Thunder

mattered most was the "emotional, irrational, barbaric, and magical imagery of great poetry, he adds (235). That appears to be the same spirit that prevails in heavy metal: a folk spirit that typifies the audience.

Norse Myth

As in J.R.R. Tolkien's Middle Earth, the ancient pre-Christian societies of Scandinavia viewed the world as if they lived in its middle. In Norse mythology this world is the Midgard and it is within the world of the gods, Asgard. Beyond this lies the treacherous and uncertain region, a wilderness of danger, deep seas, and dark forests. Utgard is the outside world. Among the gods Thor resides in *prudheim*, that is, in power and might, Odin is in Valhalla: the hall of the warriors honorably slain in battle. Balder is in splendor. Heimdall is in the high mountains of heaven. The world tree grows in the center of Asgard, reaching to the sky, holding the world.

The Volupsa observes creation and the end of the world, Ragnarok. In Ragnarok the world declines into chaos and destruction by monsters. The earth slides into the sea. Volupsa says that a new world will later emerge from the void and chaos.

The Skaldic poems, filled with Norse myth, come to us across the centuries in complex metrics, word play, and metaphors. People who are able to read this language suggest that this was all part of an oral tradition and nothing was written down until the 12th century. King sagas (*konunagasogur*) were first inscribed beginning around AD 1150. The mythic heroic sagas (*fornaldarsogur*) emerged in the 1200s. (This would make the writing of these tales more or less contemporary with the romances of the troubadours and the Arthurian tales.) The mythic heroic sagas are "openly fantastic and obviously based on folktale romances," says one critic (Lannoth, 226). Significant works include the *Gesta Danorum*, a Latin history of Denmark by Saxo, and Heimkringla, a history of the Norwegian kings from earlier sources by Snorri Sturlason. This expert in this literature calls these works "vastly different." The Gesta Danorum is a work of classical rhetoric based on Latin-Roman models of heroism. The Vikings appear statesmanlike, the critic says. Snorri, in contrast, is focused on the suspenseful Icelandic sagas in which mythical elements combine with the folk tale form. The hero is charismatic, tenacious, and endures challenges. The text, the critic says, is understated and restrained.

Myth and Magic in Heavy Metal Music

The sagas do not call their heroes Vikings (*Vikingr*). However, the heroes are cast as brave men who go on journeys (*fara i viking*). They may pillage villages or commit violence in their acts of piracy. The Viking revivals of heavy metal refer to these sagas and recall a nostalgic search that has long been part of Scandinavian society. In 1869, high Swedish society dressed as Vikings for a costume dress ball. They learned about Valhalla and the Norse myths from folk tales and through the researches of people like F.N.S. Grundtvig, who tried to bring Viking lore into the Danish schools in the 1830s. Gruntvig advocated experiential learning and learning the songs from the Eddas and oral folk tradition. There was a commercial angle as well. Norse gods names could enhance the marketability of products.[2]

Seeking the Archaic Past

In Scandinavia in the nineteenth century, recollection of the Vikings was a populist enthusiasm: a new appreciation of a mythical golden age and part of a quest for the folk spirit. Early on in the century, Denmark and Sweden were overcoming military losses. Sweden had lost Finland to the Russians in 1809. They looked to these myths and folk spirit for a new vitality. In Denmark, N.F.S. Grundtvig (1779–1872) connected Norse mythology and Germanic philosophy. Adam Oehlenschlager (1779–1850) wrote the mythological *Guldharnene* (*The Golden Horns*, 1803). In it he recalled Denmark's once glorious past that had presumably been given to it by the gods. In Sweden, nationalism also brought a turn toward myth and folklore culture. In Stockholm there was a society (*Gotiskaforbundet*, the Gothic society) that wore Gothic garb, drank mead from deer and bull horns, recited Eddic poems, used names from the Norse sagas, and practiced Viking rituals (Lonnroth, 236).

Elsewhere in Scandinavia, Viking lore entered the schools. Erik Gustag Geiger (1783–1847) was an historian-mythologist and poet who wrote on Viking culture. His *Vikingen* (*The Viking*) and *Odalbanden* (*The Yeoman Farmer*) were recited in the Swedish schools (Lonnroth, 236). Geiger believed that freedom and strength lay in recalling Old Norse ways instead of capitulating to modern ways. He would go back to the archaic pagan past, to the age of the Vikings. *The Frithiofs Saga* (1825) included 24 epic songs about Viking lore. These were derived from Iceland and became Sweden's literary contribution to Viking lore.

7. Thor's Thunder

The Norse-Teutonic myths were made well-known to modern music audiences by the composer Richard Wagner. After fleeing to Switzerland following his revolutionary activity in 1848, Richard Wagner wrote his theoretical works *The Artwork of the Future* and *Opera and Drama*. He asserted the need to reunite music-drama in which there would be a synthesis of music, words, dance, and performance. He put this into practice, creating his famed Ring cycle. In Wagner's *Ring des Nibelungen* (1852–1874) he drew upon the Teutonic myths for his subject. Siegfried, his hero, could not save the gods from cosmic disintegration in the twilight of the gods. (He and the Valkyrie Brunnhilde are the heirs of Wotan.)

This mythology later fused together with the Nietzschean Ubermensch (superman) and German imperialist dreams and racist ideas. That nationalism was rooted in ideas of soil, family, and the folk and was absorbed into party politics where Wagner and Nietzsche were appropriated to serve the National Socialist (Nazi) agenda.

In Norway, during the period of the Second World War, the images of Vikings were employed in propaganda. They were used by the Nazis when they gathered and forced a Norwegian squad to fight on their behalf. However, images and symbols of the Vikings were also used by the resistance against Nazi occupation. Holgar Danske was a group of farmers in south Denmark who were a resistance group named after an Old Norse hero.

Black Metal

Black metal from Norway emerged in the early 1990s with Mayhem, Emperor, Denmark's Mercyful Fate. It has brought the successful metal bands Dimmu Borgir and Cradle of Filth. Black metal is associated with death metal. "Death metal would work as the soundtrack to the movie version of Dante's Inferno, or at least Hell's Muszak," writes Deena Weinstein. "Its lyrics are fixated on death, decay, and the diabolical" (288). Of course, for all of Dante's grotesque imagery of starving and self-deluded souls appointed to eternal doom, his *Commedia* ultimately rises to a vision of hope. Inferno is a scathing critique of humanity's flawed desires and need to visit the underworld, guided by Virgil, the first part of the pilgrim's journey. The black metal bands of the early 1990s did not project a great deal of hope, unless one might consider the symbolic venting of hatred a desperate way of seeking attention and defining purpose in life.

Myth and Magic in Heavy Metal Music

In Sweden, Carnage and Entombed were progenitors of death metal. Entombed and Morbid Angel were enduring and influential. In the 1990s, death metal broadened in scope and variety. Bands included the symphonic. Opeth from Stockholm listened to Iron Maiden and to progressive bands like Camel and Caravan. Arch Enemy added a female vocalist in 2000, the German born Angela Gosow, who liked metal and disliked mainstream rock. She insisted on growling out her vocals as a death metal performer even while other bands, like Cannibal Corpse, offered gruesome lyrics and titles expressing direct violence against women. Norway's Emperor drew upon the influences of Bathory and Celtic Frost.

In the 1990s major record companies began to sign some death metal bands after alternative rock was successful. Morbid Angel was signed to Warner Bros. and was part of the rise of Irving Azoff's Giant label. Cannibal Corpse, however, was too extreme for Warner or Columbia. Metal Blade's Mike Faley received a phone call one day from the Morgan Creek film production company with the request that one of Cannibal Corpse's songs be included in the *Ace Ventura: Pet Detective* film. Smaller record companies that featured heavy metal like Combat and Megaforce faded by the mid–1990s. Nuclear Blast, Relapse, and Earache continued to provide death metal. The Roadrunner label took an interest in death metal and signed Deicide and Sepultura, among others.

Black metal drew upon death metal. Deicide and Morbid Angel stayed firmly death metal. Marduk and Immortal shifted from death metal into "black metal's more extreme image" (Mudrian, 219). Eventually, Emperor and Dimmu Borgir, growing in popularity, became more mainstream. Morbid Angel's sound was brought into the music of Emperor, Zyklon, and Dimmu Borgir, observes Natalie J. Purcell (18). In the 1990s the female audience for heavy metal expanded. There were more female heavy metal fans in the audience at European festivals than at American festivals, Purcell observed (31).

Purcell categorizes death metal lyrics as:

1. gore/horror/porn,
2. Satanism/occult/anti-Christian,
3. sociopolitical commentary
4. emphasizing an independence theme
5. war/apocalypse.

7. Thor's Thunder

She analyzes lyrics from death metal, such as Satanism from Deicide (42–44) and anti-female lyrics from Cannibal Corpse (44). However, she points out that the lyrics of most bands are moving into "the realm of fantasy," not reality.

Purcell, who interviewed Karl Sanders of Nile for her study of death metal, observes that "Nile's lyrics mix Lovecraft images with themes from Egyptian and Sumerian mythology" (41). Albert Mudrian says that as they developed their albums their "traditional Middle Eastern elements" became "darker and deeper" (243). This trend can be heard on *Black Seeds of Vengeance* (2000) and *In Their Darkened Shrines* (2002). Mudrian cites an October 2000 *Terrorizer* review that spoke of "the exceptional authenticity of Nile's experiment" (ctd. by Mudrian, 243). Nile brings Egyptian and Sumerian mythology to life, like a resurrected mummy, or an ancient curse, in a mix of hard-driving, modal compositions.

Nile's Karl Sanders told Albert Mudrian that he has sought innovation, not imitation. He discussed with that critic the development of musicianship in death metal. Mudrian also interviewed numerous other death metal performers, including Slipknot's Jordian (254–57), Morbid Angel's David Vincent (258), Hypocrisy's Peter Tagtgren (261), Morbid Angel's Trey Azagthoth (263), Ander Jakobson of Sweden's Nasum (269), and Alex Webster of Cannibal Corpse, who told him he wanted the audience to "feel the brutality" (268) in the band's music.

Black metal reacts against European culture in the extreme and recalls ancestral lands. The assault, against Christianity by black metal bands appears to be an argument against hypocrisy and a rejection of outward, conventional forms rather than a principled anti-theism. There is an acting out that is an expression of anger at perceived institutional limitations. Mayhem was vicious. However, that Mercyful Fate was a Satanic band was viewed by some as a commercial ploy. King Diamond's vocals ranged from growls to a piercing falsetto and he made claims to be a satanic follower. There may be a Satanic metal band but some critics have described the rhetoric and show of imagery as an act, so that they will sell more recordings. To use the tropes of dark magic or Satanism is not a commitment to them. They are symbols of rebellion. "Death Church" by Machine Head, for example, sharply criticizes the Christian church but does not subscribe to Satanism. Yet, some say that King Diamond's claim may carry a grain of truth in it.

Most accounts of black metal tend to focus on the "Black Circle" of

Myth and Magic in Heavy Metal Music

Norwegian fans and bands. They were perpetrators of arson: the burning of churches in the early 1990s. A presumed Satanic worldview was alleged along with this criminality. This acting out in violence was construed as acts of resistance to and rejection of Christianity, which represented, for the arsonists, a repressive culture. We can call the metal discourse of resistance counter-hegemonic, as Ian Reyes does. Reyes states that 1990s black metal "had become unspectacular." It was not amateurish any longer. Black metal had begun to draw upon other styles of heavy metal.[3]

Black metal, with its aggressive stance, is one of the outgrowths of thrash metal, which began between 1981 and 1983 in Los Angeles. The British band Venom might be considered a predecessor of both thrash and black metal, with their album *Welcome to Hell* (1981). Conrad Lent wrote "Son of Satan" for *Welcome to Hell* and the album used the tritone interval. Venom's record *Black Metal* referred to Satan and chaos. The band Onslaught had a pentagram on their album cover for *The Force* (1986). Nige Rockett's songs included "Flame of the Antichrist" and "Fight with the Beast." The Danish band Mercyful Fate also used these dark symbols and titles. Bathory from Sweden incorporated some demonic imagery but were not pushing that theme as heavily as Venom, Onslaught, or Mercyful Fate. In 1991–92, there was the emergence of Enslaved, Emperor, Darkthrone's *Blaze in the Northern Sky* (1991), and Satyricon with *All Evil* (1992). Swedish death metal rivaled Norway's black metal scene. The anti-Christian stance was duplicated by Finland's Black Crucifixion.

Mayhem was bitter and dark. Formed in 1984 in Oslo, its members reached depths of destructiveness in the early 1990s. One can question what alienation and disaffection, what dwelling on evil and death, led to their acts of desecration and self-destruction. Black metal had developed a cultish ideology in a group called the Black Circle. Mayhem band members hung out at Helvete record shop in Oslo. The band produced *Death Crush* (1987), *Freezing Moon and Carnage* (1990), and *De Mysteriis Dom Sathanas* (1992). Emperor drummer Bard "Faust" Eithun was also there. Deathlike Silence Productions produced albums for Mayhem, Barzum, and Merciless Fate. The shop walls were painted black and held medieval weaponry. There was Kjetil Manheim, Virkenes, Euronymous, Blackthorne, and Per Yngve Ohlin, who called himself "Dead" and soon was. After Dead's suicide, Euronymous became a central figure in the black metal scene, projecting images of hate and evil and antipathy for all

7. Thor's Thunder

organized religion, particularly the Christian church. This led to several malevolent acts and futile symbolic gestures of hate.

Flames began to climb into the Norwegian nights, destroying churches early in 1992. By 1996 there had been about fifty attacks on churches. Each arson attack was found to be connected with black metal band members or fans. This appeared to be the collective activity of a group mind: one that some observers likened to that of a cult. In Bergen, the Fantoft stave church was the first major assault on June 6, 1992. Revheim in Stavanger followed on August 1. On August 21, the day that Bard "Faust" Eithun killed a gay man in Lillehammer, the Holmekoller Church in Oslo was burned. The September arson of the Skjold Church in Vindafjord was later linked to members of Mayhem. A *Bergeus Tidende* news report in January 1993 raised public attention that spread through media around the world. Friends of Varg Vikerenes initially advertised this, seeking to obtain negative attention and Virkenes admitted to the church burning. "Our intention is to spread fear and evil," he told the interviewer. Later he said, "I exaggerated a lot." However, Vikerenes' "exaggerated" pose and actions led to more trouble. Vikerenes and Snorre "Blackthorn" Ruch killed Euronymous on August 10, 1993. They were arrested that month and convicted in May 1994. There were also convictions for arson, assault, and possessing explosives. Despite public criticisms, heavy metal itself is not responsible for the apparent psychopathology of individuals who acted out in this way.

Barzum, beginning in 1991, was Varg Virkenes' largely solo project and he played every instrument. Barzum is a Tolkien word used to describe darkness and a ring. Virkenes appealed to Tolkien's mythology and also encoded occult messages and symbols. His final record, *Hlidshjalf* on Misanthrope Records in 1999, appeared well after the murder of Euronymous. Virkenes remained in prison. Mayhem split for awhile. They returned, with Hellhammer, in 1994.

The acts of the Black Circle appear to be a search for meaning rather than strictly a matter of nihilism. It was a form of bitter protest. If there was only a depressed void there would have been no church burning. To firebomb churches was an argument and an assertion, a cry for attention, a construction of meaning. Acts of terrorism—a word originally meaning "to cause to tremble"—are often those of disenfranchised groups who hope to gain a scrap of notice from the world that they exist.

The black metal movement persisted with other bands that had become prominent. King Diamond and the Danish band Mercyful Fate appeared in the early 1980s and disbanded around 1985. King Diamond continued on with black metal occultism and satanic references. He succeeded in being repulsive and was influential for other bands. Mercyful Fate had another go at it after 1993 and concluded that run by 1999. When Darkthrone formed in 1988 in Norway they were associated with Mayhem. Nocturno Culto was their vocalist. Anders Risberget and Ivar Enger played guitars. Dag Nilsen was the bass guitar payer and Fenriz (Glyve Nagel) was the drummer. The band's material extended across punk, death metal, and black metal with occult lyrics written by Fenriz.

The black metal phenomenon of Norway continues with Dimmu Borgir. Shegrath, in a black leather coat, has his face painted white and stage blood drips from his mouth. Dimmu Borgir emerged in 1993 with Shagrath on vocals and guitar or bass, as needed. Silenoz was the guitarist and Brynjard Tristan was on bass guitar. Their first drummer was Tjodaly. They produced their first EP sung in Norwegian. With *Enthrone Darkness Triumphant* they developed a melodic, sometimes orchestrated, wall of sound. The Prague Philharmonic played on the record. From Mayhem came one of their next drummers: Hellhammer. Dimmu Borgir has been recognized at the Grammy Awards.[4]

Medievalism

Nordic and British metal have appropriated the monster lore of the early Middle Ages and the tales of epic battles in poems and sagas. The Christian religion of Europe interpreted and questioned these figures. Christianity brought its own iconography and imagery during the monastic period. This included notions of heaven and hell drawn from the earlier Patristic period and notions of thresholds or gateways to the supernatural world derived from mythology and classical sources.

Medievalism is another important aspect of some metal bands' imagery. Pictorial imagery from the 6th and 7th centuries accompanies ancient stories that arise in the Nordic and Celtic background of Viking metal. Visual imagery includes a material culture of helmets, plaques, shields, ornaments in gold and bronze. The image of Odin on his magical horse Sleipner appears on the Pict cross slab in Aberlemno in Scotland in the image of a horse and knight. The poem Gododdin tells of a battle

7. Thor's Thunder

around AD 600. The later French *chansons de geste*, or the *Song of Roland* (*Chanson de Roland*), tell of the time of Charlemagne and the period of Muslim Spain. In the Shrine of Apostle James at Compostela in Galicia, a point along the pilgrimage roads, the heroic Roland is reflected by the figure of James the Moor-slayer. The poem plays its action against a religious background and tells a story of knights and glowing banners, broken lances and shattered shields. There is the graphic imagery of piercing, violence, and death. With this comes the knight's code, their conduct of virtue in the courtly medieval *Chanson de Roland*.

The Battle of Hastings appears on the Bayeux Tapestry, a strip of linen about 70 meters in length and about fifty centimeters wide. The tapestry portrays figures with woolen thread and depicts a story, a series of scenes. On it cavalrymen face infantrymen. In other works we see more supernatural imagery. The *Book of Revelation* imagery from the Carolingian period of the 9th century appears on the dome of the chapel in Aachen with its mosaic figuring God in heaven with the elders alongside an image of the Apocalypse.

In Germanic heroic literature of the *Nibelungenlied* and in the Eddic poems and the Volsunga saga of Iceland in the 13th century gold is taken by the gods Odin and Loki from the dwarf Andvari from beneath a waterfall. The gold is possessed by Fanfir (Green, 33–34). The sword made from this metal in garnished gold is held in awe. Weland, the legendary German smith, made swords, such as "Mimming" in the poem-story *Waldere*. In the *Song of Roland* swords are also given names: Durendal, Haltedere, Almice. In the Arthurian tales is one of the most famous of named swords: Excalibur. In Norse myth Sigurd, son of Sigmund, also inherits a sword which is given a name.

The first album of Satyricon's Norwegian black metal was titled *Dark Medieval Times*. With Satyr (Sigurd Wongroven) and drummer Frost (Kjetil-Vidar Haraldstad) and Emperor's Tomas Haugen on bass, Satyricon remained solidly black metal through their first few recordings and then moved toward a somewhat more traditional metal sound with *Rebel Extravaganza* (1999). Satyricon's *The Age of Nero* (2008) explicitly recalls the time of the Roman novel Satyricon by Petronius. That text is a parody of social reality and sexual behavior which became a Fellini film. It can be classified as menippean satire and is laced with irony and eroticism. The *Satyricon* is told by a narrator who has a boy-servant lover and tells of Trimalchio, a freedman of great wealth and extravagance who was a model for F. Scott Fitzgerald's *The Great Gatsby*. The Roman text includes stories about the Sibyl of Cumae and about a werewolf and witches. Satyricon, the heavy metal band, has produced *Nemesis Divina, Volcano, Now, Diabolical* (2006), and their live album *Live at the Opera* (2013).

Monsters and Dragons

Heavy metal audiences are intrigued by epic struggles and myths. There is a deep resource of images in Western art. Relics of pre-Christian culture appeal to those who are interested in Greek myth, Nordic-Germanic myth, or Anglo-Saxon legend. We see the epic struggles of men and monster figures illustrated in early medieval art. The Hinton St. Mary mosaic shows the image of Bellerophon who rides on Pegasus to confront the beast Chimera. The image of the griffin fighting men appears on the Hereford Mappa Mundi (13th century). The story of *Beowulf* suggests that monstrous beings inhabited the earth and had to be met by courageous heroes. Beowulf sets out to fight Grendel, a fiend in hell. The dragon figures that were confronted by the Vikings appear in art at Lindisfarne dating from 793. King Hakon's ships from Norway bound for Scotland in 1263 were adorned with dragon heads. In Germanic literature the classical griffin is replaced by a beast of even more sinister shape and proportions. In the Volsunga saga the great Fanfir is transformed into a huge and cruel dragon who guards the treasure of Ardvari. The dragon spews poison. When it leaves its lair for water, Siugurd disguises himself and kills the beast. (In Beowulf we hear that Sigurd killed the dragon.)

Heavy metal adopts the dragon image for its fierce power. The dragon also has apocalyptic resonance in the Hebrew scripture and in the Christian *Book of Revelation.* In Psalm 74 the figure of Rahab is mentioned: "thou breakest the heads of the dragon in the waters." In Isaiah 51 we read: "Art thou not it that hath cut Rahab and wounded the dragon?" In Celtic culture, observes Miranda Green, "the dragon pair sword may perhaps be recorded as an apotropic symbol of special significance to people in new lands in which fierce and exotic beasts may well have protected the owner" (Green, 369–70).

Celtic Frost, a Swiss black metal band, alluded to Celtic mythology with their name. They were active from 1984 to 1996 and after a hiatus resumed performing and recording after 2000. Celtic Frost has been

7. Thor's Thunder

described as "majestic and frightening" (Philips and Cogan, 51). They have used Norse mythology and have made Satanic references. Celtic Frost has also made some use of symphonic additions to their grand and frightening creations. Beginning with *Morbid Tales* (1984) and To *Mega Therion* (1985), they became influential, using Norse myth and satanic references. *Into the Pandemonium* (1987) followed. Celtic Frost's "macabre and heavy" sound more recently appeared on *Monotheist* (2006). Their Swiss background reminds us that the Celts were a Germanic tribe that migrated across the European continent. The Scottish, Irish, and Welsh Celts and their myths and legends unfolded across centuries from that distant past.

8

Sonnets to Orpheus
Journeys to the Underworld

It is said that the bluesman Robert Johnson met the devil at the crossroads. He sold his soul to the devil so that he could brilliantly play the devil's music. Or so the myth goes. He came from the muddy, rural land, plucked from the fields of the Mississippi Delta, and he traveled that long road that went north to cut a race record. Like dozens of white boys who would follow them, the bluesmen sold their souls to the devil: a music industry cloaked in glittering garb, beckoning like Satan from the hilltop to show them, like the devil once showed Jesus, the turbulent lights of the valley below, declaring "and you can have all of this too." The voice of the blues was earthy, black, and poor. Reaching for life, the blues faced pain and turned it over for pleasure. It expressed sexuality and embraced and inverted religion. The blues lyric translated sex into puns, metaphors, and double-entendres. The blues was an underworld of the marginalized: a means of expression, of signaling resistance. It is the music of the body and of emotion. The blues are resilient and tough-minded, confronting life with realism, humor, and raunchy resolve. In all of these respects it is the direct ancestor of rock and heavy metal: the mischievous, crotchety uncle who rejects the conventions, niceties, and hollow platitudes of society and its norms. Three sure chords and sly metaphysical rebellion is rock's blues inheritance.

Heavy metal derives from the blues, which became blues-rock in players like Muddy Waters and Howlin' Wolf and with Clapton, Beck, Page, and Hendrix. Heavy metal—indeed all of rock itself—is an inheritance: one that became primarily a poor white boy's blues. For after Jimi Hendrix there were only a few blacks playing hard rock and metal: Phil Lynott of Thin Lizzy and later a few metal acts like Living Colour with

8. Sonnets to Orpheus

their funk-oriented metal. If the boys were back in town, as Thin Lizzy sang, they were mostly young, working class, and white. Before the rise of heavy metal, before many enthusiastic female metal fans joined in the metal crowd, before metal became the home of many middle class listeners, metal was principally working class, a voice of the marginalized. With its rough-edged excess and incorporation of myth it recognized on some level that the invisibles of life had been marginalized in the modern world. It forced out a challenge to the staid and the conventional. Psychologist James Hillman has written: "If a culture's philosophy does not allow enough place for the other, give credit for the invisible, then the other must squeeze itself into our psychic system in distorted form" (184).

Hell sells. A rock band can repeat images of hell with very limited claims to authenticity. The semiotics of the underworld is put to calculated use by bands for profit. Whereas Iron Maiden seriously explores mythology and history *and* makes money with their heavy metal art, bands like Poison or Skid Row have evidently posed and used these images to make money in the pop market. Poseurs are inclined toward gimmicks rather than depth. Obviously, publicity can surround the hell-bent. Hell in advertising is alluring and sells products and rock music is a commercial industry.

Heavy metal musicians have frequently enlisted images of the Underworld, or Hell, for song and album titles. The Underworld is a realm of chaos, a challenge to order, and heavy metal insists upon making us aware of it. Black metal musician Hellhammer is a case in point. Raven Lord created the album *Descent to the Underworld* (2013). The progressive metal band Symphony X devised a recording they called *The Underworld* (2015), as did the band Adagio, with their recording *Underworld* (2003). Black metal performer Shagrath wrote of "The Underworld Regime" on *Ov Hell* (2010). More than two decades ago, in death metal, the Czech band Root created their album *The Temple in the Underworld* (1992). A 1980s metal band from New Jersey called themselves Hades: the name of the Underworld.[1] Fire is lit on stages and masks and hell-mouths, inverted crosses, skulls, and devil symbols appear. Iron Maiden played a passage from Revelation over the speakers during their *Number of the Beast* tour and placed their un-dead mascot, Eddie, de-composing, on their album covers.

Heavy metal plays with disorder, suggesting monsters, mayhem, doom, and disaster, chilling us with reminders of our vulnerability. It uses religion as a source of imagery and its songs about hell have been legion. Notably, Black Sabbath gave us their recording of "Heaven and Hell." Slayer brought their listeners "Hell Awaits" On *Stained Class*, Judas Priest sang "Saints in Hell." Grim Reaper gave their fans "See You in Hell." Venom sang "Welcome to Hell" and "Sacrifice," which depicts a black mass at a dark altar and speaks of slaying a virgin to honor Lucifer. Anthrax declared "Earth on Hell." Machine Head simply said, "I Am Hell." AC/DC may get the award for the most hell titles, from their hit song "Hell's Bells" to album cuts "Hell or High Water" and "Hell Ain't a Bad Place to Be" to their hit single "Highway to Hell." Rather than reading heavy metal's references to this zone of horror literally, listeners ought to consider irony in the treatment. This dark romantic irony is a cognate of satire. Deena Weinstein observes: "most of the use of the imagery of the underworld in heavy metal is underscored by a tone that ranges from irony to burlesque" (*Heavy Metal: The Music and Its Culture*, 260).

The Underworld is the abode of the souls in the afterlife. It is a region which Circe tells Odysseus lies beyond the ocean, a place to which he must travel to hear the word of the blind prophet Tiresius. One must cross the great river to the desolate shore. Then one will enter the land of shadows. Acheron, the river of affliction, leads underground in a stream of sadness. There is Cocytus, the river of lamentation. At the gates stands Cerberus, the grizzly watchdog. In Hades is the River Lethe, the river of forgetfulness, and finally Styx, the river of hell. To cross over the soul must appeal to the ferryman Charon. Minos is the judge of souls. In later mythology the virtuous ones are in Elysian Fields, a separate region for the good. In the Underworld regions lies something darker, more sinister and vague. Hades and Persephone rule there. Hecate is a moon goddess plunged into Acheron. Thanatos is death, son of darkness and night. The Erinyes are punishers, the children of eternal night. All who dwell in the Underworld are shadows: pale, diaphanous, unsubstantial, reflections of their past on earth. They appear to be in a limbo, a vacuum rather than the place of eternal justice as in the Christian notion of hell, or Dante's *Inferno*.

Death Metal

Death metal is closely related to the anti-social hard-edged attitude of black metal. It deals in images of death and demise. Cannibal Corpse,

8. Sonnets to Orpheus

one of the more notable and vicious death metal bands has produced some serious death metal noise. They have brought medical terminology to their lyrics and have been described as "brutal and perverse" (Phillips and Cogan, 50–51). Death metal and black metal bands continue to create all over the world, not only in Scandinavia. The semiotics of the death metal subgenre are by now familiar and differentiate death metal from other genres. It is a "raw, hideous," repetitive, aggressive, down-tuned throbbing atonal music that supports the screeching or growling vocals of a demon. Phrases, rather than any extended narrative treatment, evoke themes of darkness and the vocal tone usually reaches the audience before they digest the words. When myth is used it is expressive of emotions, power, fear, and mystery.

The death metal of Cannibal Corpse and Morbid Angel is raw, fast, down-tuned, loud, intense, and characterized by chaotic guitar riffs and growling vocals. They are decidedly not mainstream (although Cannibal Corpse, a Florida based band, did have an appearance in Tom Shadyac's popular *Ace Ventura: Pet Detective* film). They insist upon a non-melodic defiance of all pop music commercial norms. With slamming deep repetitive tones and bomb-like drum crashes they express extremity.

The death metal band Morbid Angel began exploring darkness with satanic references and occultism on *Altars of Mad*ness (1989), their first album. By *Blessed Are the Sick* (1991) they had begun to express their hideous sense of chaos through Sumerian myth. Morbid Angel signed to Giant Records in 1992 and *Covenant* (1993) followed. They continued to develop songs "grounded in ancient myths," as Natalie Purcell has pointed out in *Death Metal: The Passion and Politics of a Subculture* (2003) (18). Morbid Angel has created "Gateways to Annihilation," "Abominations of Desolation" and "Angel of Disease." They have dug into Sumerian myth and have referred to the horror writer H.P. Lovecraft. The god of the skies Aruna sets a bitter tone. The strange *Simon Necromicon* (1977) alludes to Lovecraft and to Aleister Crowley. The album uses Mid-east myth, and ponders the discovery of dark secrets and magic. We hear the "Testimony of the Mad Arab" which is used as a frame story for the volume. Simon was supposedly a monk inclined toward reporting on magic and incantations and magic conjurations occur throughout the book. Morbid Angel's recording titled *Illuch Divinum [Invictus]* shows their preference for Romanizing archaic words.

On the banks of the Tigris and the Euphrates the civilization of the

Myth and Magic in Heavy Metal Music

Sumerians and the Akkadians venerated divinities and feared devils. Sumer was the region on the upper end of what is today the Persian Gulf. Akkad was north of Sumer and its people had probably migrated there from what is today Syria. It is likely that they shared their creation myths and gods. The Sumerians may have come from central Asia or the steppes of Siberia originally. They settled in between Eridu in the south and Nippur in the north. The Akkadians' cities were Agade, Borsippa, Babylon, Kish, Kutha, and Sippar. Tablets in the library at Nineveh date from the seventh century BC and indicate that the Sumerians and Akkadians imagined the creation as emerging from an abyss, or the Apsu. The oceans, or Tiamat, was the feminine force that gave birth to the world. The Anshar, or male principle, and the Kishar, or female principle, came from these beginnings. Marduk, who became the great god of Babylon, is given a central role in the creation. He let loose the winds of the hurricane, a turbulence in which the gods marched to war. He drove his chariot in an evil wind and pierced the belly of Tiamat. He took all of Taimat's assistants captive and began to organize the world. And so the earth came into being and humanity was created.

Anu, or "sky," was son of Anshar and Kishar. He lived forever in those heavenly regions, watching over the fate of the universe. Enlil, lord of the air, was more earth-bound than this and symbolized the forces of nature. Later, the Babylonians joined the image of Enlil to that of Marduk. Enlil sent forth good and evil and he could destroy the human race in a great deluge if he was angry. Marduk was the eldest son of Ea, or god of the water. In Sumer, Ea was called Enki, or lord of the earth and god of knowledge, who presided over the earth with magical incantations. Marduk, his son, would absorb all of the other gods and be the great creator of order of all things. The Assyrians looked to Asshur as warrior-god and king of the gods.

Death metal is more interested in the dark gods like Nergal, king of the underworld, and the plague demon Namtar, the fire gods Gibil and Nusku, the storm-god Adad, and the astral deity Ishtar. The great warrior goddess Ishtar (Ianna) was worshipped in Nineveh and Erbil. A cunning and voluptuous goddess, she was also revered by the Assyrians. Yet, she could be as violent and fickle as she was amorous. A cult of prostitution encircled Ishtar. Vain and powerful, she would descend into the underworld seeking more power. Upon meeting Ereshkigal, queen of the infernal, she would be cast into a prison and had to call upon Ea and magical

8. Sonnets to Orpheus

enchantment to become free. That dark underworld lay beyond the abyss of Apsu. There Nergal, a warrior god who also had the name Meshlamthea, reigned with Ereshkigal. In this bitter subterranean place lived the dark gods.

The Underground

In heavy metal, the term Underworld may also suggest the underground. Underground bands dwell in a kind of Purgatory, attracting some fans or a cult following as they travel from gig to gig. Some underground bands are signed to labels; others are not and do their own independent thing. Underground bands may be startling, or too extreme for the mainstream. Some, like Dante's souls in Purgatory, are waiting for a break. Others are as hopeless as Dante's spirits in Inferno, consigned to a hell of dive bars, backrooms, and other hellholes. They show up on college radio, in a local club, or on the Internet with a few hundred Facebook friends. They may appear at festivals and attract followings through YouTube videos or the exchanges of mp3 files. The Underground is also the place where what may be too complex, too intricate, or too deviant for mainstream pop airplay gets assigned. As Weinstein puts it, the Underground includes Dante's Purgatory of those who are waiting on commercial heaven and those self-condemned to Inferno, who "playing underground metal of an infernal sort" have no chance of the "heaven of pop stardom" and do not seek it (284). (This includes most death metal bands.) Thus, the underground is a place of novelty and immense creativity. It is, in a sense, where every band emerges from: some garage or basement or shed in some half-forgotten town, or in city rooms where friends meet and pull out their guitars.

Descending into the Underworld

In ancient Egypt, the sun god Re each evening, after he had swept across the sky, descended into a world of shadows in the far west. It was said that Re went to the world of the dead during the night and passed through the underworld before rising again into the sky each morning. The historian Herodotus wrote that the Egyptians created a myth that

Ramses III, their Pharoah, went down into the land of the dead with Isis (Demeter) and returned to earth. Osiris descended into the netherworld never to return.

Egyptology is an interest of guitarist-vocalist Karl Sanders of Nile, a second degree black belt and former roadie for Morbid Angel. Sanders' studied inquiry of Egypt was matched with the use of dropped A tunings, a minor Phrygian mode, and Arabic and Middle Eastern folk music sources on Nile's first album. In 1997, an EP featured "Ramses Bringer of War." Since then there have been numerous pseudo-myth songs, including the singles "Sarcophogus" (2002) and "Papyrus" (2007), and videos of "Papyrus Containing a Spell to Preserve Its Possessor from He Who Is in the Water" (2007) and "Permitting the Noble Dead to Descend Into the Underworld" (2010). *Ithyphallic* (2007) on Nuclear Blast and *Those Whom the Gods Detest* (2009) also were filled with Egyptian mythical references, a brutal pulsing down-tuned music, and suggestions of the underworld.

Descents into the underworld appear in the myths of many peoples. These myths of journeys to the underworld may refer to efforts to overcome the power of death. Descents are often attributed to heroes, or to seers, those who have visions or enter trances. Descents are cultivated by the shamans. They are ones who reveal something about the world that is yet to come. From Ancient Mesopotamia comes the Legend of the Descent of Ishtar and the descent of the goddess Ianna, the morning star who was not satisfied with being only the queen of heaven. Ianna wished also to rule in the underworld where her sister Ereshkigal was queen. Ianna passed the seven gates into the underworld where she was stripped naked to stand before seven judges. She was condemned and killed by them and then revenged according to instructions she had given to her servant Ninshuber. Enki creates two creatures who find a way to the underworld to revive Ianna.

There are other Sumerian stories. Kumma wished to see the netherworld. He prayed to the rulers of that region: Ereshkigal and Nergal. In a dream he is given a glimpse of the fearsome place of souls. In the epic of Gilgamesh there is reference to the story of Gilgamesh, Einkidu, and the Netherworld. When the earth shivers and a great crater appears in the earth two precious objects owned by Gilgamesh disappear. Einkidu says that he will go to get them back and Gilgamesh tells him how to act in the netherworld. However, Einkidu does not behave so well and he dies. Gilgamesh calls to the gods for assistance. The Akkadian Epic of Gilgamesh

8. Sonnets to Orpheus

says that Einkidu has a premonition in a dream. He is seized by a spirit and led down to death in the place of darkness.

From the Zoroastrian tradition of Iran comes the legend of Kadir who sought a vision of the other world. In the Uragartic myths, around ancient Syria, the descent into the underworld became symbolic of the seasons. In one tale Baal, god of the waters of chaos, noticed that Mot, the god of death, was affecting his rule and he sent messengers to insist upon the continuance of his claim. Mot challenged Baal to come down to the netherworld, where Baal died and had to be revived by his sister Anat. Baal returned to face Mot in a terrible battle. In other tales, Ahriman appears as a devil, a Zoroastrian parallel with Lucifer. Ahiriman also dwells in the netherworld.

The Old Testament Hebrews believed that one who goes down to Sheol will never return. (Job 7:9, 16:22; 2 Samuel 12:23) There are no stories of a living human traveling down to the underworld. However, metaphorically the Psalmist may experience a down-going. "When the psalmists feel themselves to be close to death ... they speak of themselves as already at the gates of the underworld" (Psalms 107:18).[2] The Psalmist says, lead me not down into Sheol (Psalms 88:6). Only God can provide deliverance to bring them up again (Psalms 9:13, 30:3, 86:13; Isaiah 38:17; Wisdom, 6:13). Similarly, in Islamic lore, Al Aaraaf is a limbo, a loss of heaven, in which souls are forever unable to see Allah. For such souls in this underworld there is no hope.

In Briton myth Ankou is a reaper who brings dread. While the protometal rock band Blue Öyster Cult may urge their listeners "Don't Fear the Reaper," this Briton figure of the reaper is one disturbing image. By the dark of the moon he drives a cart driven by the skeletons of mad horses to gather the souls of the sick and the dying. Ankou, the reaper, will drag those souls down to the underworld.

Anwnn in Celtic myth is the Kingdom of the Shades, including a region of gods and great spirits. There is a Welsh epic story, *The Spoils of Anwnn*, which tells of King Arthur and his knights and their perilous journey to get a magic cauldron in a twilight underworld. They encounter a fortress of glass in this mystical place.

It is in the mythology of the ancient Greeks that we get some of the most developed myths of journeys to the underworld. The story of Persephone's capture by Hades is a fundamental myth of the underworld. In another myth, Orpheus loses Euridice to death and seeks her in the underworld. Tiresias joins the shades in the underworld and Circe tells Odysseus that he must descend to meet with him.

The cycle of nature's seasons is represented in the myth of Persephone. One day as she gathers flowers with her mother Demeter she is seized by Hades and dragged off to the underworld. Abducted by Hades, Persephone dwelled in this region as Demeter searched for her, disguised as an old woman. The search took Demeter to Eleusis. She set aside her usual work and the crops failed. A famine threatened to sweep away humanity and Zeus intervened. Zeus sent Hermes to urge Hades to release Persephone from the underworld. However, Hades tricked Persephone into eating the pomegranate seed. This meant that Persephone would not be able to leave him forever. Persephone would spend part of the year with her on Olympus but she had to return to the underworld and to Hades each year, which created the cold season. Thus the idea of the renewal of the seasons was connected to the notion of afterlife in the underworld.

This story was told in the Homeric hymn to Demeter, which connected Persephone (also called Kore) and Demeter with the Eleusian mysteries. This was celebrated throughout the Greek isles and in Sicily. As queen of the underworld, Persephone took on an image of dread and horror. Even so, she was honored by several cults, usually in connection with Demeter.

Orpheus was the mythical singer whose song had great powers to enchant, charm, and heal. It was said that Orpheus saved the Argonauts from the Sirens, whose own song would crash sailors into the rocks. (No doubt some critics have viewed heavy metal as a Siren's song.) The song of Orpheus was present in oracles and healing rites. The most well-known tale of Orpheus concerns his journey to the underworld. The purpose of the descent of Orpheus the singer was to return his beloved Eurydice to life. The story was told by the Roman poets Virgil (in the *Georgics*, 4. 453–525) and Ovid (in *Metamorphosis*, 10.1–11). In the story Eurydice has died of a snakebite and Orpheus descended to Hades to try to retrieve her to life. Euridyce could return to life as long as Orpheus did not look back at her over his shoulder. Sadly, he did look back and Euridyce vanished back into Hades. Orpheus went away among the forests, rocks, and trees singing his lament. The Bacchic maenads overcame him, tearing him to shreds. Orphic beliefs about the Underworld spread across Greece, southern Italy, and Crete.

8. *Sonnets to Orpheus*

Throughout the Greek myths we see the heroes who travel to the underworld approaching the entrances to it: springs, rivers, lakes, waterfalls, caves. Odysseus sails his ship to the edge of the underworld and has to cloak himself with a ram's pelt to ward off the spirits as he makes his solo journey to the depths amid the beckoning shades.

Dante's Inferno

The Underworld depicted by the poet Dante Alighieri around A.D. 1300 is a region of doom, punishment, self-deception and monstrosity. It is a realm where the traveler is immediately thrown into a sense of vulnerability amid unseemly sights and sounds. Heavy metal seeks "to conjure and play with those forces" of the mythical Underworld, observes Weinstein (33). The Anthrax song "Howling Furies" quotes Dante's Canto III of the Inferno at the gates of the Underworld: "Abandon all hope all who enter here."[3] The gate of Inferno where Canto III begins is a terrible threshold. Beyond the gate are the hopeless: the souls trapped in lust, gluttony, avariciousness, and restless fury. The nine rings of Dante's Inferno is a moral realm through which Dante's character travels to remedy his own troubled soul. He encounters mythical monsters like Minos, who wraps his tail around himself to signify where a doomed soul is to be sent, and the fierce, doglike Cerberus. He is shown grotesque horrors and he is introduced to the damned and hopeless who are self-deceived and still addicted to the behaviors that landed them in this infernal place. As he travels on he enters a narrower zone where the violent curse, kick, and feed upon each other. Ultimately, he proceeds to the rings of fraud and betrayal and in the depths of this hell he sees Judas Iscariot and Cassius and Brutus, the killers of Caesar, upon whose heads the devil is feasting. The place is frozen cold, a realm of no warmth and no light other than Satan's fierce glow.

Judgment has come in Dante's *Inferno*. More than a century later, during the Italian Renaissance, Michelangelo depicted his arresting scene of the final judgment which is today upon one of the walls of the Sistine Chapel in Rome. Judgment is an ancient biblical concept. It is also one that has been worked into several heavy metal songs. Whitesnake's "Judgment Day" by David Coverdale and Adrian Vandenberg charted on November 18, 1989, and appeared on *Slip of the Tongue*. The guitar virtuoso Steve

Myth and Magic in Heavy Metal Music

Vai played on this album which reached #10 a week later. In liner notes on *The Best of Whitesnake*, Jeremy Holiday refers to their "metal epic," the song "Judgment Day," as reminiscent of Led Zeppelin's "Kashmir." If one listens to some of Whitesnake's material, including this song, one can hear suggestions of Led Zeppelin's sound.[4]

Hades in Greek mythology represents the site of an afterlife in the underworld that was not necessarily a place of torment for the wicked, as we find in Dante's Inferno, or in the Christian notion of Hell. Hades was the god of this underworld and this was his realm where dwelled the shadows. This could be seen as a place of gloom or sadness but not one of eternal despair.[5] The Hebrew concept of the afterlife was called Sheol: a term that we see in the Psalms. The Babylonian Underworld and the Greek Underworld both had gates. The Hebrew scripture of Isaiah 38:10 speaks of "the gates of death." The mention of gates also appears in Job 38:17, in Psalms 9:14 and 107:18, and in Wisdom 16:13. Descent into the Underworld appears in many myths across various cultures, along with heroic journeys. There are heroes who face the terrors, who dare to rescue someone from the Underworld, or who seek information. Descent may be psychological experiences, a coming down from a high, a trance or vision. These descents offer revelations of what is to come. They may be a prophetic voice in the Biblical world. They are the path of the shaman.

In the Sumerian myths descending into the Underworld was a perilous and fearful journey. The netherworld was a place from which no one could return. As already noted, in the legend of Enlil and Ninhil the god Enlil is banished to this region for raping Ninlil. In the descent of Ishtar, in its Akkadian version, the goddess Ianna, or morning star, does not feel satisfied as the queen of heaven. She wants to reign in the lower world too, where her sister Ereshkigal is queen. Ianna must pass seven gates, give up her jewels, and stand naked before the judges. She is condemned by them and killed. However, her message about her journey was given to Ninshubar, her servant. If she did not return a plan would be put into effect that would restore her to life.

The Babylonian epic Gilgamesh is the most famous of Assyrian-Babylonian heroes. In Assyrian-Babylonian mythology dreams are sent to men by the gods. Down beneath the earth one passes through the abyss of the Apsa to the dwelling of the spirits. This is the place of no return. In one myth Enkida passes seven gates where dwells Ereshkigal. The

8. Sonnets to Orpheus

invader Negal arrives one day and she marries him. Among the unburied souls of the dead one finds the *shedu*, the guardian spirits and the evil *utukku*.

The underworld in Sumer is known as Absu, or the abyss. It is also known as Nar Mattaru, or the great underworld ocean. Morbid Angel reads Sumerian myth through occultism. Their song "Nar Mattaru" on Covenant refers to that great underworld ocean. Morbid Angel's sound has been characterized by Pete Sandoval's fast drumming and Trey Azagthoth's fast and heavily distorted guitar lines. Michael Nielson (2013) described Trey Azagthoth's guitar playing as able to "mimic surreal horrors ... whirlpools or wildfire" ("Covenant Turns 20," *Stereogum*, June 20, 2013.) The cover image for Mobid Angel's album *Covenant* depicts *The Book of Ceremonial Magic* from Arthur Edward Waite and *The Pact of Urbain Grandier*: a pact, or promise which reflects the album's title.

Mobid Angel's song lyrics have often been the work of bassist David Vincent. Guitarist Trey Azagthoth wrote all of the music on the *Covenant* album except for "Lion's Den," which was written by David Vincent. In an interview, Vincent said that he first seeks the factual and then the fantastic and he will "create an imaginative story" for himself. He said that he prefers to explore "left hand path thoughts" and noted ideas of personal empowerment and the desire to create entertainment (www.westword.com). When Trey Azagthoth says that his songs have nothing to do with horror writer H.P. Lovecraft that apparently is a declaration of his own artistic integrity and a sign that a source for Morbid Angel's version of Middle Eastern myth is Simon's *Necronomicon* rather than a reading of Lovecraft. The *Necronomicon*, a book of occultism and magic, was supposedly assembled by a mysterious monk who called himself Simon. In *Necronomicon* there is gate symbolism, or thresholds, and a section of the celestial gate. This is followed by discussion of the great bear and the formation of the astral body. Section six discusses the primordial conflict. Attention is then given to the gates (*The Gates of Necronomicon*, New York: Avon, 2006).

One of the most striking aspects of H.P. Lovecraft's horror stories is the writer's vital and well-crafted language. The name Ctulhu may be derived from the word chthonic, meaning subterranean. Ctulhu first appeared in "The Call of Ctulhu," a 1928 story in *Weird Tales*. "The Dunwich Horror" (1928) also refers to Ctulhu. In "The Whisperer in Darkness" (1930), a character says that he knows the origin of Ctulhu. In Lovecraft's story this was a monstrous, malevolent deity, part dragon-octopus, from an underwater city. For now Ktulhu is trapped, imprisoned as a subconscious source of anxiety, but he is destined to return.

Trey Azagthoth told an interviewer, "my lyrics have nothing to do with H.P. Lovecraft" that is because his source is Simon's *Necronomicon* rather than Lovecraft. The Sumerian myths are read through this text. There is an occult interest to which the ancient myths appear to be secondary, or pseudo-myths. In the interview he mentions reading books on magic and the occult and reflects on earthly 'reality' as illusion and the movement toward pure spirit. Vincent has mentioned his familiarity with Lovecraft and with the occultism of Alesiter Crowley. (With reference to the band's mythos Azathoth says: The elder gods are actually the disease and the ancient ones are the only things that are real. The elder gods are the ego.) Vincent and Azagthoth have announced "incompatibilities" which affect the future of the band.

Keith Kahn-Harris (4), Carl Sederhom, and Gary Hill are among those who all point to H.P. Lovecraft and the Cthulhu myths. H.P. Lovecraft describes this. His character is Abdul Alhazred.

Demythologizing Hell

When the theologian Rudolph Bultmann set out to demythologize the Bible so that its message could be grasped by modern men and women, other theologians began to pursue the image of hell. In rather literalist fashion some turned to Luke 16 and asked whether there was a fire. Others attempted to make rational sense of *Revelation*, which is a highly symbolic book. Most preferred to talk about the kingdom of God rather than the depths of hell. Bultmann, for one, did not even discuss hell at all in his magisterial work *Theology of the New Testament*. However, as philosopher Walter Kaufman has pointed out, if there is the possibility that individuals will be consigned to such a place of damnation then it does not make sense to push aside notions of hell rather than to confront them (Kaufman, 257).

For the psychologist David Bakan, Protestantism focused upon human agency and Satan was a projection of "a rival task master" in which "the agentic in the human psyche is personified" (Hampden-Turner, 38). When an individual's "frantic efforts at mastery reach the limits of their effectiveness, driving the agent to despair, the individual attributes this to Satan" (38).

8. Sonnets to Orpheus

From one perspective, Satan is the rebel, the dynamic figure that intrigued Milton or Shelley. From another, there is the hell of the "dark Satanic mills" that Blake addressed, or the wheels of industry that the members of Black Sabbath saw about them in their childhoods in Birmingham. Or, this hell represents the failure of the modern world. Hampden-Turner writes in *Maps of the Mind*: "Has this overemphasis on agency spilled over into modern scientism and behavioral psychology, which ... are still cast in the Calvinist mode?" (38). That is, are we to be defined by the notion held by La Mettrie that man is a machine, or that propounded by behaviorists that we are nothing but creatures responding to stimuli and response: functions of our genes and early conditioning and reinforcements? Reflecting on Bakan's theory, Hampden-Turner writes: "The concern with ... control, habits, order and technique in a determined universe has neglected community, creativity, freedom, personality, and affections" (38). Could this not be the contemporary world that Metallica faces on their *Black Album* and System of a Down argues against on their recording *Toxicity*? This is the Temple of Syrinx that Rush's protagonist faces on their record *2112*. It is the projected demon of black metal. It is a confrontation with the restrictions of society that is cast as a journey through the Underworld.

We live, think, and speak in metaphors. We speak of the ladder of success, the corporate ladder, and of upward mobility. Less is spoken about the dark into which each person must go, the struggles that prompt a deepening of the soul. Culturally, we tend to put all the good things up high and the bad stuff down below. We face off like "Aces High" and Icarus on the heights. We are growing "up" but sometimes we dip down into "feeling like hell." We chart progress on a grading scale, according to a hierarchy, and our high-rises reach for the sky. Our subways get neglected and need repair, like the ones in New York City in 2017. Up is good. Down is bad.

Gorgoroth, for example, appeals to down deep in the Underworld. Stakes with sheep heads and crucified models adorned Gorgoroth's stage set in Krakow in February 2004. The Satanist imagery was clear to officials in the predominantly Catholic country but the legal charges were likely to be for animal abuse. Although this aspect of the display was against the law, Gorgoroth was not fined. Set within the modern world, Gorgoroth appeals to underworld mythology and an imagery of hell.

The band takes its name from the plateau of death in the land of

Mordor in J.R.R. Tolkien's *Lord of the Rings*. Their imagery and lyrics, largely supplied by founding member Infernus (Roger Tiegs) suggest devil worship and apocalyptic chaos. Gorgoroth, formed in 1992, performed with Enslaved and Cradle of Filth and were signed to Nuclear Blast Records after headlining their own tour in 1997. They have transitioned through several vocalists, including Hat (1992–1995) and Thomas "Pest" Kronenes, and have gone through many personnel changes. During the recording of their first album *Pentagram* bassist Kjettar left the band and Samoth of Emperor joined. Then the drummer, Goat, left the band and Frost from Satyricon became Gorgoroth's drummer. Tomas Asklend later became the drummer. Their second album was *Antichrist* and their third was *Incipit Satan*, written and composed by Infernus. Gaahl increasingly got involved in control of the band's music. Gorgoroth divided and experienced conflict over the ownership of the band's name. King av Hell, the bassist, and Gaahl tried to wrest this from Infernus but the courts upheld Infernus' claim in 2009. Gaahl subsequently declared his homosexuality, even as black metal has connected heterosexual masculinity with the macho-Viking image. *Instinctus Bestialus* (2015) was the band's sixth studio album. Whether Gorgoroth's Gaahl and Infernus are Satan worshippers is an open question. What is certain is that both of them are decidedly anti-Christian.

White Metal and Revelation

Christian metal has taken mythic and religious imagery in a different direction. Narnia from Sweden drew its name from C.S. Lewis's fantastic tales. Mortification has pounded out death metal in Australia with an anticipation of salvation. Christian thrash from Deliverance and Torniquet has taken on apocalyptic themes and offered a different vision. P.O.D. and Underoath are popular Christian metal bands. P.O.D.'s *Satellite* went platinum and Underoath's *Define the Great Line* rose to #2 on the charts after its release. *Revolver* in February 2007 interviewed members of Underoath, P.O.D. and As I Lay Dying and charted the continuing energy of Christian heavy metal.

A discussion of hell almost inevitably suggests its opposite: heaven. Hell is the antithesis of the afterlife of heaven that is characterized by peace, salvation, and love. That tends to be the view of what is sometimes called white metal. White metal, or contemporary Christian metal,

8. Sonnets to Orpheus

emerged in the 1980s as an evangelical alternative to secular music. These bands asserted their faith. They did not always contest the bands that played out images of hell, Satan, or violence. They asserted their own belief with apocalyptic imagery, insisting upon a salvation theme.

The notion of hell is a very powerful one for someone who believes in the invisible. Images of heaven and hell take on greater poignancy for those who believe in a spiritual realm. For Christian rock bands, which are invariably well-read in scripture, Christ is the mediator, God incarnate, a personal savior, and the living presence of the invisible and ever-available love of God. As the psychologist/mythologist James Hillman points out: "Christ becomes the only image left in the Kingdom for bringing back to our culture the fundamental invisibility upon which cultures have always rested" (110).

Christian rock appeared in the 1970s with the Resurrection Band, a Milwaukee based group that influenced other young evangelicals. Young people in Bible-based churches picked up guitars, played drums, and launched into rock music with the gospel, to reach "the unsaved." From Larry Norman to John Michael Talbot's incorporation of classical guitar to the gifted guitar player Phil Keaggy, Christian music began to be heard outside of these church circles. In the mid–1980s the band Stryper brought their heavy metal sound out of Los Angeles onto the *Billboard* charts. The band took its name from the biblical passage in Isaiah: "by his stripes we are healed." Christians viewed this passage as reflecting the passion and crucifixion of Jesus. Stryper was clear about their faith commitment and loud in making their joyful noise unto the Lord. Heavy drums, forceful guitars, and focused lyrics created a distinct heavy metal sound on *To Hell with the Devil*, which sold 2 million albums. "By 1987 there were more than a hundred Christian metal groups," observes Deena Weinstein (54).

Both white metal and black metal drew upon the apocalyptic symbols of the book of Revelation. This Biblical text gives us images of Armageddon and the Second Coming. It fosters millennialism and apocalypticism. Revelation is sometimes viewed as a work of prophecy. The scripture insists that "the time is near" (Revelation 1:3). It begins in the form of a letter (salutation, greeting, doxology). It states that this is a revelation received by "John."

The number seven is significant in Revelation and is one of the book's organizing elements. There are seven messages, seven trumpets, seven seals. (Ingmar Bergman referred to the seven seals in one of his films.)

Myth and Magic in Heavy Metal Music

The Greco-Roman thinker Philo claimed that the number seven expressed the cosmic order: a structure within the universe that orders all of reality.

The monster images and sense of impending doom appeal most to heavy metal fans. One of these images is of the beast rising from the sea (Revelation 13:1–10). The number of the beast, referred to in an Iron Maiden song, is 666 (Revelation 13:18). There is a figure of a serpent or dragon that watches this occur (Revelation 13:1): "Men worshipped the dragon for he had given his authority to the beast" (Revelation 13:4). The malevolent dragon is identified with Satan (Revelation 12:9). Theologians involved with Biblical exegesis have suggested that the beast may represent Rome, which persecuted the early Christians. They agree that this creature rebels against God. It uses words of blasphemy (Revelation 13:1, 13:5–6). Revelation makes use a mythic-symbolic language of conflict. Next, a beast arises from the earth: an anti-Christ figure. This second beast would cause those who did not worship the first beast to be slain. We read: "no one can buy or sell unless he has the mark, the name of the beast or the number of its name" (Revelation 13:17). There is a cosmic struggle of opposing powers. (Armageddon is cited in Revelation 16:12–16.)

During the Patristic period Revelation was interpreted as a symbolic narrative of a moral struggle between vice and virtue.[6] In Joachim de Fiore there was the idea of a new age, or an age of the Spirit. He read Revelation as part of salvation history. The final stage of the world in the age of the Holy Spirit would come to defeat the anti-Christ. There were millennialist readings by the Puritans in the 17th century. In the 18th and 19th centuries British and American Reformation tradition groups also had apocalyptic readings of Revelation.

Notions of imminent disaster persisted in first century Christian writings. They reflect the tension of living as a marginal sect under Roman rule and reflect tensions between sectarian Christian and Jewish communities, which were both marginalized by the dominant political-social system of the day. The use of apocalyptic themes became a literary trope, a form of literary composition.

Many Christian bands repeated apocalyptic themes. White metal ranged across a variety of styles. Deliverance, Believer, Vengeance, and Torniquet were thrash metal bands, Mortification was a death metal band. Crimson Thorn, Narnia from Sweden, and Extol from Norway embraced elements of extreme metal. After 2000 emerged Demon Hunter and

8. Sonnets to Orpheus

Underoath, Norma Jean, and P.O.D.: bands that sell fairly well. Several of these bands embrace eschatological perspectives about the end times, spiritual warfare, and humanity's fall from grace. Since the 1980s music of Stryper, Messiah Prophet, Leviticus, Whitecross, Saint, Barren Cross and others and the first Christian metal labels like Refuge Records and Intense Records, white metal has produced a wide variety of acts including X-Sinner, which sounds a bit like AC/DC and the glam metal band Holy Soldiers from California, who have been on Myrrh (Word/A&M) Records. Michael Sweet of Stryper and Jim La Verde of Barren Cross have been worship leaders in church communities. Thus, the voice of heavy metal for Christ rocks on and still the underworld, the region of hell, remains a vivid image for other heavy metal bands.

Dreams, Nightmares and Dramas

Mythic songs may be likened to dreams. "Dreaming is a complex symbolic activity" (Oswald, 267). Nightmares have been shown in some studies to be correlated with people who experience anxiety during their daylight waking hours. However, "other studies have not found a relationship between nightmare frequency and current waking life psychopathology" (267). In the ancient world the idea of dreams as revelatory was common. This view is prevalent in the Near East, particularly in the Bible and in Zoroastrian and Sumerian-Akkadian culture. We see in Homer that the interpretation of dreams among the Greeks was focused upon the idea of prophesy. Plato, Xenophon, and Demosthenes all held this view. This perspective is quite different from Sigmund Freud's approach to dreams.

Freud, of course, explored the unconscious mind and advanced many theories about the workings of the unconscious. We may sometimes think of the unconscious as a place, as if the unconscious is somehow spatially located. It is down, underneath things, like a basement. Or, perhaps it is a vast ocean with great depths. The unconscious is the realm of dreams. For Jung, who followed Freud with his own inquiries, the unconscious is the realm of myth and symbol, a collective unconscious of archetypes that arise in dreams and visions.

Freud's interest in the interpretation of dreams emerged in connection with his developing psychoanalytical techniques. In his interpretation of dreams Freud employed the method of free association. In therapy the individual would allow his or her mind to freely drift across whatever ideas or memories came up. Freud referred to these immediate responses as manifest content. Freud concluded that this manifest content concealed underlying wishes and fantasies, or latent content. Through dreamwork the dreamer could unravel these disguised fantasies that Freud termed matters infantile wish fulfillment. Freud recognized mechanisms he called condensation, displacement, and representation (or the creating of imaginative dramas). During sleep repression was relaxed and the things that might disturb the conscious mind were free to take these imaginative forms.

In contrast, C.G. Jung focused on how dreams and visions were involved with individuation: a process that he believed led to psychological wholeness and maturity. Jung made use of mythology and alchemy and symbols like the mandala in describing this. Archetypal images and symbols are experienced in dreams and cultural developments and differences alone cannot explain the power of these symbols. Rather, Jung believed, mythological themes in dreams tap into the collective unconscious: perhaps the greatest underworld of all.

9

Madness, Magic and Virtuosity

> "Imagination is not the faculty of forming images of reality, it is the faculty of forming images which go beyond reality, which turn reality into song."
>
> —Gaston Bachelard

To ignite, to blast through the ordinary, to threaten convention with theater and use the power of music to launch ecstasy and peak experience: that is a goal of heavy metal performance. The concert is a space for connection and bonding. It is the time to release Prometheus from his constraints. The heavy metal band creates pleasure and excitement, agitation and energy, moving emotions, pumping adrenaline, providing rock power and a multi-sensory experience.

Wonders and horrors, myth and magic, incantation and visceral groaning: it is time for the heavy metal band to unleash its power. Heavy metal bands explore creative alternatives in esoteric areas that they do not necessarily subscribe to. Robert Walser writes of vocalist Ozzy Osborne: "Osborne plays with the signs of the supernatural because they evoke power and mystery that is highly attractive to a lot of fans" but his song offers a critique of those experiences and "not a literal endorsement of magical practices" (*Running with the Devil,* 148). When Osborne produced *Diary of a Madman* in his solo work of the early 1980s, it did not follow that he was certifiably insane. When he sang "Suicide Solution" he was offering a critique, not an endorsement for suicide. Literalists evidently were not grasping metal's symbolic social criticism, or its enthusiasm for entertainment and fantasy.

The "madness" of metal was present in its transgression, its rebellious confrontation with society. Some artists called upon their listeners to consider consider the insanity of it all. To give attention to madness is to look for where the different voice may be found and what it might say. In *Madness in Civilization*, Michel Foucault's reflection led toward a reading of texts for silences and exclusions. In *Discipline and Punish* he explored power-discourse: who has the power to speak and how that power is used. Heavy metal seizes an opportunity to speak for the unspoken. Heavy metal has done this since its beginnings.

There was a rise of youth culture between 1967 and 1969 followed by a decline between 1970 and 1974. In the 1970s rock became more genre-specific than it had been before. These divisions were fostered as a marketing strategy by the music business. "The splintering of rock reflected a splintering of the youth culture," Deena Weinstein has observed (*Heavy Metal: The Music and Its Culture,* 13). Heavy metal can trace it origins to this period. While it drew upon myth, as did progressive rock, heavy metal determined to be direct in its approach. It remained mostly guitar-based rather than keyboard oriented. Heavy metal met an audience of the disempowered with a theme of power. With its discourse of chaos it was explicit, pointing at the existing world. When it gestured toward mythical dreamscapes it did so to summon up the grandeur and power within the mythical. In the 1980s, heavy metal rose to widespread popularity and widespread derision. By 1990 thrash metal had revised the heavy metal code, incorporating punk influences. It highlighted isolation and conflict and alienation and criticized hypocrisy, hegemonic power, and injustice. In the 1990s extreme metal needed festivals and concerts, since it would not get airplay. Heavy metal diversified further and it became a global phenomenon, even as the music industry, affected by the digital age, itself underwent changes. Heavy metal has interconnected with a variety of cultures internationally and it continues to evolve.

Heavy metal has always been controversial. A wave of criticisms and attacks on heavy metal persisted from the mid–1980s into the early 1990s. Foremost among these was the campaign launched by the Parents Music Resource Center, a group led by Tipper Gore and other wives of government officials well-connected with the U.S. Congress. Their concerns about the potential impact of heavy metal upon young minds and the family led to Congressional hearings and the proposal to place warning labels on heavy metal and hip-hop/rap record albums. The primary target was objectionable lyrics, although with the rise of MTV videos visual performance and sexual or violent imagery was a concern also.

9. Madness, Magic and Virtuosity

The 1980s was "the decade of metal's greatest popularity and influence," says Robert Walser (xiv). Heavy metal and hip-hop were "redefining American popular music" in the 1980s. Metal experienced "growth on a scale none had imagined" (11). Consequently, there was reaction to it. Heavy metal became "an important site of cultural contestation," observes Walser (x). This included concerns about alienation, community, violence, censorship, character, values, and behavior (x). Walser points out that heavy metal albums shot up the charts in 1984 to about 20 percent of the market, up from 8 percent the previous year. By 1987, heavy metal was securely among the best selling albums in America.[1] Meanwhile, the genre diversified further into thrash metal, black metal, speed metal, glam metal, punk metal. Quiet Riot, Dokken, and the thrash metal of Anthrax, Metallica, Slayer, and Megadeth became well-known. From Germany emerged the guitar driven Scorpions.

In the 1980s heavy metal drew fire from the Parents Music Resource Center. Twisted Sister's Dee Snider and other musicians who testified before Congress asserted that their work was a matter of expressing fantasy and was protected by the First Amendment asserting the right to free speech. The PMRC was expressed some legitimate parental concerns. However, there were some assumptions at work. How vulnerable were the children to certain uses of language, or violent imagery, or sexual content in songs and performances? Could it be assumed that they were only suggestible, passive receptacles for recorded material and that they would take all of this literally rather than as expressions of fantasy? What evidence was there that heavy metal music mentally or ethically disabled anyone? As other critics joined the fray, much was made of the lyrics and imagery and little was said about the music: the epicenter of heavy metal. One heard no references to Plato's ancient critiques of poetry or musical modes and their presumed effects on the Republic. One heard in these complaints no references to Mozart's histrionics, Berlioz' drug use, Schumann's alcoholism and mental decline, Scriabin's insanity, Tchaikovsky's depressions, or Wagner's affairs. Classical music was honorable and elite. Heavy metal was deviant and abhorrent.

Much of the derision of heavy metal by its critics in the mid to late 1980s focused on visuals. The rise of attention to the visual aspects of a band's image or performance is attributable to the rise of MTV and videos. Music, after all, is an auditory art and little was said by metal's critics that was, in any sense, musicological. At issue were the visuals and then the lyrics. It is a stretch to assume that teenage heavy metal fans are at home scrutinizing song lyrics. Far more central to heavy metal is its sound, its music. Perhaps even stranger were the claims that records were being listened to played backwards to listen to lyrics. Such criticism begged the question of how listeners listen and how they interpret music. These criticisms were generally launched by individuals who had learned to read literally, such as fundamentalists, rather than people who were comfortable with reading symbolically.

By now the arguments of the PMRC have receded into the past and heavy metal has expanded into a global phenomenon. However, it is helpful to recall past tensions about popular culture forms as metal expands amid globalization today. Metal was reviled in some sectors of American society in the 1980s. Similarly, in the nineteenth century Victorian respectability was threatened by the sensation novels of the 1860s, the penny dreadful of cheap literature, and fin de siècle decadence. Instead of realism the sensation novel provided destabilizing challenges to narrative omniscience and objective mimesis, or the mirror-image of a presumably empirical reality. Robert Louis Stevenson's Jekyll and Hyde were a shadowy double of the author. Hyde wanders dangerously on a borderland of bohemian artistic license between the scientific and the alchemical, the civilized and the uncivilized. Stevenson wrote on the border of realism and romance; he was part engineer and part creative writer. Oscar Wilde, whose art challenged the culture, announced a curious doubleness in *The Picture of Dorian Gray* and there was the "poisonous" book in his story. The late Victorian period was one of the divided self we see in the writings of Joseph Conrad and several other authors. For George Gissing the very idea of a popular literary culture for the masses was an improbable reality he wrestled with in The *Unclassed* (1884), *The Netherworld* (1889), and *New Grub Street*, in which "vulgarity defeats culture" (Brantlinger, 181).

Among the most notable charges against heavy metal was the case against Judas Priest. It was claimed that their album *Stained Class* (1978) motivated two teens to attempt suicide.[2] In Reno, Nevada Ray Belknap, 18, and Jay Vance, 20, made a suicide pact. Belknap died and Vance survived but, after years of reconstructive surgery, eventually overdosed on drugs. Neither of the two was particularly stable to begin with. Vance ran away from home thirteen times, sometimes to escape beatings. Reports claim that he was violent and alcoholic before ever listening to Judas Priest. Belknap rejected the born-again Christian ideas of his mother who was

9. Madness, Magic and Virtuosity

separating from her fourth husband. Vance was laid off when a General Motors plant closed. Belknap had left his job with a local contractor.

Clearly, Judas Priest was not the villain. Their lyrics were a mythic, symbolic fantasy discourse. An artist is responsible for what he or she produces. However, a listener is also responsible for how he or she interprets the product. According to the plaintiff, *Stained Class* allegedly had masked backwards messages like "try suicide" and "do it." Supposedly, listeners who were perverse enough to spin the vinyl backwards were given the exhortation to "sing my evil spirit." Rob Halford, Judas Priest's vocalist, played parts of his record backwards at the trial and the result was a string of absurdities. In one line listeners could hear the vocalist asking for a peppermint.[3]

The year 1990 brought not only this celebrated case but major events like German reunification, the release of Nelson Mandela in South Africa, the Iraqi invasion of Kuwait, and the further dissolving of the Soviet Union. Heavy metal reached out across Europe and to Asia and Latin America. In popular music it was time a time of the rise of grunge. It burst into the veins of American culture like an injection from the space needle of Seattle. Meanwhile, with their platinum best-selling self-titled album, Metallica began to be heard on radio often. *Load* and *Re-Load* connected metal and alternative. Metallica had gone mainstream. The 1990s was a time of pop/rock lite-metal bands like Bon Jovi that attracted both male and female audiences. There was the return of the decadent Mötley Crüe and the face-painted rockers Kiss. Meanwhile, punked out metalcore bands like Machine Head and Pantera made a strong showing. Industrial metal emerged with Nine Inch Nails. Thrash originators Anthrax and Megadeth persisted. Black metal took hold in Scandinavia. Death metal dropped the bass lower, smashing about with double-bass drums and knife-edged Listerine user vocals that sang of death and doom.

Enter Grunge

The big story was grunge, bringing Nirvana and Pearl Jam, Stone Temple Pilots, Soundgarden, and Alice in Chains to new listeners. Grunge was distorted, forceful, and earnest. It combined elements of punk and metal with Seattle rain and fog and a Generation X sense of alienation. Heavy Metal diversified even further into speed and thrash metal, black metal and death metal, nu-metal and other forms. Metal remained mythical while bands directed their concern and disdain at the contemporary world. Grunge met metal in themes of authenticity, angst, introspection, and socially conscious lyrics. However, by the end of the 1990s it had already crested in popularity. Bands like Smashing Pumpkins and Pearl Jam, with their charismatic front-man Eddie Vedder, were selling a bit less than they used to.

Metal diversified further in the 1990s, becoming a variety of subgenres from thrash and speed metal to black metal and death metal and from progressive metal to combinations of metal with punk and alternative. Alice in Chains combined metal, post-punk alternative, and grunge with heavy guitars and harmonies. They were marketed by Columbia Records as an alternative band. Jerry Cantwell created their guitar sound and Lagne Staley sang. The rhythm section was comprised of Mike Starr and then Mike Inez on bass and Sean Kinney, the drummer. *Facelift, Dirt, Jar of Flies*, and the self-titled *Alice in Chains* all appeared between 1990 and 1995. The band produced two live albums and their *Nothing Safe* (1999) studio album. They played nothing safe and sang more of drugs and addiction than of anything mythological. Staley died in 2002.

From the 1990s to the New Century

The originators of metal persisted in the final decade of the Twentieth century, although there were some changes along the way. Ozzy Osborne had recorded five studio albums across the 1980s before his 1991 platinum *No More Tears* and by now he was a metal icon. In 1991, charismatic vocalist Rob Halford of Judas Priest left the band. He was replaced by Tim Owens, who was drafted into his favorite band from a tribute group called Winter's Bane. Iron Maiden persisted, although vocalist Bruce Dickinson went on hiatus. Hard rock bands like Aerosmith drew upon the heavy metal sound. Progressive bands, like Rush and Dream Theater, brought metal edges to their sound and toured widely. The thrash metal of Metallica went mainstream.

By the late 1990s more critics were doubting the authenticity of heavy metal bands who ventured in the direction of myth—or who copied underworld themes or Satanic gestures. Even so, metal continued to sell formidably. *Spin* did an issue on nu-metal (Summer 1998) and *Rolling Stone*

9. Madness, Magic and Virtuosity

featured a cover with musician and filmmaker Rob Zombie (February 1999). Bruce Dickinson returned to Iron Maiden. Manowar endured, venturing large mythical themes and asserting the importance of authenticity. Their version of metal continued to offer active dreams, a subconscious tapping into the primal mind, and references to Greek mythology. They produced their compilation album, *Kingdom of Steel* (1998) to highlight their best. Meanwhile, across the northern Atlantic myth-driven young Norwegian bands raised their voices. With ice in their veins and fire in their eyes, Norway's disaffected youth sent shivers up listener's spines with black metal. Both Norse myth and J.R.R. Tolkien's mythology found root in Norway. In the midst of Norway's black metal scene Gorgoroth took their name from Tolkien's *Lord of the Rings*. Gahl ritually drank blood and the band members took stage names: Hat, Infernus, Samoth, Ares the King of Hell, Satyricon, and Grim. Dark myth and anti-Christianity reigned and Norway's churches burned.

In 1999 Black Sabbath reunited and went on tour. They received extensive press and strong ticket sales. Their *Reunion* album went gold. This was not only because of the claim of nostalgia for a pivotal creator of heavy metal. It was also due to the rise and continuing success of the heavy metal genre itself.

Vocalist Ronnie James Dio, who sang with Black Sabbath, was at the top of his game in the 1990s. There was his band Elf, early in his career, Deep Purple and Black Sabbath along the way, and Dio, toward the end of it. He is credited with creating the devil's horns hand gesture. Dio's lyrics, in both his earlier work and his later work with his own band, Dio, were at times mythical, or filled with imaginative expression. In his lyric for "Heaven and Hell" the singer is a bringer of evil and there are references to the devil and hellfire. In "Rainbow in the Dark" he cries out for magic. There seems to be a bit of the Italian-American lapsed Catholic hidden in this lyric that, like Dante, ponders sin and the moral complexity of humanity. He asks his listeners if their demons ever bother them. Is a human being evil or divine, the singer wonders. Here we have been tossed on our crosses. Is that an angel approaching or is it a beast? His lyric to "Strange Highways" suggests a yearning for a different 'institution' where people can be free to play: a place where the road is open and things are not forbidden. "Egypt (The Chains Are On)" tells another story, drawing upon biblical references to milk and honey and reflecting upon a lost horizon and a queen that is alone. "The Temple of the King" tells a story from the year of the fox, in which a bell is ringing, a young man is searching, and an old man is singing before the dawn. The song refers to stories that have been told and heard. The circle of people suggests the audience of listeners to the song, to a story being told and a ritual being re-enacted. Dio passed away in 2000, leaving a rich legacy of vocal performances and imaginative lyrics.

After 2000, came rock groups which descended from grunge, like the popular band Nickelback. Among those bands is the Foo Fighters with Dave Grohl, who had played drums with Nirvana. Grohl emerged from the Washington, D.C., punk scene in the early 1980s and was drawn toward metal by bands like Motörhead. On his solo record *Probot* (2004) Grohl included guest appearances by Cronos (Conrad Lant) from Venom and Lemmy from Motörhead. The Foo Fighters have combined blues rock, punk, and metal into a successful mainstream rock career.

After 2000, dozens of metal bands merged myth and metal with contemporary concerns and new sounds across the past two decades. With the rise of nu-metal came the eclectic mix of styles in Limp Bizkit and Korn. Bagpipes open Korn's *Issues* (1999) album. There is distortion in the guitars, rim shots on the tom-toms. On "It's Gonna Go Away," the seventh cut an anguished voice calls out as if from a circle of Inferno. The tormented voice is consumed by other voices and superseded by this chorus that diminishes and buries it. A heavy bass line follows, with percussive punches. Fieldy on bass, Munky on guitar, Head on guitar, and Dave Silveria on drums provide an unmistakably hard, distorted, pulse-driven recording.

Heavy metal bands that first appeared in the 1980s and 1990s have developed followings and have endured into the new century. Some have gone through a number of changes. Others have disbanded and later reunited. For example, Testament was formed in San Francisco by Eric Peterson who was joined by Alex Skolnick (who had studied guitar with Joe Satriani), Chuck Billy, Gene Hogan on drums, and bass guitarist Steve Di Giorgio. The lineup has changed a few times but the band lives on. Testament spent time performing in Los Angeles. Their first album was *The Legacy* in the 1980s. Their *albums The New Order, Practice What You Preach*, and *Souls of Black* (1990) followed. With *The Ritual* (1992), which tended to move away from thrash metal, Skolnick left the band. More recently, Testament has produced *Dark Roots of Earth* (2012) and *Brotherhood of the Snake* (2016).

9. Madness, Magic and Virtuosity

Tool

Tool was formed in Los Angeles in 1990 and emerged with their album *Undertow* (1993) and their follow-up *AEnina* (1996). The band is Maynard James Keenan (vocals), Danny Corey (drums), Adam Jones (guitar) and Justin Chancellor (bass), who followed Paul D'Amour who played bass for the band until 1995. Early on in their recording career, "Sober" was a single in 1994. The song "Prison Sex" was censored. Tool was first described as alternative metal. Jon Pareles in the *New York Times* stated that Tool had the sound of "Led Zeppelin ... battering guitar riffs and Middle Eastern modes." Tool taps into the archetypal unconscious through the artwork of Adam Jones and stereoscopic photography. Their first album *Undertow* appeared with a design based on a ribcage and Jones's visual art has continued to be a dimension of the band's creativity. *Lateralus* (2001) and *10,000 Days* (2006) also made use of visual arts. *Lateralus* including the song "Schism," was considered closer to art rock-progressive rock by some fans and critics. *AEnine* earned platinum status for its sales. By then the band had earned a solid cult following. During a time when Keenan took some time off from the band the others recorded a cover of Led Zeppelin's "No Quarter." Returning to action they became increasingly commercially successful with the 10,000 Days album. Patrick Donovan in *New Age* called them both "cerebral and visceral ... melodic and abrasive."

Lamb of God

Classification of music is always a curious game. After all, most musicians like a lot of different kinds of music. Bands may create a unique eclectic mix in developing their sound and the lines between genres and subgenres are somewhat fluid. Some heavy metal fans will define Lamb of God as metal and others will call them a punk band that incorporates some metal. They have been called "groove metal," by those willing to create another descriptive label and category. With eight albums to date and over two million copies sold they are a band which has made an impact. They are not shy about using and inverting religious terms in their titles. Their second album was called *New American Gospel*. It was heavy and filled with one critic, Patrick Kennedy, insisted were Pantera riffs. *Sacrament* (2006) tends toward speed metal. The Grammy nominated song

"Wrath" (2009) may also. Earlier albums were slightly mythological, with *As the Palaces Burn* (2003) and *Ashes of the Wake* (2004). In *Rolling Stone*, Kirk Miller called *As the Palaces Burn* an album that was "meticulous crafted metal assault" (*Rolling Stone*, May 6, 2003). (Alex Skolnick of Testament played guitar on the opening track for *Ashes of the Wake*.) *Sacrament*, also on Epic Records, drew a comment from Jon Pareles, who called the record a "speed rush all the way through" (*Blender*, August 8, 2006). *Walk with Me in Hell* (2008) and *Wrath* (2009), with the Grammy nominated title song, earned further critical acclaim and strengthened Lamb of God's popular fan base. "Hit the Wall" was a single in 2010. Sometime after a fan rushed the concert stage and singer Randy Blythe pushed him away, fatally injuring the fan, Blythe, enmeshed in a legal case, took a break. Lamb of God returned with marked strength with *VII: Sturm und Drang* (2015).

Mastodon

Mastodon came out of Atlanta, Georgia, after 2000 with Troy Sanders on bass, Brann Dailor on drums, Brent Hinds and Bill Kelliher on guitars. They have brought a heavy sound to each album they have recorded: *Remission, Leviathan, Blood Mountain,* and *Crack the Skye*. Mastodon created a concept album from one of America's great myths: the story of *Moby Dick* by Herman Melville. The story of the fierce great white whale and the vengeance of Captain Ahab has echoed across the past century and a half. *Moby Dick* has been studied for its symbols, its sense of a cosmic struggle between good and evil, whiteness and darkness, heroism and doom. Mastodon's *Leviathan* recasts the story in powerful music and vivid imagery. The album cover by artist Paul Romano shows the whale rising up in a wave, tipping a ship and reflects the art of Hokusai's illustration of the great wave. The name Leviathan itself has ancient Biblical echoes. It was the title of the philosopher Thomas Hobbes' most significant work: one with an empirical perspective and an atomistic vision of perpetual competition in this world, a treatise telling of a war of all against all in a life that is nasty, brutish, and short.

Mastadon's *Leviathan* begins with "Blood and Thunder" in the voice of Ahab who declares that he thinks someone is trying to kill him. He is bitter from past encounters with the great whale and angered by the loss

9. Madness, Magic and Virtuosity

of his leg to it. No one will stop him from his determined quest to kill the great whale. Ahab says that he is covered in darkness. He walks on board with his ivory leg surrounded by men with harpoons. That first dramatic pronouncement is followed by "I Am Ahab" which recognizes a magic in the water that attracts men to go to sea. The sailors are captivated by the sea and anticipate a fight with the beast. "Seabeast" is the third song and like the novel it relies upon associations with monstrous sea creatures in myth. The character Queequeg, a Native American Indian, is mentioned in this dramatic lyric. So too is the Norse god Odin and Thor's hammer, which connects this band's concept album with an array of heavy metal Norse mythology. The song lyric for "Iron Tusk" is constructed in double-syllables, or words of two syllables set side by side. There are images of destruction and one of a poisonous Fiji mermaid. "Megaloden" follows with its reference to myths and legends and tales of nymphs. "Aqua Dementia" repeats the band's focus on the fundamental element of water. It begins by welcoming listeners to the extra-sensory perception of clairvoyance. This develops into an intricate lyric in which we hear the singer say that the sailors like to breathe an ancient wind that leads them to their destiny. Three heavy metal fanzines voted *Leviathan* the album of the year in 2004.

From Europe have emerged many more innovative metal bands. Avatar, for example, is a Swedish metal band from Gothenburg that first appeared in 2001. Among their recent albums is *Flesh and Feathers* (2016). "New Land" was on the U.S. charts in May 2017. Avatar also performed "Hail the Apocalypse." Avatar features Jonas Jarsby on guitar. John Alfredsson is the drummer. The first Avatar album was one with an apocalyptic sounding title: *Thoughts of No Tomorrow* (January 25, 2006). Their second album, *Schlacht,* included "Letters from Neverland" with Bjorn Gelotte on guitar. The third album was the self-titled *Avatar.* In January 2010 the band signed with Sony. The song "Queen of Blades" draws upon the imaginative imagery of the video game *Starcraft,* with the character Sarah Kerrigan. Vocalist Johannes Echerstrom wore white face paint and brought his energy to a tour with Five Finger Death Punch, Gemini Syndrome, and September Mourning. On *Flesh and Feathers* Avatar presents the image of an eagle crushing its adversary on their "The Eagle Has Landed" single.

Toxicity by System of a Down immediately voices a political protest against building a prison system that entraps any user of drugs and critiques the hypocrisy the band sees in this institution. Daron Malakian (guitar/vocal), Serj Tankian (vocal/keyboard), Shavo Dordjan (Odadjan) (bass), and John Dolmayan (drums) continue their critique of the modern world with "Deer Dance," which appears to gaze into a haunted world of Los Angeles and finds a contemporary world that feels totalitarian. Beyond the Staples Center is a world and they attack it with the fierce, distorted power chord and bass bottom of their sound. All of this drives on relentlessly, with clever musical changes. In "Jet Pilot" there is a strong pulse, little lead guitar, just rhythm. The vocal carries the only sense of melody and there is a rhythmic chant. "Forest," the eighth track on the album, begins with percussion and bass racing. Then a thrash metal mood with harder bass and rhythm guitar enters. The song refers to a forest of denial. The voice dips, with quieter dynamics, but can also be explosive. The vocal repeats the question: why don't you know you are my child? "Chop Suey" brings acoustic guitar chords joined by rapid drums. Then the music breaks out, including chorus vocals, and the lyric quotes Christ's call from the cross: "why have you forsaken me?" The lead vocals are more prominent here than on some of the other cuts on the album. "Science," the tenth track of fourteen, insists that science has failed us and has failed the mother earth. The single most important element of human existence is faith. Letting go to faith and the spirit that moves through all things seems to a way out from the disturbed environment that Toxicity presents in the first few songs. "Science" stays anchored in one key and races along. The title track "Toxicity" refers to computer software and to the city, its modern myths and disorder, the sacred silence and the contemporary world.

Heavy Metal Creativity and the Future

In exploring heavy metal's voice in contemporary society, we need to investigate what Robert Walser pointed to as the "significance of mysticism, horror, and violence in metal" (137). Myth is used by heavy metal musicians to address contemporary needs and concerns, even when they employ ancient stories and symbols on their recordings. Of course, in each metal performance there is entertainment, mystery, or excitement. However, at the root of it all is free expression that energizes and reaffirms the heavy metal community. Power and empowerment remains possibly the most important single factor in the experience of heavy metal. We

9. Madness, Magic and Virtuosity

may look at heavy metal as a social signifying system that draws upon, utilizes, and transforms mythical stories and images, producing social meanings and a public discourse (Walser, xiv-xv). Heavy metal is indeed, as Walser has pointed out, "engaged with the deepest of contemporary desires and tensions" (170). It intersects with our present history. The way that we respond to its sound and imagery says much about who and where we are in the present in our attitudes and perceptions. Different listeners approach metal from within different life experiences and contexts. Whereas one person hears a threat to family values and to civilization another person hears a critique of that civilization, or has experiences of energy, or of wonder.

We can approach heavy metal and myth as a symbolic discourse. Songs as discourse are open to a variety of interpretations and meanings. Listeners may respond to signs differently. They represent what Mikhail Bahktin called heteroglossia, or the many-voiced possibilities of a text.[4] This is a dialogical framework in which the music, imagery, lyrics, and other signs of heavy metal are negotiated by performers, fans, critics, and meanings are, as Walser says, "multiple, fluid, and negotiated" (Walser, 21).

If "man is a symbolic animal," and "art may be defined as a symbolic language" as the philosopher Ernst Cassirer contended, then heavy metal's future depends upon recalling its roots, not forgetting them (Cassirer, 168). Metal may need to enter what has been called "a second naivete": an openness to possibility and to the unknown that the poet John Keats called "negative capability." The leading edge of art cannot be just a reiteration of the tropes and patterns of the past. To evolve, heavy metal has to develop new symbols, new sounds, and bend genre categories with renewed creativity.

Heavy metal is a commercial form and commercial contexts organize production and consumption. However, listeners and concert-goers have a lived atmosphere and experience, social activity, and personal response. In the heavy metal music business there may be pretense and there is imitation and the sheer novelty and spectacle that spurs capitalist consumption. However, heavy metal originality is more than merely commodified fantasy. Music can encourage narratives and produce new meanings. Pop music provides a social field for constructing meanings and contesting them. The heavy metal audience is an interpretive community.

Heavy metal is deeply embedded in our culture. If the psychologist

Myth and Magic in Heavy Metal Music

Carl Jung is to be believed, with archetypes metal performers draw upon the mythic mind, even when they don't know a lot about myth. That is because they are creative artists. Myths are also deeply anchored in our minds. Art has power and wants to make contact. Storytelling and music making are natural human impulses. Heavy metal lyricists often aim at concise, creative narratives with a strong voice. Writing against the grain, drawing upon myth and fantasy, they give voice to a vision that rejects colonization by the structures, world-view, and stories of a dominant culture. They resist being made subaltern to the master language and framework by inventing their own way of speaking out, or shouting out. Their resistance makes use of their native language and symbols: those of the heavy metal genre.

In his classic work *The Anthropology of Music* (1964) ethnomusicologist Alan Merriam defined ethnomusicology as "the study of music in culture." Music, he wrote, is a symbolic form of expression that reflects the organization of society. Thus, music can be a means for understanding a culture and its people. "The functions and uses of music are as important as those of any other aspect of culture for understanding the workings of society," he wrote (13).

There is a long tradition in Western culture in which the musician, viewed as a maker of seductive music, has been considered a servant of demons. The musician can conjure sounds that entice and wreck the listener. This was perhaps an unconscious tradition that lay behind the anxieties of the PMRC. This magical and mythological thought lies in the past behind the cloak of several centuries. In the Middle Ages, when the Christian Church became a dominant force in Western society, God and the angels stood over and against a realm of the devil that was sometimes portrayed as a realm disposed toward cacophony. Heaven was about harmony; hell was about discord. That trope extended into the twentieth and the twenty-first centuries. Pandemonium is characterized by noise, shrieks, thunder, blustery wind, growls, groans, and powerful volume: all of which have become qualities of heavy metal.

When we speculate on the future of heavy metal we have to keep its interactions with contemporary culture in mind. Our world today is replete with cultural myths and our daily routines often include little rituals. Rock music creativity builds upon the past—but also needs to break with it to be truly innovative and set forth new trends and new possibilities. Rock functions in a context that has been changing since the advent

9. Madness, Magic and Virtuosity

of the digital age and heavy metal music is widely available in a variety of styles via Internet and other electronic sources. Rock is an entertainment form within a world-wide commercial economy. It is within this context that one will ask the question: what will the future of heavy metal music be? How will generational differences affect the future of heavy metal? This is a question for sociologists and for anyone pursuing heavy metal studies. Will audience expectations and reception be different? Will music makers create differently, constructing new sounds or conveying their work in interactive ways? How will genres or subgenres shift as styles mix, combine, overlap, and change?

No entire generation is ever the same and no generation can be uniformly typed and categorized. There are always variations in culture across location, family background, gender, race and ethnicity, socioeconomic class, and other variables. There are also "cusps" between generations in which some of the same general patterns overlap. The dates given for generations are fluid and not rigid. However, generational theory does develop conceptual frameworks to try to gain understanding. William Straus and Neil Howe wrote *Generations: The History of America's Future, 1584 to 2069* back in 1992. Since then they have viewed the emerging millennial generation—the oldest born after 1982—as a new "great generation" (*Millennials Rising: The Next Great Generation*, 2000.) They tend toward cooperative work confidence and optimism, those researchers say. However they measure high on ratings of conventionality and on over-reliance on parents the researchers say. If that is so, where will creativity come from? How will willingness to risk and the ability to mature and make a contribution take shape?[5]

These generational researchers call the millennials the "largest and healthiest generation in American history." Yet, they are, on the whole, more sheltered despite great access to the Internet and much media exposure. They are a "sunshine" generation in comparison with Gen X. Their so-called "helicopter parents" tend to fuss over them. They are a more conservative generation. Straus and Howe say that millennials are "a direct reversal from boomers" (44–45) and "a sharp break from traits associated with Gen X" (44–45). If these trends have any weight, it is up to sociologists and heavy metal enthusiasts to sort out what this might mean for heavy metal in the heart of the audience.

If we view the audience for heavy metal and the creators of heavy metal through the lens of generational cohorts, the so-called baby boom generation members were among the originators (Black Sabbath, Led Zeppelin, Deep Purple, and hard rock bands). Metal crystallized and became popularized in the 1980s thanks to late baby boom generation artists (Judas Priest, Iron Maiden, Slayer, Manowar). Then came speed and thrash, black metal, and other forms and popular listening among Gen X, who built upon metal into the 1990s. There was also the Internet and PCs. Millennials, born after 2000, never had to splice tape. They were born in times that were fully digital and information savvy. So, we might ask, how do they respond to the sounds of the 1980s, 1990s, and after 2000? How does globalization affect this generation? How have events since 2000—recession, 9/11—affected this generation? Have they any concern with rock music of the previous generation? Are the pundits who have seen less concern with politics, sustainability and savings, and more of a sense of entitlement correct in their assessments? Research suggests that this cohort has more openness to change but places less emphasis than a previous generation on self-transcendence. They are more flexible within a disposable society, yet tend to be more conservative those pundits say. Are there generational differences in basic human values? What music may the sensibility of this emerging generation produce?

Heavy Metal and Postmodernism

Heavy metal music has become a diversity of styles and approaches. Its audience has become similarly diverse. If metal was once the province of working class white male teenagers and young adults, it is no longer only that. Heavy metal has become a world-wide phenomenon and it has a strong female following, a broad base across all socio-economic groups, and it need not be white or working class. At the end of the 1990s, sociologist Deena Weinstein concluded her book on heavy metal with the recognition that heavy metal connects with "prole leanings ... tabloid news ... pro-wrestling ... radio shock jocks" (294). That remains true but the audience has widened, even as heavy metal has moved in many directions: fragmented, some would say. "Metal is not dying but rather ... it has become incoherent" Keith Kahn-Harris pointed out in 2013.

This incoherence may be reflective of the times. Postmodernism is part of a re-reading and re-envisioning of history within Western tradition and our encounter with a multiplicity of voices and perspectives.

9. Madness, Magic and Virtuosity

Postmodernism is said to be characterized by fragmentation, superficiality and surfaces, a jumbling of styles (or bricolage), the blurring of mediation and reality, relativism, presentism and a lost sense of history, construction of identity, a rejection of grand narratives (in Jean-François Lyotard's sense), and a tendency to emphasize the visual over the verbal. Over the past forty to fifty years the postmodern turn has included questions about the relationship of works of art to social context, the presumed collapse of traditional philosophical foundations, and the power of art, language, and political action in relation to the dominant social order. Today we live amid a proliferation of information which affects us in what Jean Baudrillard has called "an implosion of meaning" (142). The question arises whether we will express this implosion and whether we will re-construct meaning. Baudrillard underscores the central significance of artistic production when he asks the important question of who is producing cultural images and information. Who has information power and what agendas are attempting to shape our world-view? Opposition requires art as well as rational communication. Baudrillard argues that the masses (and we each do belong to the masses in some respects) tend to be resistant to rational communication—to articles, books, and discussion—and simply want to be entertained. In postmodernism Baudrillard says of the pop audience: "They are offered meaning when they want entertainment. They are given messages when they want only signs" (142–43).

So, what is next? If metal remains "resilient" and "defiant" and willing to explore darkness and transgression, as Keith Kahn-Harris puts it, what will be "metal beyond metal": the future beyond the present phase of heavy metal creativity? How will its "wit and playfulness," its promotion of bonds of fellowship be sustained in the next decades of the twenty-first century?[6] Tom O'Boyle and Niall Scott have suggested that heavy metal can embrace progress and that it does not have to be louder and darker and heavier. Heavy metal scenes persist and the digital age has made circulation of music increasingly available via mp3s, music streaming, Internet blogs, and other media. Heavy metal has moved into fine art, in iconography, painting, and design. For years it joined with punk, sometimes with progressive rock, often with alternative, in a variety of intersections of styles. More recently, genre fusion has been part of nu-metal. Metal has overlapped with rap and hip-hop. Heavy metal has continued to bond audiences or create a community of interest. It has served as a kind of ritual or liturgy, as O'Boyle and Scott (2014) and others have pointed out.

Myth and Magic in Heavy Metal Music

Heavy metal is "serious." It is not "light" pop entertainment. The musical content of heavy metal raises questions about society, identity, and community in this global information age. Heavy metal is a site for debate about modernity's dynamics and the shifts in culture in our time. The metal audience has developed beyond being predominantly youth/teen, working class, white, and male. Today it is young and older, male and female, and it includes middle class fans and extends across a wide variety cultures. Even so, a case could be made that the industrial base remains an important factor. Deindustrialization has affected much of heavy metal's audience and it has had an impact on their sense of their prospects in life. The insights of Weinstein, Walser, and Berger about heavy metal's mostly working class audience remain in place in America, the U.K., and in Europe. In this picture heavy metal's listeners live within modernity but are not necessarily receiving its benefits. There is social frustration, economic insecurity, job displacement resulting in some people feeling social and psychological displacement.

Myth, whether drawn from Romanticism, ancient cultures, or from Norse medievalism, engages with modernity in heavy metal music. The use of myth is a creative step along the way toward reframing the picture of the modern world and articulating present needs and a new vision. In this sense, the use of myth is progressive. Myths, models, and religious or metaphorical imagination can be transformative. "No part of the modern escapes an ongoing grounding in myth," Milton Scarborough has written (7). "Man is a symbol making animal," philosopher Ernst Cassirer once asserted. Heavy metal is a forum for symbol-making.

Myth is an exemplar or a model, Mircea Eliade has observed (23). Myths help us to structure our sense of the world. We tell stories to each other to explain the changes we see occurring. Marjorie Ferguson pointed out that some of our current myths are that bigger is better and that growth and "more" is always better. There is the myth of a new world order. There is also the myth of cultural homogeneity. However, we are not necessarily creating a meta-culture via shared popular culture materials (30).

We live today amid a shifting paradigm. We have inherited from Descartes and from the Enlightenment the modern agenda that all "superstition" would end and we would become fully rational. The cosmological function of myth could not fit with scientific rationality, so myth was discredited (Scarborough, 12). So, we are left with the ontological dualism

9. Madness, Magic and Virtuosity

of Descartes, for whom the "outside" world beyond his mind (cogito, his "inner" life) was "extended substance." The rationality insisted upon by science has served humanity well in advancing science and technology and institutions. However, the overemphasis on a type of rationality—an instrumental rationality—and the illusion of technique and managerial ethos has also led to forms of dehumanization. Against these forms of dehumanization and against the institutions or hypocrisies that perpetuate it, heavy metal music rebels.

Heavy metal's audience is experiencing the seismic shifts of postmodern change. Among the signs of the times, we can see several trends that have drawn forth an audience that seeks community and connection and a renewed sense of meaning:

- With the shift from local, intimate connections to more impersonal organization, bureaucratization, urbanization, and modern fragmentation there arose a longing for community.
- The growth of advanced capitalism has resulted in economic globalization which affects world cultures and has affected peoples' work and livelihoods. The post-industrial environment can no longer sustain many of the industrial jobs of previous times. The economic priorities of businesses call them to seek profit and lower production costs where possible. Businesses have turned to automation, outsourced jobs overseas, and reduced workforce. Consequently, more workers become unemployed or under-employed and their families face the strain and struggle that comes with that.
- With the secularization of Western society came the dwindling of attendance and participation in mainstream churches. Yet, people seek human bonds and a transcendent point of reference. They seek meaning in their lives and a sense of community. If *"religare"* is a word that means "to bind" then disenfranchised individuals in a fragmented society need some alternative. Heavy metal music has become one of those alternatives.

Heavy metal has also become global. As heavy metal and its use of myth enters different cultures around the world this raises questions. How does metal provide a source of meaning in these varied circumstances? Heavy metal has been an outcast as well as a popular culture wonder, being censored, encountering social disapproval, or not being critically valued. Will heavy metal have any social-political-cultural impact in the various milieu in which it is played and listened to? Do popular culture materials have the capacity to change cultures? What are the effects of the insertion of pop media like film, television, and rock music across borders? This is being studied by empirical social science. Is pop culture's global extension just a matter of connectivity, or is it also introducing new ideas, images, myths, and products and influencing cultural change?

To recall heavy metal's past prepares it for the future. O'Boyle and Scott call for "eliminative transgression"—a phrase that sounds Nietzschean in spirit. To go beyond what has been created in the past the new creators of metal must "forget" enough to go deep. To renew metal they have to go beyond their predecessors and have an openness to reconfigure heavy metal. This always occurs in a transaction with culture and society. Postmodernist bricolage, parody, and pastiche, and the abundant availability of metal music are factors of our time. Heavy metal is "arguably a postmodern music form," as O'Boyle and Scott have recognized and writers on metal from Walser to Kahn-Harris have also pointed out. However, if literary and musical history teaches us anything it is that to renew heavy metal artists have to renew symbols and myth. One cannot simply repeat the same tropes in the same way. One who appropriates and juxtaposes materials must avoid having one's own creativity overwhelmed by them. The artist stands on the shoulders of the giants of the past and then—perhaps with some anxiety of influence—carves out a new direction. Heavy metal music does need its history—to begin to conceptualize how to break from it toward new horizons. The goal is not erasure. To just live on a postmodern surface that forgets that history in the service of immediacy is inadequate. To draw creatively from the depths in new ways, to allow for the fluid movement into new musical genres is the way to evolve. This is what it means to be "authentic." Or, to use Keith Kahn-Harris's words, this is what it means to aspire toward a "thoroughgoing articulation" of "true" (Kahn-Harris, "Coming Out," 27).

Heavy metal can be regarded in connection with ancient and modern myths and the creative depths of the human psyche. In heavy metal studies, metal ought to be positioned in relation to popular culture broadly and within the context of rock music. Meanwhile, it remains valuable to recognize how heavy metal challenges popular culture itself. Reflexivity and a future orientation are important for heavy metal enthusiasts, creators, and researchers, as Kahn-Harris has pointed out. To speculate about

9. Madness, Magic and Virtuosity

our cultural future will extends the discussion of heavy metal's place and role in society beyond the important discussions of technology that have taken place and beyond writings on the commercial aspects of the music business. Part of this exploration might include creative investigations into how heavy metal might refresh and create new music and new symbols. In an age of stimulation and simulation, mythology remains an abiding resource.

A band's ability to distribute its work is no longer entirely contingent upon a record company's outlets for this. However, there will always be the exigencies of the market and the pressure of commercial needs. The cultural influences and experiential inputs of life are ever-changing. However, at the level of archetypes and myth and dreams there is material available for reshaping. It is time again to prepare for the journey into the underworld and draw in new ways, with new sounds, from that repository of myth, from the guts and soul of rock and from those possibilities of the mind and the human spirit.

Heavy metal responds to our current world, not only to some misty, mythical past. It is created by artists that create or appropriate symbols and sounds to address our contemporary world. Rock draws upon a blues sensibility. It engages with audiences and the entertainment industry, with economics, social and political conditions, and with institutional structures, including the music business. Features of Romanticism like rebellion, emotion, nostalgia, and the search for new forms only partly begin to explain the persistence and power of myth in the heavy metal genre. Heavy metal has become one of the most popular of forms of rock music. It has contributed to the realization, in part, of new kinds of togetherness in an age that is often short on community. Metal energizes and invigorates its listeners. It is a vehicle for social critique that is engaged with present dreams and social tensions. It is a self-conscious entertainment, a force in society that recasts and revives the symbolic. When the power of metal meets the power of myth, imagination and wonder are restored. Metal lives and in myth remains transformational, challenging, entertaining—and ever alive and well.

Selected Discography

AC/DC. *High Voltage*, Atco, 1976.
____. *Highway to Hell*, Atlantic, 1979.
____. *Back in Black*, Atlantic 1980.
____. *For Those about to Rock We Salute You*, Atlantic, 1981.
____. *Blow Up Your Video*, Atlantic, 1988.
____. *The Razor's Edge*, Atco, 1990.
Annihilator. *Alice in Hell*, Roadrunner, 1989.
Anthrax. *Spreading the Disease*, 1985.
____. *State of Euphoria*, Megaforce/Island, 1988
____. *Persistence of Time*, Megaforce/Island, 1990.
____. *For All Kings*, Metalcore, 2016.
Avatar. *Thoughts of No Tomorrow*, Sony, 2006.
____. *Schlacht*, Sony, 2007.
____. *Avatar*, Sony, 2008.
____. *Feathers and Flesh*, Sony, 2016.
Avenged Sevenfold. *Avenged Sevenfold*, Warner, 2007.
Bathory. *Under the Sign of the Black Mark*, Black Mark/Under One Flag, UK, 1987.
Black Sabbath. *Black Sabbath*, Warner, 1970.
____. *Paranoid*, Warner, 1970.
____. *Sabbath, Bloody Sabbath*, Warner 1974.
____. *Never Say Die*, Warner, 1978.
____. *Heaven and Hell*, Warner, 1980.
Blue Cheer. *Vincebus Eruptum*, Philips, 1968.
Blue Öyster Cult. *Agents of Fortune*, Columbia, 1976.
Bon Jovi. *7800 Degrees Fahrenheit*, Mercury, 1985
____. *Slippery When Wet*, Mercury, 1986.
____. *New Jersey*, Mercury, 1988.
Cannibal Corpse. *Butchered at Birth*, Mills, 1991.
Celtic Frost. *Into the Pandemonium*, Combat, 1987.
Cinderella. *Long Cold Winter*, Mercury, 1988.
Cradle of Filth. *Cruelty and the Beast*, 1998.
Deep Purple. *Made in Japan*, Warner, 1972.
____. *Deep Purple in Rock*, Harvest 1970.
____. *Machine Head*, Warner, 1972.
____. *Perfect Strangers*, Polydor, 1984.

Selected Discography

Def Leppard. *Pyromania*, Mercury, 1983.
____. *Hysteria*, Mercury, 1987.
Deicide. *When Satan Lives*, Roadrunner, 1990.
Dimmu Borgir. *Enthrone Darkness Triumphant*, Nuclear Blast, 1997.
____. *Abrahadabra*, Nuclear Blast, 2010.
Dio. *Holy Diver*. Warner, 1983.
____. *The Last in Line*, Warner, 1984.
Disturbed. *Immortalized*, Reprise, 2015.
Dokken. *Tooth and Nail*, Elektra, 1984.
____. *Back for the Attack*, Elektra, 1987.
Dream Theater. *Images and Words*, Atco, 1992.
Einherjer. *Odin Owns Ye All*, Napalm, 1998.
Emperor. *Anthems to the Welkin at Dusk*, Norman UK, 1997.
Exodus. *Bonded by Blood*, Legacy, 1985.
Forbidden. *Forbidden Evil*, Sony, 1988.
Gorgoroth. *Pentagram*, Embassy, 1994.
____. *Destroyer*, Nuclear Blast, 1998.
____. *Instinctus Bestialis*, Soulseller, 2015.
Guns n' Roses. *Appetite for Destruction*, Geffen, 1987.
____. *GN'R Lies*. Geffen, 1988.
Hammerfall. *Glory to the Brave*, Nuclear Blast, 1997.
Helloween. *Keeper of the Seven Keys, Part II*, RCA, 1987.
Hypocrisy. *Osculum Obscenum*, Nuclear Blast, 1993
Iron Maiden. *The Number of the Beast*, EMI, 1982
____. *Powerslave*, Capitol, 1984.
____. *Live After Death*, Capitol, 1985.
____. *Seventh Son of a Seventh Son*, EMI, 1988.
____. *No Prayer for the Dying*, Epic, 1990.
____. *Brave New World*, EMI, 2000.
____. *The Final Frontier*, EMI, 2010.
____. *The Book of Souls*, Parlophone, 2015.
Judas Priest. *Sin After Sin*, Columbia, 1987.
____. *Stained Class*, Columbia, 1978.
____. *Unleashed in the East*, Columbia, 1979.
____. *British Steel*, Columbia, 1980.
____. *Point of Entry*, Columbia, 1981.
____. *Screaming for Vengeance*, Columbia, 1982.
____. *Defenders of the Faith*, Columbia, 1984.
____. *Turbo*, Columbia, 1986.
____. *Ram It Down*, Columbia, 1988.
____. *Painkiller*, Columbia, 1990.
Kiss. *Hotter Than Hell*, Casablanca, 1974.
____. *Dressed to Kill*, Casablanca, 1975.
____. *Alive*, Casablanca, 1975.
____. *Destroyer*, Casablanca, 1976.
Korn. *Issues*, Immortal, 1999.
Lamb of God. *Sacrament*, Prosthetic, 2006.

Selected Discography

Led Zeppelin. *Led Zeppelin I*, Atlantic, 1969.
_____. *Led Zeppelin II*, Atlantic, 1969.
_____.*Led Zeppelin III*, Atlantic, 1970.
_____. *Led Zeppelin IV (ZOSO)*, Atlantic, 1971.
_____. *Houses of the Holy*, Atlantic, 1973.
_____. *Physical Graffiti*, Swan Song, 1975.
_____. *Presence*, Swan Song, 1976.
Living Colour. *Vivid*, Epic, 1988.
_____. *Time's Up*, Epic, 1990.
Machine Head. *Unto the Locust*, Roadrunner, 2011.
_____. *Catharex*, Nuclear Blast, 2018.
Manowar. *Into Glory Ride*, Atlantic, 1983.
_____. *The Triumph of Steel*, Atlantic, 1992.
Mastodon. *Crack the Skye*, Reprise, 2004.
Megadeth. *Peace Sells...but Who's Buying?* Combat/EMI, 1986.
_____. *So far so good...so what?* Combat/Capitol, 1988.
_____. *Rust in Peace*, Combat/Capitol, 1990.
Mercyful Fate. *Don't Break the Oath*, Roadrunner, 1984.
Metallica. *Kill 'Em All*, Important, 1983.
_____. *Ride the Lightning*, Megaforce/Elektra, 1984.
_____. *Master of Puppets*, Elektra, 1986.
_____. *And Justice for All*, Elektra, 1988.
_____. *Metallica*, Elektra, 1991.
_____. *Load*. Elektra, 1996.
_____. *Re-Load*. Elektra, 1997.
_____. *Death Magnetic*. Vertigo, 2008.
_____. *Hardwired to Self-Destruct*, Warner/Blackened, 2016.
Michael Schenker Group. *MSG*, Chrysalis, 1981.
_____. *Assault Attack*, Chrysalis, 1982.
Ministry. *Psalm 69*, Sire, 1992.
Morbid Angel. *Altars of Madness*, Combat, 1989.
Mötley Crüe. *Shout at the Devil*, Elektra, 1983.
_____. *Theatre of Pain*, Elektra, 1984.
_____. *Girls, Girls, Girls*, Elektra, 1987.
Motorhead. *Live: No Sleep til Hammersmith*, Mercury, 1981.
_____. *No Sleep At All*, Enigma/GWR, 1988.
Nazareth. *2XS*, A&M, 1982.
Osborne, Ozzy. *Blizzard of Ozz*, Jet/CBS, 1981.
_____. *Diary of a Madman*, Jet/CBS 1981.
_____. *Just Say Ozzy*, CBS, 1990.
_____. *No More Tears*, Epic, 1991.
Pantera. *Vulgar Display of Power*, Atco, 1992.
Poison. *Look What the Cat Dragged In*, Enigma, 1986.
Possessed. *Beyond the Gates*, Combat, 1986.
Queensrych. *Operation Minderime*, EMI, 1988.
Quiet Riot. *Mental Health*, Pasha, 1983.
Rainbow. *Ritchie Blackmore's Rainbow*, Polydor, 1975.

Selected Discography

_____. *Difficult to Cure*, Polydor, 1981.
Rush. *2112*, Mercury, 1976.
_____. *Clockwork Angels*, Anthem, 2012.
Saxon. *Wheels of Steel*, Parlophone, 1980.
Scorpions. *In Trance*, RCA, 1976.
_____. *Love at First Sting*, Mercury, 1984.
_____. *Savage Amusement*, Mercury, 1988.
Slayer. *The Reign of Blood*, 1986.
_____. *South of Heaven*, Def Jam, 1988.
_____. *Seasons in the Abyss*, Def American, 1990.
Slipknot. *Slipknot*, Roadrunner, 1999.
_____. *Iowa*, Roadrunner, 2001.
_____. *All Hope Is Gone*, Roadrunner, 2008.
_____. *The Gray Chapter*, Roadrunner, 2014.
Stryper. *To Hell with the Devil*, Hollywood, 1986.
Suicidal Tendencies. *How Will I Laugh Tomorrow When I Can't Even Smile Today?*, Virgin, 1988.
System of a Down. *Toxicity*, Columbia, 2001.
Testament. *Souls of Black*, Megaforce, Atlantic, 1990.
_____. *The Ritual*, Megaforce, Atlantic, 1992.
_____. *Dark Roots of Earth*, Atlantic, 2012.
_____. *Brotherhood of the Snake*, 2016.
Thin Lizzy. *Jailbreak*, Island/Def Jam, 1976.
Tool. *Undertow*, Zoo, 1993.
_____. *AEnina*, Zoo, 1996.
_____. *Lateralus*, Volcano, 2001.
_____. *10,000 Days*, Volcano, 2006.
Twisted Sister. *Under the Blade*, Roadrunner, 1982.
_____. *Stay Hungry*, Atlantic, 1984.
UFO. *Obsession*, Chrysalis, 1978.
Van Halen. *Van Halen*, Warner, 1978.
_____. *Van Halen II*, Warner, 1979.
_____. *Diver Down*, Warner, 1982.
_____. *1984*, Warner, 1983.
_____. *5150*, Warner, 1986.
_____. *OU812*, Warner, 1988.
Venom. *Black Metal*, 1982.
Whitesnake. *Whitesnake*, Geffen, 1987.
_____. *Slip of the Tongue*, Geffen, 1989.
Yngwie Malmsteen's Rising Force. *Rising Force*, 1984.
_____. *Odyssey*, Polydor, 1988.

Chapter Notes

Introduction

1. Mircea Eliade was a significant mythologist and explorer of comparative religion. Readers can also gain much insight into mythology from Joseph Campbell's *The Hero with a Thousand Faces* (Princeton, 1949) and his conversations with Bill Moyers recorded in *The Power of Myth* (Doubleday, 1988), both valuable resources for anyone who wishes to explore mythology.

Chapter 1

1. Page commented in an interview that the hermit is a seeker aspiring to the light of truth. See Chapter 13, George Case, *Led Zeppelin FAQ: All That's Left to Know about the Greatest Hard Rock Band of All Time* (London: Backbeat Books, 2011).
2. In an interview with Page he says that ZOSO was drawn from Rudolph Koch's *Book of Signs* (1955), a collection of symbols from around the world. Jones chose three ovals meeting in a circle and Bonham chose three circles meeting in an oval. Plant's symbol included a feather in a circle. Page's symbol was a creative composite of several symbolic images.
3. William S. Burroughs and Jimmy Page had a conversation. The abstract to the article noted that Page had bought the Loch Ness home of Aleister Crowley, the occultist. Page says that he awaits the day of holograms, and a Van Der Graff Generator, like in old horror films. Burroughs refers to infra-sound that is below the level of hearing (163) and Page speaks about music with riffs that "will have a trancelike effect" (164). He reflects on "rhythms within the audience." Burroughs responds that mantras set up vibrations.
4. On September 27, 1968, Led Zeppelin went into Olympic Studios in London and in about 35 hours across two weeks recorded *Led Zeppelin I*. Led Zeppelin was signed by Jerry Wexler at Atlantic Records. *Led Zeppelin II* appeared during the same year. On *Led Zeppelin I*, "Dazed and Confused" was composed by Jake Holmes for a 1967 album. "Babe, I'm Gonna Leave You," by Anne Bredon, appeared on a Joan Baez recording.
5. Robert Plant is quoted by critic Robert Walser early on in his discussion of the challenge in defining heavy metal. See *Running with the Devil*, p.6. The interview appeared in *Musician* (September 1984), p. 53.
6. Page played several guitars on the recording of "Stairway to Heaven," including a Fender 12 string, a guitar solo on a 1958 Telecaster, and the final riff on a 1959 Les Paul. In performance he played a custom made Gibson EDS 1275 which combined a 6-string and a 12-string. The lead includes blues based runs and Aeolian intervals (E-C-A hammer on triplets at 17th fret on the Telecaster). Page's lead rises above the A minor, G, F chord structure of the concluding section.
7. Sandy Denny of Fairport Convention sings with Robert Plant on "The Battle of Evermore."
8. "No Quarter" on *Houses of the Holy* (1973) has the mythical Nordic god Thor

on a mission. See Bennett's discussion in "Paganism and the Counterculture," Chapter Two of *Pagan Pop*.

9. See Theodore Gracyk, *Listening to Popular Music, or How I Learned to Stop Worrying and Love Led Zeppelin* (Ann Arbor: University of Michigan Press, 2007), p. 32.

10. Paul Ricoeur, *The Symbolism of Evil* (Boston: Beacon, 1967).

Chapter 2

1. Andrew L. Cope, *Black Sabbath and the Rise of Heavy Metal Music* (London: Ashgate/Routledge, 2010). Paul Ricoeur writes that in the Hebrew tradition the symbol of *shagah* indicates the alienated one who has gone astray and feels lost. "But if the image of revolt is more forceful, the image of having gone astray is more radical, for it directly envisages a total situation, the state of being astray and lost." Paul Ricoeur, *The Symbolism of Evil* (Boston: Beacon, 1967), p. 73.

2. Candace Grissom comments on seeing the name "Ozzy" sketched on a water tower as a young girl in Alabama. (See her essay in Alex Di Blasi and Robert McParland, eds., *Finding God in the Devil's Music*. Jefferson, NC: McFarland, 2018.) Cutting through the park after taking a bus from the city of Paterson, where I was teaching at the time, I witnessed the "Ozzy Is God" graffiti on the wall in Passaic, New Jersey, in the mid-1980s.

3. Greg Kot of the *Chicago Tribune* observes that Ozzy "morphed" from "evil incarnate to party monster." "The Satanists Who Changed Music," On the Record, BBC Culture (November 3, 2015), www.bbc.com/culture/story/20151027/the-satanists-who-changed-music.html.

4. Among the best thinkers about these presumed binaries in rock music with respect to theological studies is Sabbatino DiBernardo. For his thoughts on Black Sabbath, see his essay "Heavy Metal's Ironic Edge: Distortion, Demonization, and Noise" in Scott Wilson's *Music at the Extremes: Sounds Outside the Mainstream* (Jefferson, NC: McFarland, 2015). Di Bernardo sees in Black Sabbath as "ironic doubleness" (209). They raise questions of "religio-political and socio-political values and beliefs" (208). He cites Claire Colebrook's reference to "the destabilizing force of irony" (197).

5. In the Reformation period, Martin Luther recognized the power of a sacred music to assist in exorcism. Invert the letters of sacred and you have "scared." The sacred contests with the infernal.

6. See *Essentials of Demonology* by E. Langton (1949), *By the Finger of God* by V. McCaslin (1951), *Possession: Demonological and Other* by T.K. Oesterreich (1930).

7. In Jesus' ministry he casts out demons (Matt. 12:25–29, Mark 3:23–27, Luke 11:17–22). He encourages his disciples to do likewise (Matt 10:8, Mark 3:13–19, 6:7–13, Luke 9:1–2).

Chapter 3

1. To overlook the music is a serious flaw in some rock music writing, Robert Walser notes in *Running with the Devil*, p. 38.

2. Morris Dickstein's comments appear in "The Age of Rock Revisited" (183–210) in *Gates of Eden*.

3. Robert Walser identifies this as an eighth and two sixteenths figure. See *Running with the Devil*, p. 156.

4. CBS was sued by the families of teens who were said to have committed suicide after listening to Judas Priest's *Stained Class* (Vance v. CBS, 1985). CBS was then sued in cases against Ozzy Osborne's "Suicide Solution" (McCollum v. CBS. 1988, Waller v. CBS 1991).

5. It seems to me that bands like Aerosmith, Guns n' Roses, Mötley Crüe, Kiss, Alice Cooper, or Bon Jovi, all of which have had widespread pop radio airplay, are best classified as hard rock rather than as metal, although they may incorporate some aspects of metal and could be called lite metal.

6. In April 1974, bassist Rob Bailey and drummers Peter Clack recorded with them their first single: "Can I Sit Next to You, Girl?"

Chapter 4

1. *Masks of Gods* by Joseph Campbell was published between 1959 and 1968 and appears in four volumes. In literary theory archetypal criticism, prominent during the period when it was practiced by Northup Frye, has somewhat faded. However, we will return to this approach for what it has to contribute in an investigation of archetypes, mythic motifs, and recurrent patterns.
2. Anthropologist Jane Harrison wrote *Themis*, which was published in 1912.
3. This is Andrew Elkins' phrase. See Elkins, p. 243.
4. Thomas Moore, *Care of the Soul: A Guide for Cultivating Depth and Sacredness in Everyday Life* (New York: Harper Perennial, 1992).
5. See Peter Beresford Ellis, *The Druids* (London: Constable, 1994; Grand Rapids: Eerdsmans, 1995).

Chapter 5

1. Robert Pattison's *The Triumph of Vulgarity* (1987), considers parallels with Romanticism. Danny Sugerman notes the connection in his book on Guns n' Roses, *Appetite for Destruction*. There are several claims on death metal.org that death metal draws upon gothic Romanticism's themes. Keir Keightly points out that Modernist and Romantic tendencies may appear in the same artist (*Cambridge Companion to Pop and Rock*, p. 138). See James Rovira's blog at rockandromanticism, which features some of William Blake's mythical illustrations among discussions on the subject.
2. In "Fled Is That Magic: The Uses of Enchantment in John Keats and Led Zeppelin," Jenna Ruggiero, in a fascinating senior undergraduate project at Bard College (2011), focuses on Led Zeppelin in relation to that most musical of poets John Keats. While she does not spend time on Keats's poetics per se, Ruggiero, who is now a creative manager at Jason Flom's Lava Records in New York, makes connections between the music and lyrics of Led Zeppelin and the art of the Romantic poet. Jason Flom, while with Atlantic Records, signed Twisted Sister, White Lion, Stone Temple Pilots, and the mythically named Antigone Rising. On Lava Records are Lorde, Trans-Siberian Orchestra and several other acts.
3. In Jungian psychotherapy, to break down the persona to attain individuation is a necessary goal.
4. Among the key works of Novalis is his novel *Heinrich von Ofterdingen* (1799), which is about a miner. Novalis drew upon a myth of the Middle Ages. He claimed to see social, political and religious unity in them: a utopia.
5. Goethe's first period is usually known as the *Sturm und Drang*. Johann Gottfried von Herder encouraged him to cast aside neo-classicism and to embrace Shakespeare and to seek the "inner form" rather than rationalism's artificial categories. Goethe then entered his classical phase, in which he reflected on genre.

Chapter 6

1. Mick Wall, *Run to the Hills* (London: Sanctuary, 2004), pp. 10–15.
2. Robert Walser, *Running with the Devil: Power, Gender and Madness in Heavy Metal Music* (Middletown: Wesleyan University Press, 1993), pp. 53–54.
3. Deena Weinstein, *Heavy Metal: The Music and Its Culture* (New York: Da Capo, 2000), p. 214.
4. Walser, p. 55.
5. Weinstein, p. 41.
6. Weinstein, p. 88.
7. Eduard Hanslick, *On the Beautiful in Music*, p. 110.
8. Thomas MacFarland, *Coleridge and the Pantheist Tradition* (Oxford: Clarendon Press, 1969), pp. 383–87, 400–01.
9. Robert Penn Warren, "Coleridge," (1946), in *Selected Essays of Robert Penn Warren* (New York: Random House, 2000).
10. Weinstein, p. 232.
11. Weinstein, p. 42.
12. Walser, p. 151.
13. Richard Holmes, *Coleridge, Early*

Visions, 1772–1804 (New York: Pantheon, 1999), p. 33.

14. Weinstein, pp. 262–63.
15. Weinstein, p. 289.
16. For another transformation of Bruce Dickinson's vocal, in a work influenced by science fiction, listen to the song "Into the Black Hole" on *Universal Migrator: Part Two, Flight of the Migrator* (2000). Dickinson, of Iron Maiden, lends his vocal to this work by Areyon, the Dutch composer Arjon Anthony Lucaasen. The narrative concerns a time travel dream sequencer. This is a journey through space, encountering a pulsar and ending up in a black hole.

Chapter 7

1. This image is discussed by Simon Trafford and Aleks Pluskowski, "Anti-Christ Superstars: The Vikings in Hard Rock and Heavy Metal," in *Mass Market Medieval: Essays on the Middle Ages and Popular Culture*, ed. David Marshall (Jefferson, NC: McFarland, 2007), pp. 57–59. They note Alexandra Service's thesis in 1998 in which she describes the Vikings, pp. 196, 211.
2. See Lars Lannoth, "The Vikings in History and Legend," *Oxford Illustrated History of the Vikings*, ed. Peter Sawyer (New York and Oxford: Oxford University Press, 1999), pp. 225–249.
3. Ian Reyes, "Blacker Than Death: Recollecting the Black Turn in Metal Aesthetic," *Popular Music and Culture*, Vol. 25, No. 2 (June 20, 2013): 240–257.
4. Extreme metal has been viewed by some critics as a branch of thrash metal. Bands include Bathory, Venom, Celtic Frost.

Chapter 8

1. Some people may have considered the shopping malls of Paramus, New Jersey, a kind of hell at times. Paramus Park, the Bergen Mall, and the Garden State Plaza were fixtures on Route 4 or Route 17 but that suburban town seems an unlikely place for Paul Smith and Dan Lorenzo to have met and have formed a heavy metal band with the ominous name Hades. Hades opened for New Jersey's hair-metal band Twisted Sister. They continued rocking out until about 1988 and later had some reunion gigs. It was a sign that heavy metal had arrived in the neighborhoods of America.
2. *Anchor Bible Dictionary II*: 148.
3. See Iced Earth, *Dante's Inferno, Burnt Offerings*, 1995.
4. "Here I Go Again" on the *Saints and Sinners* album was Whitesnake's biggest radio hit.
5. The Orphic-Pythogorean ideas brought the sense that there could be an afterlife of rewards and one of souls that were punished. In the Hebrew Bible the place to which the dead go is mentioned in 2 Macabees 6:23, 1 Enoch 102:5, Ezra 7:32.
6. The Patristic period refers to the writings of the Church fathers, from the time of St. Augustine in the AD 300s to about AD 1100.

Chapter 9

1. Robert Walser notes that in June 1987 U2 held the #1 album spot and this was followed by five heavy metal recordings: Whitesnake, Bon Jovi, Poison, Mötley Crüe, and Ozzy Osborne (*Running with the Devil*, p.13).
2. Ozzy Osborne was also later cited twice in lawsuits against his record company CBS/Columbia for the alleged role of the song "Suicide Solution" in the deaths of two other teens.
3. Robert Walser, *Running with the Devil*, p. 146; Ivan Solataroff, *The Village Voice* (September 4, 1990): 24–34.
4. You and I may have unique and different responses. These variant meanings are negotiated. See Walser's comments, p. 33.
5. Critics of the Straus and Howe study point out limited attention to ethnicity and race, or to demographics.
6. Keith Kahn-Harris explores this question (2013). O'Boyle and Scott have responded to Kahn-Harris in "The Future

of Metal is Bright and Hell Bent on Genre Destruction," in *Global Metal Music and Culture*, eds. Andy Brown, Karl Sprecklen, Keith Kahn-Harris, and Niall W.R. Scott (New York and London: Routledge, 2016). "Metal can be read as a kind of collectively constructed myth," Kahn-Harris has written elsewhere. In this constructed myth our complex world is focused into "a set of idealized symbols, aesthetics and stories." Heavy metal, paradoxically, seeks "trueness" through these mythological formulations and "what links the fantastic to the real is a kind of vitalism," he says. See "Coming Out: Realizing the Possibilities of Metal" (26–38) in *Heavy Metal Gender and Sexuality: Interdisciplinary Approaches*, ed. Florian Heesch and Niall Scott (New York and London: Routledge, 2016), pp. 26–27.

Bibliography

Books and Articles

Adams, Hazard. *Philosophy of the Literary Symbolic*. Tallahassee: University Press of Florida, 1983.
Alighieri, Dante. *The Inferno*. Trans. Robert Pinsky. New York: Farrar, Straus and Giroux, 1997.
Aristotle. *The Poetics*. Trans. T.S. Dortsch. London: Penguin, 1965.
Ashkenazi, Abraham. *Modern German Nationalism*. New York: John Wiley; Cambridge: Harvard University Press, 1976.
Attali, Jacques. *Noise: The Political Economy of Music*. Trans. Brian Masumi. Minneapolis: University of Minnesota Press, 1985.
Auxier, Randall. "Magical Pages and Mythic Plants." In *Led Zeppelin and Philosophy*. Ed. Scott Calef. Chicago: Open Court, 2009. 111–130.
Bachelard, Gaston. *L'Eau et les reves. Essais sur la imagination de la matiere*. [*Water and Dreams: An Essay on Imagination and the Material*.] Paris, 1942; rpt. Paris: J. Corti, 1971.
Bakhtin, Mikhail. *The Dialogic Imagination*. Eds. Caryl Emerson and Michael Holquist. Austin: University of Texas Press, 1981.
Bangs, Lester. "Bring Your Mother to the Gas Chamber: Are Black Sabbath Really the New Shamans," Part One. *Creem* (June 1972): 40 ff.
_____. "Bring Your Mother to the Gas Chamber: Black Sabbath and the Straight Dope on Blood Lust Orgies," Part Two. *Creem* (July 1972): 47 ff.
_____. "Heavy Metal." In *The Rolling Stone Illustrated History of Rock and Roll*. Ed. Jim Miller. New York: Random House, 1976.
_____. *Led Zeppelin III* Review. *Rolling Stone* (November 26, 1970).
_____. *Main Lines: Blood Feasts and Bad Taste: A Lester Bangs Reader*. Ed. John Morthland. New York: Knopf/Doubleday, 2002.
Bashe, Philip. *Heavy Metal Thunder: The Music, Its History, Its Heroes*. Garden City: Doubleday, 1985.
Baudrillard, Jean. *Simulacra and Simulations*. Trans. Paul Voss, Paul Paton, and Philip Beitchman. New York: Semiotext(e), 1983.
Baumlin, James S., Tita French Baumlin, and George H. Jensen. *Post-Jungian Criticism: Theory and Practice*. Albany: State University of New York Press, 2004.
Berger, Harris M. *Metal, Rock, and Jazz: Perception and the Phenomenology of Musical Experience*. Hanover, NH: Wesleyan University Press, 1999.
Blake, William. *Selected Poems*. New York: Penguin, 1989.
Bloom, Allan. *The Closing of the American Mind*. New York: Simon & Schuster, 1987.
Bloom, Harold. "Freud and the Poetic Sublime: A Catastrophe Theory of Creativity," 1978.

Bibliography

In *Freud: A Collection of Critical Essays*. Ed. Perry Meisel. Englewood Cliffs, NJ: Prentice Hall, 1981. 218.
Booker, Christopher. *The Seven Basic Plots: Why We Tell Stories*. New York: Continuum, 2008.
Borowitz, Hank. *Led Zeppelin on Led Zeppelin: Interviews and Encounters*. Chicago: Chicago Review Press, 2014.
Brantlinger, Patrick. *The Reading Lesson*. Bloomington: Indiana University Press, 1998.
Breen, Marcus. "A Stairway to Heaven or a Highway to Hell? Heavy Metal Rock Music in the 1990s." *Cultural Studies* 5.2 (May 1991): 191–203.
Brontë, Emily. *Wuthering Heights*. New York and Oxford: Oxford University Press, 1983.
Brown, Andy, Karl Spracklen, Keith Kahn-Harris, and Niall W.R. Scott, eds. *Global Metal Music Culture*. New York and London: Routledge, 2016.
Burke, Edmund. *A Philosophical Enquiry into the Origin of Our Ideas of the Sublime and Beautiful* (1757). New York and Oxford: Oxford University Press, 1998.
Burroughs, William S. "Rock Magic: Jimmy Page, Led Zeppelin, and a Search for the Elusive Stairway to Heaven." *Crawdaddy* (June 1975): 150.
Caesar, Julius. *De Bello Gallico*, 52–51 BC In *The Gallic Wars*. Trans. John Warrington. Norwalk: Easton, 1993.
Calef, Scott. *Led Zeppelin and Philosophy*. Chicago: Open Court, 2009.
Campbell, Iain. "From Achilles to Alexander: The Classical World and the World of Metal." In *Heavy Metal Music in Britain*. Ed. Gerd Bayer. Burlington, VT: Ashgate, 2009, 111–128.
Campbell, Joseph. *The Hero with a Thousand Faces*. Princeton: Princeton University Press, 1949.
_____. *The Masks of Gods*. 4 vols. New York: Viking, 1959–1964.
_____. *The Power of Myth*. Ed. Betty Sue Flowers, Bill Moyers. New York: Doubleday, 1988.
Case, George. *Led Zeppelin FAQ: All That's Left to Know about the Greatest Hard Rock Band of All Time*. London: Backbeat, 2011.
Cassirer, Ernst. *The Philosophy of Symbolic Forms*. Vol. 2, 4 vols. New Haven: Yale University Press, 1955–1966.
Cicero. *Selected Political Speeches*. New York: Penguin, 1977.
Coleridge, Samuel Taylor. *Samuel Taylor Coleridge: Selected Poems*. London: Folio, 2003.
Cope, Andrew L. *Black Sabbath and the Rise of Heavy Metal Music*. Burlington, VT: Ashgate/Routledge, 2010.
Craig, Gordon. *The Germans*. New York: Meridian, 1991.
Davies, Sioned. *The Mabinogion: Celtic Tales*. Oxford and New York: Oxford University Press, 2008.
Davis, Erik. *Led Zeppelin IV*. 33 and 1/3 Series. New York: Continuum/Bloomsbury, 2005.
Davis, Oliver. "Theorizing Writerly Creativity: Jung with Lacan?" In *Post-Jungian Criticism*. Ed. James Baumlin, Tita French Baumlin, George Jensen. Albany: State University of New York Press, 2004.
Davis, Stephen. *Hammer of the Gods*. London: Sidgwick and Jackson, 1985.
De Maio, Joey. Interview (member of Manowar). www.wortraub.com.
Di Bernardo, Sabatino. "Heavy Metal's Ironic Edge: Distortion, Demonization, and Noise." In *Music at the Extremes: Sounds Outside the Mainstream*. Ed. Scott Wilson. Jefferson, NC: McFarland, 2015.
Dickstein, Morris. *Gates of Eden: American Culture in the Sixties*. New York: Penguin, 1977, rpt. 1989.
Djurslev, Christopher Thrue. "The Metal King; Alexander the Great in Heavy Metal Music." *Metal Music Studies* Vol. 1, No. 1 (October 2014): 127–141.

Bibliography

Doctorow, E.L. "Standards." In *Jack London, Hemingway and the Constitution: Selected Essays, 1977–1992*. New York: Harper, 1994.
Durkheim, Emile. *The Elementary Forms of Religious Life*. New York: Free, 1965.
Eagleton, Terry. *After Theory*. New York: Basic, 2003.
Eliade, Mircea. *Myth and Reality*. New York: Harper, 1963.
_____. *The Sacred and Profane*. New York: Harper and Row, 1957.
Eliot, T.S. *Ulysses, Order, and Myth*. New York: Dial, 1923.
Elkins, David. *Beyond Religion: A Personal Program Outside the Walls of Traditional Religion*. Quest, 1998.
Ellis, Peter Beresford. *The Druids*. London: Constable, 1994; Grand Rapids: Eerdsmans, 1995.
Euripedes. *The Bacchae and Other Plays*. New York: Penguin, 2006.
Farley, Helen. "Demons, Devils, and Witches: The Occult in Heavy Metal Music." In *Heavy Metal Music in Britain*. Ed. Gerd Bayer. Burlington, VT: Ashgate, 2009.
Fast, Susan. *In the Houses of the Holy*. New York and Oxford: Oxford University Press, 2001.
Ferguson, Marjorie. "The Mythology about Globalization." *Journal of Communication* (2005): 23–45.
Flynn, Robb. Foreword. *The Complete History of Black Sabbath*. Joel McIver. New York: Race Point, Quarto Group, 2016.
Foucault, Michel. *Discipline and Punish*. Trans. Alan Sheridan. New York: Vintage, 1979.
_____. *Madness and Civilization: A History of Insanity in the Age of Reason*. Trans. Richard Howard. New York: Vintage, 1971.
Frazer, James. *The Golden Bough*. London: Macmillan, New York: St. Martin's, 1922.
Freud, Sigmund. *Civilization and Its Discontents* (1930). trans. James Strachey. New York: W.W. Norton, 1961.
_____. "The Uncanny." *The Standard Edition of the Complete Psychological Works of Sigmund Freud*, ed. James Strachey. London: 1953–1974, Vol. 17, 237–243.
Fricke, David. "Heavy Metal Justice: The Thrash Superstars Metallica Make It to the Top with Their Integrity Intact." *Rolling Stone* (January 12, 1989).
Fruman, Norman. *Coleridge: The Damaged Archangel*. New York: George Braziller, 1971.
Frye, Northrop. *Anatomy of Criticism: Four Essays*, Princeton: Princeton University Press, 1957.
_____. "Conclusion." In *The Literary History of Canada*. Ed. Carl F. Kinck. Toronto: University of Toronto Press, 1965, rpt. 1976.
_____. *Fearful Symmetry: A Study of William Blake*. Princeton: Princeton University Press, 1947.
_____. *The Secular Scripture: A Study of the Structure of Romance*. Cambridge: Harvard University Press, 1976.
Goethe, Johann von. *Werke*. Ed. Erich Trunz, 14 vols. Munich: Beck, 1948–60.
Gowensmith, William Neil, and Larry J. Bloom. *Journal of Music Therapy* Vol. 34, No. 1 (Spring 1997): 33–45.
Granholm, Kennet. "Ritual Black Metal: Popular Music as Occult Mediation and Practice." *Correspondences* Vol. 1, No. 1 (2013): 5–33.
Graves, Robert. *The Greek Myths*. 2 vols. Harmondsworth: Penguin, 1948.
_____. *The White Goddess*. London: Faber & Faber, 1948.
Green, Miranda, ed. *The Celtic World*. London: Routledge, 1995.
Gross, Robert. "*Heavy Metal: A New Subculture in American Society.*" *Journal of American Popular Culture*, Vol. 24, No. 1 (Summer 1990): 119–130.
Guirand, F., and J. Viaud, et al. *New Larousse Encyclopedia of Mythology*. Introduction, Robert Graves. London and New York: Hamlyn, 1959, rpt. 1968.

Bibliography

Hagen, Ross. "Musical Style, Ideology, and Mythology in Norwegian Extreme Metal." *Metal Rules the Globe: Heavy Metal Around the World*. Ed. Jeremy Wallach, Harris M. Berger, Paul D. Greene. London: Berg/Bloomsbury, 2011. 180–199.
Hamilton, Edith. *Mythology*. Boston: Little, Brown, 1942.
Hammerstein, Reinhold. *Dictionary of the History of Ideas*, Vol. III, 266. New York: Charles Scribner's Sons, 2005.
Hampden-Turner, Charles. *Maps of the Mind*. New York: Collier, 1981.
Harrell, Jack. "Poetics of Destruction: Death Metal Rock." *Popular Music and Society* Vol. 18, No. 1 (1994): 91–103.
Harris, Chris. MTV Interview, Joey De Maio of Manowar. February 2007. MTV.com/news/1552016/metal-file-manowar-a-life-once-lost-origin-news-that-rules.
Hart, D.S. "Heavy Metal Thunder: White Metal Is the New Grassroots Movement." *Contemporary Christian Music* 18 (January 1988): 20.
Heesch, Florian. "Metal for Nordic Men: Amon Amarth's Representation of Vikings." *The Metal Void* (2017).
Herzog, Edgar. *Psyche and Death: Death-Demons in Folklore: Myths and Modern Dreams*. Dallas: Spring, 1983.
Hesiod. *Theogony*. Trans. M.L. West. Oxford and New York: Oxford University Press, 1988.
Hill, Rosemary, and Karl Spracklen, eds. *Heavy Fundamentalisms: Music, Metal, and Politics*. Oxford: Inter-Disciplinary, 2010
Hillman, James. *Blue Fire: Selected Writings*. New York: Harper, 1989.
_____. *The Dream of the Underworld*. New York: Harper and Row, 1979.
_____. *The Essential James Hillman: A Blue Fire*, ed. Thomas Moore. New York and London: Routledge, 1990.
_____. *The Soul's Code: In Search of Character and Calling*. New York: Warner, 1996.
Hinds, Elizabeth Jane Wall. "The Devil Sings the Blues: Heavy Metal, Gothic Fiction, and Postmodern Discourse." *Journal of Popular Culture*, Vol. 26, No. 3 (December 1992): 151–164.
Holmes, Richard. *Coleridge: Early Visions*. London: Hodder and Stoughton, 1989.
Homer. *The Iliad*. Trans. Robert Fagles. New York: Penguin, 1990.
_____. *The Odyssey*. Trans. Robert Fagles. New York: Penguin, 1997.
Hornblower, Simon, and Anthony Spawforth. *The Oxford Companion to Classical Civilization*. New York and Oxford: Oxford University Press, 1998.
Hughes, Henry Mayric. *Cambridge Companion to German Romanticism*, ed. Nicholas Saul. Cambridge: Cambridge University Press, 2009.
Huxley, Aldous. *The Doors of Perception*. London: Chatto and Windus, 1954.
Iommi, Tony. *My Journey Through Heaven and Hell with Black Sabbath*. New York: Da Capo, 2005.
Irwin, William. *Black Sabbath and Philosophy*. Oxford: Blackwell, 2012.
Janz, Curt Paul. "Is Zarathustra a Symphony?" In *Nietzsche*. Munich: Hanser, 1978.
Jensen, George, "Introduction: Situating Jung in Contemporary Critical Theory." In *Post Jungian Criticism*, ed. James Baumlin, Tita French Baumlin, George H. Jensen. Albany: State University of New York Press, 2004.
Jung, Carl G. *Archetypes and the Collective Unconscious*. Vol. 9. London: Routledge, Kegan Paul, 1953–1979, Princeton: Princeton University Press, 1953–1979.
_____. *Collected Works*. London: Routledge, Kegan Paul, 1953–1979, Princeton: Princeton University Press, 1953–1979.
_____. *Psychological Types*. Vol. 6. London: Routledge, Kegan Paul, 1953–1979, Princeton: Princeton University Press, 1953–1979.
_____. *Symbols of Transformation*, Vol. 5. London: Routledge, Kegan Paul, 1953–1979, Princeton: Princeton University Press, 1953–1979.

Bibliography

Jung, Carl, and Carl Kerenyi. *Essays on a Science of Mythology.* Trans. R.F.C. Hull. (1949) rpt. Princeton: Princeton University Press, 1969.
Kahn-Harris, Keith. *Extreme Metal: Music and Culture on the Edge.* London: Berg. Bloomsbury, 2006.
Kaufman, Walter. *The Faith of Heretic.* Garden City, NY: Doubleday, 1961.
Keats, John. *The Selected Poetry of John Keats.* New York: Signet Classics, 2008.
Kerenyi, Carl. *The Heroes of the Greeks.* London: Thames and Hudson, 1959.
Koch, Rudolph. *The Book of Signs.* London, 1930, New York: Dover, 1955.
Kot, Greg. "The Satanists Who Changed Music." On the Record, BBC Culture. www.bbc.com/culture/story/20151027/the-satanists-who-changed-music.
Lamroth, Lars. "The Vikings in History and Legend." In the *Oxford Illustrated History of the Vikings.* Ed. Peter Sawyer. New York and Oxford: Oxford University Press, 1999. 225–249.
Langer, Susanne. *Feeling and Form.* New York: Macmillan, 1953.
_____. *Philosophy in a New Key.* Cambridge: Harvard University Press, 1957.
Leppert, Richard, and Susan McClary. eds. *Music and Society: The Politics of Composition, Performance and Reception.* Cambridge: Cambridge University Press, 1987.
Levi-Straus, Claude. *The Raw and the Crooked.* Chicago: University of Chicago Press, 1964, rpt. 1970.
_____. *The Savage Mind.* Chicago: University of Chicago Press, 1966.
_____. "The Structural Study of Myth." In *Myth: A Symposium.* Ed. Thomas Sebeok. Bloomington: Indiana University Press, 1955.
Lewis, Matthew. *The Monk* (1796). New York: Penguin Classics, 1998.
Lief, Jason. *Christianity and Heavy Metal as Impure Sacred Within the Secular in the Secular West.* Lanham: Lexington, 2017.
_____. "Some Kind of Monstrosity: What Youth Ministry Can Learn from Heavy Metal." *Journal of Youth and Theology,* Vol. 12, No. 2 (2013): 7–22.
Lindow, John L. *Norse Mythology: A Guide to Gods, Heroes, Ritual, and Beliefs.* New York and Oxford: Oxford University Press, 2001.
Lonnroth, Lars. "Structural Divisions in the Njada Manuscripts." *Njada Saga: A Critical Introduction.* Berkeley: University of California Press, 1976.
Lovecraft, H.P. *H.P. Lovecraft: Collected Stories.* New York: Library of America, 2005.
Lowes, John Frederick. *The Road to Xanadu: A Study in the Ways of the Imagination.* New York: Houghton Mifflin, 1927.
Lyotard, Jean François. *Postmodern Condition: A Report on Knowlesge.* Ed. Geoff Bennington and Brian Massumi. Minneapolis: University of Minnesota Press, 1979.
Mann, Thomas. "Appeal to Reason." In *Essays of Three Decades.* New York: Alfred A. Knopf, 1947, rpt. 1976.
_____. *Doctor Faustus.* Trans. H.T. Lowe-Porter. London: Secker and Warburg, 1949.
_____. "Sufferings and Greatness of Richard Wagner." In *Essays of Three Decades*, New York: Alfred A. Knopf, 1947, rpt. 1976. 346.
McClary, Susan. *Feminine Endings.* Minneapolis: University of Minnesota Press, 1991.
McDonald, Chris. *Rush, Rock Music, and the Middle Class.* Bloomington: Indiana University Press, 2009.
McIver, Joel. *The Complete History of Black Sabbath.* New York: Race Point, Quarto Group, 2016.
Meachem, Rebecca. "The Sun's Children: Shadow Work in the Poetry of LeRoi Jones/Amiri Baraka." In *Post-Jungian Criticism*, ed. James Baumlin, Tita French Baumlin, George H. Jensen. Albany: State University of New York Press, 2004.
Menand, Louis. "The Defense of Poetry." *The New Yorker* (July 31, 2017).
Merriam, Alan P. *Anthropology of Music.* Evanston, IL: Northwestern University Press, 1964.

Bibliography

Meyer, Leonard. *Emotion and Meaning in Music.* Chicago: Unversity of Chicago Press, 1956.
Milton, John. *Paradise Lost.* Oxford: Oxford University Press, 2013.
Moberg, Marcus. "The Darker Side of Alternative Spirituality: Popular Culture and the Case of Metal Music." In *Postmodern Spirituality* (2009).
____. "Religion and Popular Music, or Popular Music as Religion? A Critical Review of Scholarly Writing on the Place of Religion in Metal Music and Culture." *Popular Music and Society* Vol. 35, No. 1 (2012).
Moore, Thomas. *Care of the Soul: A Guide for Cultivating Depth and Sacredness in Everyday Life.* New York: Harper Perennial, 1992.
Moretti, Franco. *Signs Taken for Wonders.* London: Verso, 1988.
Morris, David B. "Gothic Sublimity." *New Literary History: A Journal of Theory and Interpretation.* Vol. 15, No. 2 (Winter 1985): 299–320.
Moynihan, Michael, and Didrick Soderlind. *Lords of Chaos: The Bloody Rise of the Satanic Metal Underground.* Vancouver: Feral House, 1998.
Mudrian, Albert. *Choosing Death: The Improbable History of Death Metal and Grindcore.* Brooklyn, NY: Bazillion, 2016.
Nietzsche, Friedrich. *Basic Writings of Nietzsche.* Ed. Walter Kaufman, New York: Random House, Modern Library, 1968.
____. *Thus Spake Zarathrusta.* Trans. Walter Kaufman. New York: Penguin, 1968.
Novalis [Friedrich Hardenburg]. *Hymnen an die Nacht [Hymns to the Night].* Trans. Dick Higgins. Kingston, NY: McPherson, 1988.
O'Boyle, Tom, and Niall Scott. "The Future of Metal Is Bright and Hell Bent for Genre Destruction: A Response to Keith Kahn-Harris." In *Global Metal Music and Culture: Current Directions in Metal Studies,* ed. Andy R. Brown, Karl Spracklen, Niall Scott, Keith Kahn-Harris. London and New York: Routledge, 2016.
Oswald, Ian. "Dreaming." In *The Oxford Companion to the Mind.* Ed. Richard L. Gregory. New York: Oxford University Press, 2004.
Pagels, Elaine. *The Origins of Satan.* New York: Random House, 1995.
Pattison, Robert. *The Triumph of Vulgarity: Rock Music in the Mirror of Romanticism.* New York: Oxford University Press, 1987.
Peck, M. Scott. *The People of the Lie: The Hope for Healing Human Evil.* New York: Simon & Schuster, 1983.
Phillips, William, and Brian Cogan. *Encyclopedia of Heavy Metal.* Westport: Greenwood, 2009.
Pillsbury, Glenn J. *Damage Incorporated: Metallica and the Production of Musical Identity.* New York and London: Routledge, 2006.
Piotrowska, Anna G. "Scandinavian Heavy Metal as an Intertextual Play with Norse Mythology." In *Music at the Extremes: Essays on Sounds.* Ed. Scott A. Wilson. Jefferson, NC: McFarland, 2015.
Plato. *The Republic.* Trans, H.D.P. Lee. London: Penguin, 1955.
Plutarch. *Lives.* 9 vols. New York: Penguin, 2004–2014.
Poe, Edgar Allan. *Essays and Reviews,* ed. G.R. Thompson. New York: Library of America, 1984.
Polybius. *Histories.* Trans. F.W. Walbank. New York: Penguin, 1957.
Purcell, Natalie J. *Death Metal: The Passion and Politics of a Subculture.* Jefferson, NC: McFarland, 2012.
Reese, David George. *The Anchor Bible Dictionary* II. New York: Doubleday, 1992. 142.
Reich, Charles. *The Greening of America.* New York: Random House, 1970.
Reyes, Ian. "Blacker than Death: Recollecting the Black Turn in Metal Aesthetics." *Journal of Popular Music Studies,* Vol. 25, No. 2 (June 20, 2013): 240–257.

Bibliography

Ricoeur, Paul. *The Symbolism of Evil*. Boston: Beacon, 1967.
Rohde, Erwin. *Psyche: The Cult of Souls and Belief in Immortality Among the Greeks* (1893). Eugene, OR: Wipf and Stock, 2006.
Ross, Anne. *Pagan Celtic Britain*. London: Routledge and Kegan Paul, 1967; New York: Columbia University Press, 1967.
Roszak, Theodore. *The Making of the Counter-Culture*. Garden City, NY: Anchor, 1969, rpt. Berkeley: University of California Press, 1995.
Ruggeiro, Jenna. "Fled Is That Magic: The Uses of Enchantment in John Keats and Led Zeppelin." Bard College, 2011. www.digitalcommons.bard.edu.
Scarborough, Milton. *Myth and Modernity: Postcritical Reflections*. Albany: State University of New York Press, 1994.
Scruton, Rogers. *Aesthetics of Music*. Oxford and New York: Oxford University Press, 1997.
Seaford, Richard A.S. *Oxford Companion to Classical Literature*. Oxford: Oxford University Press, 2013.
Sebeok, Thomas. *A Sign Is Just a Sign*. Bloomington: Indiana University Press, 1991.
Shakespeare, William. *The Tempest: The Complete Works of William Shakespeare*. Oxford: Oxford University Press, 1952.
Sharpe, John C. "The Viking Expansion: Climate, Population, Plunder." Dissertation, www.scholarworks.umt.edu/visual/content.
Shelley, Mary. *Frankenstein* (1818). Oxford: Oxford University Press, 2008.
Shelley, Percy Bysshe. *Percy Bysshe Shelley: Selected Poems*. London: Folio, 2004.
Shepherd, John. *Music as Social Text*. Cambridge: Polity, 1991.
Siculus, Diodorus. *History*. Library of History, ed. and trans. C.H. Oldfather. Cambridge: Harvard University Press, 1935.
Sinclair, Gary. "Heavy Metal Rituals and the Civilizing Process." In *Critical Issues: Can I Play With Madness? Metal Dissonance, Madness, and Alienation*. Ed. Colin A. McKinnon, Niall Scott, and Kristin Sollee. Oxford: Interdisciplinary Press, 2011. 93–100.
Soghomanian, Talia. "Interview with Corey Taylor." *N.Y. Rock* (2002).
Sophocles. *Antigone* in *Greek Tragedy*. Mark Griffith, David Grene and Richard Lattimer. Chicago: University of Chicago Press, 2005.
Spenser, Edmund. *The Faerie Queene* (1590). Oxford: Clarendon Press, 1998.
Spracklen, Karl, Caroline Lucas, and Mark Deeks. "The Construction of Heavy Metal Identities Through Heritage Narratives: A Case Study in Extreme Metal Bands of Northern England," *Popular Music and Society* Vol. 37, No. 1 (2014): 48–64.
Stevenson, Robert Louis. *The Strange Tale of Dr. Jekyll and Mr. Hyde* (1886). New York: Signet, 2003.
Sugerman, Danny. *Appetite for Destruction: The Days of Guns n' Roses*. New York: St. Martin's, 1991.
Tolkein, J.R.R. *The Lord of the Rings* (1937). London: Folio, 1976.
Trafford, Simon, and Aleks Pluskowski. "Antichrist Superstars: The Vikings in Hard Rock and Heavy Metal." *Mass Market Medieval: Essays on the Middle Ages and Popular Culture*. Ed. David W. Marshall. Jefferson, NC: McFarland, 2007. 57–73.
Tuve, Rosamund. *Elizabethan and Metaphysical Imagery*. Chicago: University of Chicago Press, 1947.
Tylor, Edward Burnett. *Researches into the Development of Mythology, Philosophy, Religion, Art, and Custom. Primitive Culture*, Vol. 1. London: J. Murray, 1871, rpt. Cambridge: Cambridge University Press. 2010.
Umurthan, Osman. "Heavy Metal Music and the Appropriation of Greece and Rome." *Syllecta Classica*, Vol. 23 (2012): 127–152.
Varas-Diaz, Nelson and Niall Scott. eds. *Heavy Metal and the Communal Experience*. Lanham, Md.: Lexington, 2016.

Bibliography

Venkatesh, Vivek, Jeffrey S. Podoshen, Kathryn Urbaniak, Jason J. Wallin, "Eschewing Community: Black Metal." *Community and Applied Psychology*, Vol. 25, No. 16 (2015): 66–81.
Vilhjalmsson, Bjorn., "Coming in from the Cold: Icelandic Punk Rock and Sites of Cultural Memory." In *Resounding Pasts*. Ed. Drago Momcilovic. Newcastle-on-Tyne: Cambridge Scholars, 2011.
Von Helden, Imke. "Barbarians and Literature: Viking Metal and Its Links to Old Norse Mythology." *The Metal Void, First Gatherings* (2010). www.interdisciplinary.net.
_____. "Scandinavian Metal Attack: The Power of Northern Europe in Extreme Metal." In *Heavy Fundamentalisms*. Ed. Rosemary Hill and Karl Spracklen. Interdisciplinary Press. 33–41. www.interdisciplinary.net
Wagner, Richard. *The Artwork of the Future* (1850). Trans. William Ashton Ellis. Lincoln: University of Nebraska Press, 1993.
Waksman, Steve. *This Ain't the Summer of Love: Conflict and Crossover in Heavy Metal and Punk*. Berkeley: University of California Press, 2009.
Walker, D.P. *Spiritual and Demonic Magic from Ficino to Campanella*. London: Warburg Institute, 1958.
Wall, Mick. *When Giants Walked the Earth: A Biography of Led Zeppelin*. New York and London: Macmillan, 2007.
Wallach, Jeremy, Harris M. Berger, Paul D. Greene, eds. *Metal Rules the Globe: Heavy Metal Music Around the World*. Durham: Duke University Press, 2011.
Walser, Robert. "Eruptions: Heavy Metal Appropriations of Classical Virtuosity." *Popular Music* Vol. 11, No. 3 (1992): 263–308.
_____. *Running With the Devil: Power, Gender, and Madness in Heavy Metal Music*. Middletown, Ct.: Wesleyan University Press, 1993.
Walsh, Ashley Anne. "A Great Heathen Fist from the North: Vikings, Norse Mythology, and Medievalism in Nordic Extreme Metal." www.duo.uio.no, *Vikingtid og nordisk middelaider*, University of Oslo Library.
Walzel, Oscar. F. *German Romanticism* (1932). New York: Capricorn, 1966.
Weinstein, Deena. *Heavy Metal: A Cultural Sociology*. New York: Lexington, 1991.
_____. *Heavy Metal: The Music and Its Culture*. New York: Da Capo, 2000.
_____. "Pagan Metal." In *Pop Pagans: Paganism and Popular Music*. Ed. Donna Weston and Andy Bennett. London: Routledge, 2014.
_____. *Rock 'n' America: A Social and Cultural History*. Toronto: University of Toronto Press, 2015.
Wiener, Philip, et al., eds. *Dictionary of the History of Ideas*. New York: Charles Scribner's Sons, 1973.
Wilde, Oscar. *The Picture of Dorian Gray* (1890). London: Folio, 2012.
Wilson, Scott. *Great Satan's Rage: American Negativity and Rap Metal in the Age of Supercapitalism*. Manchester and New York: Manchester University Press, 2008.
_____. *Music at the Extremes: Sounds Outside the Mainstream*. Jefferson, NC: McFarland, 2015.
Wordsworth, William. *William Wordsworth: Selected Poems*. London: Folio, 2002.
Yeats, William Butler. *A Vision* (1925). New York: Colliers, 1966.

Index

AC/DC 15, 57, 137
Ace Ventura 128, 139
Achilles 2, 11, 24, 52
Adams, Eric (Manowar) 51
Aerosmith 7, 50, 160
Aeschylus 92
Agincourt 24
Agrippa, Cornelius 26
Akurlund, Jonas (Bathory) 119
Al Aaraaf 143
Alan Parsons Project 91
Albion 23–24, 81, 87–88
alchemy 26–27, 69, 107
Alice Cooper 14, 50, 55
Alice in Chains 159
alienation 36
Altamont 34
Amon Amarth 121
Amorphis 15
Anthrax 3, 53, 55, 145, 157
Antigone (Sophocles) 78
Aphrodite 79
apocalypse 15, 36, 83, 150–152
Apollo 27
Arch Enemy 128
archetypes 4, 9, 19, 22, 37, 44, 62–63, 69–70, 122, 175
Arentium Astrum (Crowley) 26
Ares King of Hell (Gogoroth) 161
Aristotle 66, 77
Arnim, Achim von 97
Artemus 79
Arthurian myth 80
Arturus 57
Assyrian myth 66
astrology 26, 107
Athena 79
Atlas 24
Auden, W.H. 115

Augustine of Hippo 60
Avalon 23, 81
Avatar (band) 164
awe 71
Azagthoth, Trey 129, 147–148
Azoff, Irving 128

Baal 143
The Bacchae (Euripedes) 78
bacchanalian festival 78
Bacchic cult 78, 144
Bacon, Francis 66
Bakan, David 148
Bakhtin, Mikhail 38, 167
Bangs, Lester 17, 35
Barren Cross 153
Barrie, James M. 58
Basche, Philip 103
Bastian, Alfred 62
Bathory 14, 118–119, 128
"The Battle of Evermore" (Led Zeppelin) 19, 22–23
Baudelaire, Charles 59, 91
Baudrillard, Jean 171
The Beatles 31
Beck, Jeff 49, 136
Beethoven, Ludwig van 100, 117
Believer 151
Beowulf 66
Berger, Harris 2, 172
Bergson, Henri 59
Berlioz, Hector 157
The Bible 40–42, 48, 66, 107, 145–146, 151
Billboard 8, 151
Birch, Martin 108
Birmingham 14, 89
Black Circle 129–130
Black Crucifixion 130

Index

black metal 7, 118–119, 127, 130, 161
Black Sabbath 3, 7, 12–13, 31–43, 56–57, 80, 88, 96, 137, 161
Blackmore, Ritchie (Deep Purple) 49, 51
Blackthrone 130
Blake, William 24, 36, 68, 84, 87
Blondie 91
Blue Cheer 14, 35
Blue Oyster Cult 49, 143
blues 13, 18–19, 25, 136
Bloom, Allan (*The Closing of the American Mind*) 77
Blythe, Randy 164
Boethius 60
Bonham, John (Led Zeppelin) 29, 39
Bon Jovi 56, 159
Booker, Christopher 1, 65, 122
Bosch, Hieronymous 25, 40
Botticelli, Sandro 66
Brentano, Clemens 97
Brontë, Charlotte 85
"Bron-y-aur Stomp" (Led Zeppelin) 21
Brothers Grimm 35, 97
Browning, Robert 20
Bruno, Giordano 26
Bultmann, Rudolph 32, 148
Burgess, Colin (AC/DC) 57
Burke, Edmund 14, 71, 85
Burke, Kenneth 115
Butler, Geezer (Black Sabbath) 31–43, 47

Caesar, Julius 81–82, 145
"The Call of Cthulhu" (H.P. Lovecraft) 147
Campbell, Joseph 10, 61–62, 113, 116
Cannibal Corpse 128–129, 138–139
Cantwell, Jerry (Alice in Chains) 160
Captain Ahab 164
Carnage 128
carnival 38
Cassirer, Ernst 9, 167, 172
CBGB 52
Celtic Frost 80, 128
Celtic myth 3, 23, 80–81
Cereberus 138, 145
Cervantes (*Don Quixote*) 35
Charon 1, 23, 138
"Christabel" (Coleridge) 34, 84, 90
Christian metal 8, 56, 150–151
Christianity in Norway 124
Cicero 82
Cinderella 50
Cipher Manuscripts 26

Circe 136, 144
Clapton, Eric 49, 57, 136
Clarke, Arthur C. 104
Cocytus 138
Codex Regius 123
cognitive psychology 69
Coleridge, Samuel Taylor 34, 68, 84, 99, 104, 106, 106–117
collective unconscious 68
Columbia Records 55, 128, 160
Columbus, Scott (Manowar) 51
Combat Records 128
community 59
Comte, August 64, 67
concert 6, 9, 56, 63, 78
Condorcet, Marquis Marie Jean Antoine 67
counterculture (1960s) 17–18
Coverdale, David (Whitesnake) 52, 145
Cradle of Filth 127, 150
Cream 14, 31, 49
Crimson Thorn 152
Cristgau, Robert 35
Cronos (Venom) 80, 162
Crosby, Stills, Nash, and Young 25
Crowley, Aleister 25–26, 33, 57, 104, 139, 148
Cyfarwyddyd 82

Daedelus 48, 104
Dante's *Inferno* 8, 40, 52, 127, 138, 141, 145–146, 161
Darkthrone 15, 118
The Da Vinci Code 61
death metal 7, 56, 140
Dee, John 26
Deep Purple 12, 14, 56, 161
Def Jam Records 54
Def Leppard 15, 50
Deicide 57, 128
Deism 67
Deliverance 150
della Mirandola, Pico 26
De Maio, Joey (Manowar) 12, 47, 50, 101–102
Demeter 144
Demon Hunter 152
demons 40–41
Derrida, Jacques 91
deSaussure, Ferdinand 63
Descartes, Rene 172–173
devil 11, 23, 32, 34–35, 39–40, 42–44, 88–89, 136, 143, 145; *see also* Satan

Index

Di Anno, Paul 103
Dickinson, Bruce (Iron Maiden) 8, 12, 47, 103–104, 106–107, 109–112, 161
Dickstein, Morris 45
Dimmo Borgir 12, 127–128
Dio, Ronnie James (Dio, Black Sabbath) 34, 37, 47, 50–51, 161
Dionysian 5, 6, 22, 45, 78–79, 92–93, 100, 115
Dismember 15
dissonance 14
Disturbed 12
Doctorow, E.L. 70
Dodds, E.R. 78
Dokken 15, 50, 157
Dolmayan, John (System of a Down) 166
doors of perception 89
Dordjan, Shavo (System of a Down) 166
Downing, K.K. (Judas Priest) 44
downtuning 31
Dracula (Bram Stoker) 85, 104
dragon 22, 29, 120
dreams 1, 153–154, 175
Dreamtheater 8, 47, 160
Druids 81
Dumas, Alexandre (*Man in the Iron Mask*) 103
Durand, Gilbert 63
Durkheim, Emile 59, 63

The Eagles 34
Eagleton, Terry 2
Earth 31
Easy Rider (film) 35
ecstasy 43
The Eddas 14, 67, 122–123
Eddie (mascot) 104
Egyptian Book of the Dead 105
Egyptian myth 3, 25, 27, 41, 48, 55, 105–106, 129, 141–142
Einherjer 12, 118–119
Eithon, Bard Faust 130
Electric Light Orchestra (ELO) 34
Eliade, Mircea 6, 33, 61, 64, 68, 172
Eliot, T.S. 47
Elizabethan 66
Elliott, Joe (Def Leppard) 50
Elysian fields 105, 138
emotion 9–11
Emperor 15, 118, 127, 128
Enlightenment 67, 172
Enslaved 118–120, 150
"Enter Sandman" (Metallica) 54, 59

Entombed 15, 128
Entwistle, John (The Who) 105–106
esoteric 17, 26
Euripedes 34, 78, 92
Euronymous 130
Eurydice 15, 80, 143
Evans, David (AC/DC) 57
evil woman figure 34
Exodus 53, 55
The Exorcist (William Peter Blatty) 41

fantasy of escape 43
Fast, Susan 2, 18, 28
fate 48
Faust (Goethe) 98–100
fear 72
festivals 8
Finnegans Wake (James Joyce) 62
Five Finger Death Punch 16, 165
Flynn, Rob (Machine Head) 39–40
Foo Fighters 162
Foucault, Michel 156
The Four Zoas (William Blake) 88
Frankenstein (Mary Shelley) 85
French Revolution 85
Freud, Sigmund 61, 68, 71–72, 153–154
Freyja 122
Frye, Northrop 87
Funicello, Ross "The Boss" 52

Gahl (Gogoroth) 161
The Game of Thrones 29, 61
Geb 105
Geertz, Clifford 65
Geffen Records 52, 55
Geiger, Erik Gustag 126
generations 169
Germanic myth 19
Gesta Danorum 125
Giant Records 139
Gilgamesh 66, 146
Glam metal 8
Gluck, Christof 80
gnosis 33, 67, 69
Godwin, William 85
Goethe, Johann von 65, 67, 98–99
Gogoroth 159, 161
The Golden Dawn 26
Golem 19
Gosow, Angela 128
Gothic 14, 38, 68, 71–72, 84–85, 103, 117
Greek myth 3, 51–52, 60, 64, 143–144, 161

197

Index

Grim (Gogoroth) 161
Grim Reaper 137, 143
Griswold, Rufus 91
Grohl, Dave 162
grotesque imagery 73
grunge 7, 159–160
guitar solos 46, 58, 108
Guns n' Roses 7

Hades 79, 137, 143–144, 146
Haphaestus 79
Halford, Rob (Judas Priest) 8, 49, 160
Hanslick, Eduard 111
Hanzik, Donnie (Manowar) 51
Harris, Steve (Iron Maiden) 4, 12, 14, 47, 50, 88, 103–104, 106–113
Harrison, Jane 59, 64
Hat (Gogoroth) 161
Hawkwind 44, 80
Hawthorne, Nathaniel 39
Haydn, Joseph 80
Hebraic myth 15, 66
Hebrew Bible 40–41
Hecate 138
Hector (*The Iliad*) 24
hedonism 7
Hell 15; *see also* underworld
Hendrix, Jimi 14, 57, 136
Henry V 24
Hera 79
Herbert, Frank (*Dune*) 104
Herder, Johann von 65, 67–68
Hermes Trismegistus 27
hermeticism 25–26
hermit in tarot 15
Herodotus 141
heroism 9, 11, 44, 47, 52, 70, 72, 107, 118
Hesiod (*Theogony*) 79
Hetfield, James (Metallica) 57
hierophany 33
Hillman, James 1, 36, 38, 59, 70, 137, 151
Hinduism 26, 81
hip-hop/rap 46, 54
Hoffmann, E.T.A. 54, 68
Holderlin, Friedrich 68
Homer (*The Iliad, The Odyssey*) 73
horror 7, 13, 43, 71, 91, 103, 128
horror films 7
Horus 105
Houses of the Holy (Led Zeppelin) 21, 23–24
Howlin' Wolf 136
Hugo, Victor (*Les Miserables*) 33

Hume, David 67
Huxley, Aldous 89, 104
hypocrisy 129

Icarus 1, 48, 104, 107
iconography 3, 6, 35
The Iliad 24, 52
industrialism 35
Inez, Mike (Alice in Chains) 160
Infernus (Gogoroth) 161
The Interpretation of Dreams (Sigmund Freud) 71
Iommi, Tony (Black Sabbath) 31–43
Iron Butterfly 14
Iron Maiden 7, 11–12, 14, 44, 47–48, 50, 53, 56, 80, 88, 91, 103–117, 128, 137, 160–161, 170
"Iron Man" (Black Sabbath) 36, 40
irony 35, 84

Jacobson, Ander (Nasum) 129
Jagger, Mick (Rolling Stones) 78
Jane's Addiction 8
Johnson, Brian 58
Johnson, Robert 25, 136
Jones, John Paul (Led Zeppelin) 29
Jordian (Slipknot) 129
Jourgensen, Al 57
Joyce, James 62
Judas Priest 8, 14, 49, 56, 137, 158–159, 160, 170
Judgement Day 145
Jung, Carl Gustav 38, 59, 61–62, 68–71, 92, 153–154, 168

Kahn-Harris, Keith 3, 47, 148, 170–171, 174
Kant, Immanuel 90
"Kashmir" (Led Zeppelin) 29, 43, 80
Kaufman, Walter 148
Keaggy, Phil 151
Keats, John 19, 167
Kilmister, Lemmy 44, 49, 162
King Arthur 143
King Diamond 129
The Kinks 14, 44, 49
Kiss 8, 14, 69, 159
Korn 8, 15, 162
Kothar (Bathory) 119
"Kublai Kahn" (Coleridge) 84, 89–90

Lacan, Jacques 91
Lamb of God 7, 164

198

Index

La Mettrie, Julien Offray de 149
Lang, Andrew 64
Langer, Susann (*Philosophy in a New Key*) 9, 63
Led Zeppelin 3, 12, 14, 17–30, 38–39, 43, 80, 146, 163
Leonardo da Vinci 66
Lethe 138
Levi-Straus, Claude 10, 63–64
Leviathan 164
Levy-Bruhl, Lucius 59
Lewis, C.S. 104, 150
Lewis, Matthew "Monk" (*The Monk*) 85
Liberty Records 52
Limp Bizkit 56, 162
Liszt, Franz 111
Living Colour 136
Locke, John 88
Logan, Karl (Manowar) 51
Loki 118, 122
Lord of the Rings 19, 23, 29
Lovecraft, H.P. 32, 129, 147–148
Lowes, John Livingston 89
Lynnot, Phil 136
Lyotard, Jean François 171

Machine Head 39, 129, 137, 159
madness 155–156
maenads 144
magic 25, 28–29, 33, 155
magus 15
Malakian, Daron (System of a Down) 166
Mallarme, Stephen 59, 91
Mallet, Paul Henri 67, 124
Manichean dualism 38–39, 41
Mann, Thomas 99–100
Manowar 2, 11–12, 14, 47, 50–51, 101–102, 118, 161, 170
Manson, Marilyn 69
Marvel comics 29
masks 69, 92
Mastodon 164
mathematics 59–60
Mayhem 15, 127, 129–130
MC 5, 14, 44
McBrain, Nikko 103, 107
McDonald, Chris 3
McGann, Jerome 116
mechanism 35
Medea (Euripedes) 34
medievalism 19, 22, 82
Megadeth 3, 7, 11, 53, 93, 157, 159

Megaforce Records 53, 128
Menand, Louis 2, 27
Merciful Fate 52, 127, 130
Merriam, Alan 168
Metal Blade Records 128
metal core 56
Metallica 3, 7, 8, 11, 13, 53, 93, 159
Michelangelo 66, 145
Milton, John 35, 88–89, 148
mimesis 77
Minos 138
minstrel 25
Mitchell, Joni 25
Mogg, Phil 49
monomyth 10
Monteverdi, Claudio 80
Moore, Thomas (*Care of the Soul*) 73–74
Morbid Angel 57, 128–129, 142, 147
Moretti, Franco 85
Morris, William 20
Mortification 150
Motley Crue 7, 15, 47, 50, 58, 159
Motorhead 44, 49–50, 56, 162
Mountain 12, 57, 157
Mozart, Wolfgang Amadeus 157
MTV 8, 50, 156–157
Mudrian, Albert 129
Munch, Edvard ("The Scream") 54, 72
Murray, Dave (Iron Maiden) 106
Muses 73
music-drama 93
Musset, Alfred de 91
Mustaine, Dave (Megadeth) 53
Mythology (band) 30
mythopoeic (mythopoetic) 59

Narnia 150, 152
nationalism 96–98, 102
The Necronomicon 147
Neo-classicism 72
Nestor (*The Iliad*) 24
New Age 69
New York Dolls 8
The New York Times 163
The New Yorker 2, 27
Newsweek 5
Newton, Isaac 88
Nibelungenlied 19
Nickelback 162
Nietzsche, Friedrich 78, 93–96
Nile (band) 129
Nine Inch Nails 159

Index

Nirvana 7, 159–160, 162
Nordic myth 4, 12, 14–15, 19, 51–52, 67, 97, 121
Norman, Larry 151
Novalis (Friedrich Hardenberg) 91, 96
Nuclear Blast Records 128, 143
nuclear war 38
Nugent, Ted 52

Oakenshield 80
O'Boyle, Tom 171, 174
occultism 13, 25
Odin 12, 14, 52, 67, 118–119, 121, 164
Odysseus 15, 24, 111, 117, 136
The Odyssey 11
Oedipus 72
Old Corpse Road 80
Onslaught 130
operatic vocals 55
opium 99
orchestrated metal 12
Ordi Templi 25
Orpheus 15, 80
Osborne, Ozzy (Black Sabbath) 8, 31–43, 56, 85, 155, 160
Osiris 105, 142
Ovid 144

Page, Jimmy (Led Zeppelin) 17–30, 43, 49, 80, 136
painting 20, 25–26, 40, 47, 54, 73, 119
Pan 79
pandemonium 40
Pantera 159, 163
Paradise Lost (John Milton) 40
Parales, Jon 163–164
Paranoid (Black Sabbath) 32, 35
paranormal 26, 69
Parents Music Resource Center (PMRC) 60, 85, 156–158, 168
Patroclus (*The Iliad*) 24
Pearl Jam 7, 160
Persephone 138, 143–144
Persian myth 15, 41
Pharmakon 33
Philo 152
Picasso, Pablo (*Guernica*) 38
Plant, Robert (Led Zeppelin) 17–30
Plato 60, 73, 77, 153, 157
Plotinus 60
Plutarch 105, 107
P.O.D. 150, 153
Poe, Edgar Allan 90, 104

poetry 2
Poison 15, 137
Polidori, William 92
Polybius 82
Poseidon 79–80
Pre-Raphaelites 20
Primordial 80
progressive metal 56, 156
Prometheus 6, 79–80, 155
Propp, Vladimir 65
protest 40, 53
Proteus 84, 86
Psyche 69
psychological issues 57
punk rock 49,
Purcell, Natalie J. 3, 128, 139
Puritanism 67
Pythagoras 59–60, 66

Quadrivium 60
Queen Mab 85
quest 1, 10, 63, 86
Quiet Riot 15, 50, 157
Quorthon 119

Radcliffe, Ann 85
Ragnarock 123, 125
Ramses III 105
Rare Breed 31
rebellion 11, 13, 48
Red Cross Knight 26
Reed, Lou 57, 91
Refuge Records 153
Reich, Charles (*The Greening of America*) 18
Relapse Records 128
Renaissance 20, 66
repression 72
Resurrection Band 151
Revelation 108, 151–152
Rhoads, Randy 8, 43
Rhode, Erwin 78
Ricouer, Paul 28, 48
Rime of the Ancient Mariner (Coleridge) 2–3, 11, 14, 68, 84, 104, 106–117, 124
ritual 5, 63
Roadrunner records 128
Robbins, Michael 2
Rolling Stone 35, 55, 58, 160–161, 164
The Rolling Stones 35
Romanticism 3, 14, 67–68, 72, 83–85, 172, 175
Root 137

Index

Rosicrucian 26
Roth, David Lee (Van Halen) 58
Rousseau, Jean-Jacques 83
"Running with the Devil" (Van Halen) 43
Rush 8, 47, 56, 60, 77, 149, 160

Salem witch trials 39
Sanders, Karl (Nile) 129, 142
Santana 34
Satan 11, 23, 32, 34–35, 39–40, 42–44, 88–89, 136, 143, 145; *see also* devil
Satanism 43, 54, 119, 128–130, 160
Satriani, Joe 162
satyr 37
Satyricon 130, 161
Saxo Grammaticus 123
Schelling, Friedrich 99
Schenker, Michael (Scorpions, Schenker Group) 49
Schlegel, August 68
Schlegel, Friedrich 35, 68, 99
Schoenberg, Arthur 100
Schopenhauer, Arthur 101
Schultz, Max F. 117
Scott, Walter 116
science fiction 104
Scorpions 15, 50, 56
Scott, Bon (AC/DC) 57
Scott, Niall 171, 174
Scriabin, Alexander 157
Scruton, Roger 10
Sentenced 15
Sepultura 128
Set 105
shadow 38, 69
Shadyac, Tom 139
Shagrath 137
Shakespeare, William (*The Merchant of Venice*) 60–61
shaman 15
Shelley, Mary (*Frankenstein*) 85
Shelley, Percy Bysshe 35, 84–85, 148
"Shout at the Devil" (Motley Crue) 58
Sirens 60, 144
Sixx, Nikki (Motley Crew) 47
Skaldic poems 125
Skid Row 137
Skolnick, Alex 162
Slayer 3, 8, 53–54, 57, 157, 170
Slipknot 16, 69, 92, 129
Smashing Pumpkins 160
Smith, Adrian 106

Smith, W. Robertson 64
Snider, Dee 157
Song of Roland 66
Soundgarden 7, 159
speed metal 159–160
Spenser, Edmund (*The Faerie Queene*) 26, 66
Spin 160
Spinal Tap 80
spiritualism 26
Squier, Chris (Yes) 105
"Stairway to Heaven" (Led Zeppelin) 21–22, 27, 29
Staley, Lagne (Alice in Chains) 160
Starr, Mike 160
Starr, Ringo 37
Steppenwolf 14, 35, 49
Stevenson, Robert Louis 158
Stoker, Bram 85, 92
Stone Temple Pilots 159
Stonehenge 80
storytelling 29, 59
Stravinsky, Igor 100
Stryper 8, 50, 151
Sturlason, Snorri 125
Styx (river) 137
sublime 14, 68, 71
Sumerian myth 3, 66, 139–140, 142, 146–148, 153
Swedenborg, Emanuel 26
Sweet, Michael (Stryper) 150
symbols 6, 17, 30, 48, 69, 87
Symphony X 127
System of a Down 16, 149, 165–166

Talbot, John Michael 151
Tankian, Serge (System of a Down) 166
tarot 15, 26
Taylor, Corey (Slipknot) 92
Tchaikovsky, Peter Illych 11, 157
Temple of Syrinx (Rush) 77
Tennyson, Alfred 20, 107, 112
terror 71
Thanatos 138
Theban plays (Sophocles) 78
theosophy 69
Thin Lizzy 136
Thor 14, 52, 121–122, 164
thrash 7, 53, 119, 159–160
Tieck, Ludwig 35
Tiresius 15, 138, 144
Titan 79
Tolkein, J.R.R. 19, 80, 125, 150, 161

Index

Tool 15, 163
Torniquet 150
Triton 84, 86
tritones 13
Trojan War 24
Turner, Martin (Wishbone Ash) 106
Twisted Sister 15, 50, 157

UFO 51, 56
Ugaritic myth 143
Ulster Cycle 82
uncanny 71–72
underground 141, 145
Underoath 150, 153
underworld 15, 79, 141, 145
Uriah Heep 12
Urizen 87

Vai, Steve 145–146
Valery, Paul 91
Valhalla 122
Vanderberg, Adrian (Whitesnake) 145
Van Halen 7, 43, 49, 58
Van Halen, Eddie 43
Vanilla Fudge 14
Vedder, Eddie (Pearl Jam) 160
Velvet Underground 57
Venom 15, 56, 130
Victorian respectability 158
Vidar 122
Viking metal 118–126
Vincent, David 129
Virgil 127, 144
Virkenes, Varg 123, 130
volume 51, 56
Volupsa 124–125

Wagner, Richard 14, 53, 68, 93, 100–102, 127, 157
Waksman, Steve 2
Wales 82, 143
Wall, Mick 115

Walser, Robert 2, 13, 27, 37, 42–43, 46, 53, 58, 65, 106, 108, 114, 155, 166–167, 172
war 7, 22–23, 38, 107, 122, 128
"War Pigs" (Black Sabbath) 7, 34, 36, 39
Ward, Bill (Black Sabbath) 31–43
Warner Brothers Records 128
Warren, Robert Penn 116
Waters, "Muddy" 136
Waylander 80
Webster, Alex (Cannibal Corpse) 129
Weinstein, Deena 2, 6, 17, 34–35, 46, 50–51, 63–64, 85, 92, 115–117, 141, 170–172
Welles, Orson 52, 156
West, Leslie (Mountain) 49
Whiplash 54
white metal 8, 56; *see also* Christian metal
Whitesnake 15, 50, 146
The Who 31
Wilde, Oscar 158
Windham, John 104
Winterfelleth 80
Winters Bane 160
wizard 32–33
Wodensthrone 80
Woodstock 34
Wordsworth, William 68, 84, 86, 90
Wotan 119

Yardbirds 14, 49
Yeats, William Butler 26, 59
Young, Angus (AC/DC) 57–58
Young, Edward 91
Young, Malcolm (AC/DC) 57–58

Zarathrusta 93–96
Zeus 78, 144
Zombie, Rob 161
Zoroastrian 15, 41, 143, 153
Zyklon 128

www.ingramcontent.com/pod-product-compliance
Ingram Content Group UK Ltd.
Pitfield, Milton Keynes, MK11 3LW, UK
UKHW042006140426
5217IPUK00015B/1003